GW00808722

KETO DIET COOKBOOK AFTER 50

The Ultimate Guide for Seniors to Lose Weight and Boost Metabolism | 500 Affordable, Quick and Easy Recipes | 28-Day Meal Plan Included

Deborah Faragher

CONTENTS

Introduction

Life after you turn fifty is quite different. Your body suddenly starts experiencing behaviours that start off as weird. They are inconvenient but after a while, you accept them and throw them under the 'I'm getting old' table. However, that is not always the case. Some of these negative symptoms are actually a result of our habits. At 50, it is more important than ever that you eat more healthy foods. Unlike decades earlier, you cannot get away with careless and unplanned meals; each calorie and carb matters. When you eat healthily, you not only gain health but you also lose weight easier and your body feels much younger. Fifty is also the age when you need to stay in shape but find it more difficult to do so. At this age, one of the best things you can do for yourself is to eat healthily. Your body will appreciate every healthy meal you give it and you are sure to enjoy the benefits extensively.

Unfortunately, eating healthily is one of the hardest things to do. There are tons of diets out there but few of them are actually practical. The Keto diet is one of those few. In this book, I'll take you on a journey of discovery through everything you need to know about Keto after 50 plus 101 awesome recipes that I live by. Eating healthily has never been easier!

General overview of the Keto diet

What is Keto diet?

The word keto is short for ketogenic. The Ketogenic diet focuses on consuming very low amounts of carbohydrates, high levels of fat, and adequate levels of protein. In simple terms, with the Keto diet, you replace carbohydrates with fat. In case you haven't figured this out, carbohydrates are known as carbs, for short. You're probably wondering: The aim of a diet is to lose weight and not to gain more. How does that happen if I'm replacing carbs with fat? It is quite simple, really. When the levels of carbs in your body start to dwindle, your body goes into a metabolic state. This metabolic state is referred to as ketosis. The ketosis state is one in which the body burns fat much more rapidly to convert it into energy. The fat is not only turned to energy but is also turned into ketones. Ketones located in the liver also boost energy. In summary, Keto changes your body's mode of operation. Rather than converting your carbohydrates into energy, the fats you want to rid your body of are converted and burned off instead. The end result of a Keto diet is burned fat, boosted energy, reduced insulin levels, and reduced blood sugar.

Advantages of the Keto diet

The Keto diet has been proven to have many advantages for people over 50. Here are some of the best.

Strengthens bones

When people get older, their bones weaken. At 50, your bones are likely not as strong as they used to be. However, you can keep them in really good condition. Consuming milk to get calcium cannot do enough to strengthen your bones. What you can do, is to make use of the Keto diet as it is low in toxins. Toxins negatively affect the absorption of nutrients and so with this, your bones can take in all they need.

Eradicates inflammation

Few things are worse than the pain from an inflamed joint or muscle. Arthritis, for instance, can be extremely difficult to bear. When you follow the ketosis diet, the production of cytokines will be reduced. Cytokines cause inflammation and therefore, their eradication will reduce it.

It eradicates nutrients deficiency

Keto focuses on consuming exactly what you need. If you use a great Keto plan, your body will lack no nutrients and will not suffer any deficiency.

Reduced hunger

The reason we find it difficult to stick to diets is hunger. It doesn't matter your age; diets do not become easier. We may have a mental picture of the healthy body we want. We may even have clear visuals of the kind of life we want to lead once free from unhealthy living but none of that matters when hunger enters the scene. However, the Keto diet is a diet that combats this problem. The Keto diet focuses on consuming plenty of proteins. Proteins are filling and do not let you feel hungry too easily. In addition, when your carb levels are reduced, your appetite takes a hit. It is a win-win situation.

Weight loss

Keto not only burns fat, but it also reduces that craving for food. Combined, these are two great ways to lose weight. It is one of the diets that has proven to help the most when it comes to weight loss. The Keto diet has been proven to be one of the best ways to burn stubborn belly fat while keeping yourself revitalized and healthy.

Reduces blood sugar and insulin

After 50, monitoring blood sugar can be a real struggle. Cutting down on carbs drastically reduces both insulin levels and blood sugar levels. This means that the Keto diet will benefit millions as a lot of people struggle with insulin complications and high blood sugar levels. It has been proven to help as when some people embark on Keto, they cut up to half of the carbs they consume. It's a treasure for those with diabetes and insulin resistance. A study was carried out on people with type 2 diabetes. After cutting down on carbs, within six months, 95 percent of people were able to reduce or totally stop using their glucose-lowering medication.

Lower levels of triglycerides

A lot of people do not know what triglycerides are. Triglycerides are molecules of fat in your blood. They are known to circulate the bloodstream and can be very dangerous. High levels of triglycerides can cause heart failures and heart diseases. However, Keto is known to reduce these levels.

Reduces acne

Although acne is mostly suffered by those who are young, there are cases of people above 50 having it. Moreover, Keto is not only for persons after 50. Acne is not only caused by blocked pores. There are quite a number of things proven to cause it. One of these things is your blood sugar. When you consume processed and refined carbs, it affects gut bacteria and results in the fluctuation of blood sugar levels. When the gut bacteria and sugar levels are affected, the skin suffers. However, when you embark on the Keto diet, you cut off on carbs intake which means that in the very first place, your gut bacteria will not be affected thereby cutting off that avenue to develop.

Increases hdl levels

HDL refers to high-density lipoprotein. When your HDL levels are compared to your LDL levels and are not found low, your risk of developing a heart disease is lowered. This is great for persons over 50 as heart diseases suddenly become more probable. Eating fats and reducing your intake of carbohydrates is one of the most assured ways to increase your high-density lipoprotein levels.

Reduces ldl levels

High levels of LDL can be very problematic when you attain 50. This is because LDL refers to bad cholesterol. People with high levels of this cholesterol are more likely to get heart attacks. When you reduce the number of carbs you consume, you will increase the size of bad LDL particles. However, this will result in the reduction of the total LDL particles as they would have increased in size. Smaller LDL particles have been linked to heart diseases while larger ones have been proven to have lower risks attached.

May help combat cancer

I termed this under 'may' because research on this is not as extensive and conclusive as we would like it to be. However, there is proof supporting it. Firstly, it helps reduce the levels of blood sugar which in turn reduces insulin complications which in turn reduces the risk of developing cancers related to insulin levels. In addition, Keto places more oxidative stress on cancer cells than on normal cells thereby making it great for chemotherapy. The risk of developing cancer after fifty is still existent and so, Keto is literally a lifesaver.

May lower blood pressure

High blood pressure plagues adults much more than it does young ones. Once you attain 50, you must monitor your blood pressure rates. Reduction in the intake of carbohydrates is a proven way to lower your blood pressure. When you cut down on your carbs and lower your blood sugar levels, you greatly reduce your chances of getting some other diseases.

Combats metabolic syndrome

As you grow older, you may find that you struggle to control your blood sugar level. Metabolic syndrome is another condition that has been proven to have an influence on diabetes and heart disease development. The symptoms associated with metabolic syndrome include but are not limited to high triglycerides, obesity, high blood sugar level, and low levels of high-density lipoprotein cholesterol.

However, you will find that reducing your level of carbohydrate intake greatly affects this. You will improve your health and majorly attack all the above-listed symptoms. Keto diet helps to fight against metabolic syndrome which is a big win.

Great for the heart

People over the age of 50 have been proven to have more chances of developing heart diseases. Keto diet has been proven to be great for the heart. As it increases good cholesterol levels and reduces the levels of bad cholesterol, you will find that partaking in the Keto diet proves extremely beneficial for your health.

May reduce seizure risks

When you change your intake levels the combination of protein, fat, and carbs, as we explained before, your body will go into ketosis. Ketosis has been proven to reduce seizure levels in people who suffer from epilepsy. When they do not respond to treatment, the ketosis treatment is used. This has been done for decades.

Combats brain disorders

Keto doesn't end there, it also combats Alzheimer's and Parkinson's disease. There are some parts of your brain that can only burn glucose and so, your body needs it. If you do not consume carbs, your lover will make use of protein to produce glucose. Your brain can also burn ketones. Ketones are formed when your carb level is very low. With this, the ketogenic diet has been used f r plenty of years to treat epilepsy in children who aren't responding to drugs. For adults, it can work the same magic as it is now being linked to treating Alzheimer's and Parkinson's disease

Helps women suffering from polycystic ovarian syndrome (pcos)

This syndrome affects women of all ages. PCOS is short for polycystic ovarian syndrome. Polycystic ovarian syndrome is an endocrine disorder that results in enlarged ovaries with cysts. These cysts are dangerous and cause other complications. It has been proven that a high intake of carbohydrates negatively affects women suffering from polycystic ovarian syndrome. When a woman with PCOS cuts down on carbs and embarks on the Keto diet, the polycystic ovarian syndrome falls under attack.

It is beyond doubt that the Keto diet is beneficial in so many ways that it almost looks unreal. If you are to embark on the Keto diet, there are several things you must know. We'll refer to this section as 'Caution for Keto'

Caution for Keto

Yes, Keto is beneficial and yes, it has a lot of benefits but it is no small thing and so, it must be approached with caution. Here are some tips you should keep in mind before embarking on Keto.

Make use of recipes you can trust

Keto involves a lot of meal planning and this single phase is where a lot of people get it wrong. Your meals are no longer allowed to be careless and you must note everything that goes into your mouth. If you are embarking on a Keto diet, you must use recipes you can trust. The recipes must be beneficial, safe, and delicious. Keto should not take out the enjoyment in your meals. Luckily, you have your hands on the best book for Keto aspirants under 50.

You may need a doctor

If you have had any issue with blood sugar, insulin levels or diabetes, consult your doctor before embarking on Keto. Do not make any dietary changes as large as Keto to your diet without first informing your doctor. He or she is in the best position to guide you properly. See your doctor.

It will be hard at first

Keto is no walk in the park. However, people continue on the path of Keto despite the initial difficulty because the results are evident after a short while. When you kick-start Keto, you may suffer from low blood sugar, sluggishness, and constipation, However, they will all wear off in a few days if you are religious about it.

Can Keto have side effects?

Yes. Keto can have side effects. Keto can have negative side effects if it is wrongly done. Keto cuts down on carbs and replaces them with fat. However, if the replacement is not adequately carried out, a lot of negative side effects may occur. This is why it is extremely important to begin the Keto diet armed with the right information and recipes which are all included in this book.

If you do not make use of quality meal plans and recipes, you'll lack nutrients that your body needs. With Keto, you must not lack proteins and so, your meals must be planned.

How to reach ketosis

Reaching the state of ketosis is not so straightforward for many people. In order to effectively reach ketosis, there are some steps you must take.

Eat the right food- Ketosis relies a lot on what you eat. To reach ketosis, you need to first cut down on the carbohydrates you take in. Secondly, you need to take in much more fats in your diets. However, you should just take in any fat, you should make sure to take in healthy fat. Taking in unhealthy fats can cause more harm than good.

Exercise- To efficiently reach ketosis, you should make sure to exercise. It doesn't have to be intensive, however, long walks, jugs, biking, and other exercises can help your body reach ketosis.

Try intermittent fasting- Some people combine intermittent fasting with ketosis. The reason is that, as you progress, your hunger pangs are reduced greatly and you will find intermittent fasting easy. In fact, even when you do not plan to, you'll find yourself doing it. It is definitely not compulsory but if you are making use of ketosis to lose weight, intermittent fasting is a great bonus.

Take lots of fruits and vegetables- Fruits and vegetables for snacks will keep your body healthy and help revitalize your skin.

Include coconut oil in your diet- Coconut is compulsory if you want to reach ketosis. Coconut oil contains healthy fat. It helps the body reach ketosis and contains four types of MCTs. It is one of the best tools for inducing ketosis. If you have never made use of coconut oil before, start slowly and increase your intake gradually.

General overview of macros

What are macros?

'Macros' is short for macronutrients. These macronutrients are the important nutrients your body needs. These nutrients are-

Carbohydrates: In this group, we have sugars, fibers, and starches. Carbohydrates are broken down into glucose or blood sugar. Your body can then use it as energy or store it as glycogen in your liver or in your muscles.

Proteins: Proteins are found in fish, meat, eggs, and lentils such as beans. Proteins are necessary for a lot of functions such as cell signaling, the building of tissues, building of enzymes, as well as hormones. It is also necessary for various immune functions.

Fats: Fat is found in oils, butter, nuts, meat, fatty fish, and avocado. Fat is used for a lot of important things in the body. It helps maintain body temperature and produce hormones. It also helps the body absorb nutrients.

The Keto diet focuses on providing adequate levels of protein and substituting carbs for healthy fat.

Although some foods have the nutrients you need, they may also have a high level of carbs. This is why it is important to check the nutritional composition of any food before incorporating it into your diet

Getting started with keto over 50

There are various types of Keto diets. At 50 and above, you cannot just make use of the normal Keto diet. This is because at this age, each and everything you eat matters. You literally become what you eat and so, it is essential that you make use of the right variation of Keto.

You cannot make use of the traditional Keto diet as it is not suitable for older persons. Whatever Keto diet you'll be on must be suitable for your age and take into consideration that your body doesn't metabolize as fast as previously. It isn't what we want to hear, but it is what we need.

What not to eat when Ketoing
- X   Sugar
- X   Starches and food high in carbohydrates
- X   Too much fruit as it contains sugar when in large quantities.
- X   Beer and Alcohol

Keto diet for below 50 versus Keto for above 50

Those who are younger than 50 years of age find that they can stick to traditional Keto diets with no problems. They have schedules, cheat days, and other tools that help them. Missing a day or two does not have too serious repercussions as they can make up. However, one over 50, Ketoing has to be taken more seriously simply because it is harder to lose weight.

Due to the fact that it becomes harder to lose weight, a lot of over 50's have made Ketoing the 'rule' and not the exception. A careful study of this book will show that all the great recipes have been converted to Keto forms. Carbs were taken and replaced with fats and proteins are highly favored.

When 50 or above, your Keto diet must be followed religiously. This used to be a problem as most of the things we loved just involved a lot of carbs. Luckily, that is no longer the case. With the right recipe book, you will find it much easier to do without carbs.Remember to run any dietary changes by your doctor.

28-Days Meal Plan

Day 1
Breakfast – 4 Keto Almond Cereal
Launch - 356 Saucy and Crispy Chicken
Dinner – 350 Cucumber Salad

Day 2
Breakfast – 13 Keto Fruit Cereal
Launch – 334 Vanilla Frozen Yogurt
Dinner – 263 Mexican Tofu Scramble

Day 3
Breakfast – 1 Green Banana Pancake
Launch – 264 Goat Cheese Figs Pizza
Dinner – 336 Shrimp Pepper Soup

Day 4
Breakfast – 18 Lemon Blueberry Muffins
Launch – 259 Jackfruit Burger
Dinner – 345 Tri-Tip Roast

Day 5
Breakfast – 11 Cranberry Oatmeal Cups
Launch – 347 Quinoa Cauliflower Bites
Dinner – 329 Gingered Ham

Day 6
Breakfast – 44 Swiss Chard Bowl
Launch – 383 Egg Chilada
Dinner – 331 Backed Chicken with Bacon

Day 7
Breakfast – 31 Keto Open-Face Bagel Breakfast Sandwich
Launch – 428 Lobster Bisque
Dinner – 432 Turkey Salad

Day 8
Breakfast – 42 Veggie Mix of Colors
Launch – 377 Greek Burger with Feta Dressing
Dinner – 434 Beef Stew

Day 9
Breakfast – 24 Keto Omelet
Launch – 355 Creamy Chicken soup
Dinner – 380 Classick Duck à l'orange

Day 10
Breakfast – 32 Avocado Egg Bake
Launch – 283 Poulet Grand Mère
Dinner – 270 Buffalo Chicken

Day 11
Breakfast – 37 Winter Berry Smoothie
Launch – 244 Keto Catfish Soup
Dinner – 281 Chicken AND Waffles with Hollandaise

Day 12
Breakfast – 60 Keto Pumpkin Smoothie
Launch – 193 Air Fried Falafel
Dinner – 242 Keto Breast Salsa

Day 13
Breakfast – 49 Almond Pancake Rolls with Apple Syrup
Launch – 183 Keto Burger
Dinner – 186 Keto White Rice

Day 14
Breakfast – Keto Coconut Porridge
Launch – 358 Chicken Divan
Dinner – 177 Goat Cheese Watermelon Salad

Day 15
Breakfast – 40 Pan
Launch – 390 Braised Turkey Legs with Creamy Gravy
Dinner – 352 Smoked 321 Ribs

Day 16
Breakfast – 21 Mango Chia Pudding
Launch – 425 Halibut with Creamy Sauce
Dinner – 436 Tuna Burger

Day 17
Breakfast – 35 Bean Sprout Salad
Launch – 437 Carnivore Meatloaf
Dinner – 422 Cheese Tuna Casserole

Day 18
Breakfast – 33 Peach Berry Parfait
Launch – 236 Coconut Crabs Cakes
Dinner – 303 Chicken Cauliflower Alfredo

Day 19
Breakfast – 39 Apple Chips
Launch – 245 Chcken Salad
Dinner – 240 Keto Fish Cake

Day 20
Breakfast – 5 Feta Asparagus Poached Egg Toast
Launch – 379 Garlic and Rosemary Rack of Lamb
Dinner – Easy Buffalo Wings

Day 21
Breakfast – 41 Zucchini and Egg Bowl
Launch – 373 Filet Mignons Florentine
Dinner – 365 Chicken Cordon Bleu

Day 22
Breakfast – 30 Chicken Breast Fillets and Peppers
Launch – 435 Meatlof
Dinner – 374 Meatballs with Brown Gravy

Day 23
Breakfast – 23 Keto Flasxseed Bread
Launch – 362 Chicken Pot Pie
Dinner – 330 Lamb Potato Hotpot

Day 24
Breakfast – Keto Savory Cheese Muffins
Launch – 278 Tangy Classic Chicken Drumettes
Dinner – 358 Chicken Divan

Day 25
Breakfast – 75 Chaffle Sandwich with Eggs and Bacon
Launch – 181 Keto Lasagna
Dinner – 286 Vegan Cheddare Garlic Wings

Day 26
Breakfast – 20 Keto Meatballs
Launch – 238 Chicken Spinach Salad
Dinner – 235 Cauliflower Chicken Broth

Day 27
Breakfast – 15 Egg Bagel
Launch -199 Air Fryed roasted Okra
Dinner – 237 Grilled Lamb

Day 28
Breakfast – 16 Golden Porridge Overight
Launch – 179 Baked Salmon
Dinner – 206 Keto Prime Rib

Breakfast

1. Green Banana Pancakes

Serves: 4 — Preparation Time: 20 minutes — Meal Type: Breakfast.
Nutritional Value Per Serving: Calories 224 kcal — Cholesterol 224mg; — Total Fat 32g — Total Carbs 5g

Ingredients
- 2 large peeled bananas
- 2 eggs
- 6 tablespoons of coconut flour
- 2 teaspoons cassava flour or arrowroot starch
- Pinch of salt
- ¼ teaspoon stevia powder
- 1 tablespoon of baking powder
- Coconut oil or grass-fed butter

Directions
- Puree the banana until smooth.
- Mix the coconut flour, stevia, arrowroot or cassava, baking soda, and a pinch of salt in a mixing bowl to make a powder form.
- Whisk egg very lightly in a small bowl, then pour into the banana, mix well.
- Then add in the powder mixture in it. If the mixture is too thick, add some water with a spoon to make it slightly thin; do not overwater.
- Preheat a skillet along with butter, ghee, or oil.
- Pour in the batter in the skillet with a spoon.
- When it is golden brown from the top, flip it, cook until brown, and take out in a plate. Serve hot.

2. Berry bread spread

Serves: 3 — Preparation time: 15 minutes — Meal Type: Breakfast.
NUTRITIONAL VALUE PER SERVING: Calories 285 kcal — Total Fat 18g — Total Carbs 5.5g — Protein: 6.8g

Ingredients
- 2 cups of coconut cream
- 2 ounces of strawberries
- 1 ½ ounce of blueberries
- 1 ½ ounce of raspberries
- ½ teaspoon coconut extract

Directions
- Dice three of each berry in small pieces separately.
- Blend the remaining strawberries, blueberries, and raspberries in a blender until smooth.
- Mix in the coconut extract and coconut cream.
- Blend again until smooth, then add in the diced berries.
- Serve chilled.

3. Chocolate Bread Spread

Serves: 3 — Preparation time: 15 minutes — Meal Type: Breakfast.
NUTRITIONAL VALUE PER SERVING: Calories: 257 kcal — Total Fat: 19g — Total Carbs:7.5g — Protein: 11.8g

Ingredients
- 4 cups of sweet cream
- 2 ounces of coconut oil
- 3 ounces of chocolate
- 1 teaspoon of coconut extract
- 1 tablespoon of powdered cacao
- Groundnuts [optional]

Directions
- Put sweet cream in a microwavable bowl and heat for 10-15 seconds
- Add in coconut oil and mix, then mix in the chocolate and powdered cacao, mix well.
- Heat the mixture in the microwave for a minute or so.
- When it is warm, add groundnuts, if desired.
- Pour in fridge bowls, and chill.
- Serve as you desire.

4. Keto Almond Cereal

Serves: 3 — Preparation time: 20 minutes — Meal Type: Breakfast
NUTRITIONAL VALUE PER SERVING: Calories 104 kcal — Fat 15g — Carbohydrates 4g — Protein 5g

Ingredients
- 3 cups of unsweetened coconut flakes
- 1 cup of sliced almonds
- ¾ tablespoon of cinnamon
- ¾ tablespoon of nutmeg

Directions
- Preheat oven to 250 degrees F.
- Mix the almonds and coconut flakes together, then add nutmeg and cinnamon. Mix well.
- Spread the nut mixture on a baking tray, and bake for 3-5 minutes.
- Take out, when slightly brown.
- Enjoy with milk.

5.Feta Asparagus Poached Egg Toast

Preparation Time: 5 minutes— Cook time: 15 minutes— Servings: 1 person

Ingredients
- Eggs: 2
- Asparagus: 12
- Sourdough bread: 2 slices
- Feta cheese: 90 gm
- Mint leaves: 1 tsp chopped
- Olive oil
- Almonds: 1 tbsp (roughly chopped)
- Chives: 1 tsp chopped
- Lemon zest: of one lemon
- Parsley: 1 tsp chopped
- Salt & pepper: as per your taste

Directions
- Turn on the grill
- Crumble feta and chop herbs and set aside
- Take a small saucepan and add water with a small amount of vinegar and allow it to boil then lower the heat
- Roast the asparagus in the baking tray and brush olive oil on top for 5 minutes and don't let them burn
- Prepare pouched eggs by adding one egg in a small bowl
- Whisk water fast as it will create a whirlpool and add an egg to the water
- Poach the egg for 3 minutes and remove from the water using any perforated spoon
- Repeat it again with the second egg
- Toast the bread in between
- Put feta on each bread slice and arrange 6 asparagus on top
- Top each slice with mixed herbs, lemon zest, sliced almonds, and poached eggs
- Season with salt, pepper, and olive oil and serve

6. Chocolate Oats Overnight

Preparation Time: 10 minutes— Servings: 2

Ingredients
- Oats: 100 g
- Chia seeds: 2 tbsp
- Cocoa powder: 2 tbsp
- Cardamon powder: ¼ tsp
- Vanilla extract: ½ tsp
- Dairy-free milk: 2 cups or 500 ml
- Maple syrup: 3 tbsp
- Pear: 1
- Raspberries: a handful
- Almond butter: 2 tbsp
- Dark chocolate: grated

Directions
- Take a large jar and add oat, cocoa powder, chia seeds, and cardamom and combine well
- Add dairy-free milk and vanilla extract and blend well
- Cover the jar and place in the fridge overnight
- In the morning, add maple syrup if you like it sweet
- Divide equally into two bowls and top with the servings items

7. Almond and Apricot Granola

Preparation Time: 10 minutes— Cook time: 40 minutes — Servings: 2

Ingredients
- Coconut oil: 6 tbsp melted
- Rolled oats: 300 gm
- Clear honey: 4 tbsp
- Pumpkin seeds: 3 handfuls
- Almonds: 1 cup with skin
- Sunflower seeds: 3 handfuls
- Salt: ¼ tsp
- Raisins: 2 handfuls
- Ground cardamom: 1 tsp
- Vanilla extract: 1 tbsp
- Ground ginger: 1 tsp
- Chopped apricots: 2 handfuls

Directions
- Preheat the oven to 160C
- Take a pan and add coconut oil and honey at slow heat and mix well
- Combine rolled oats with pumpkin seeds, almonds, sunflower seeds, cardamom, vanilla and ginger
- Now add the heated mixture of coconut oil and honey
- Mix them all together
- Line a large baking tray with the baking sheet and add the granola but don't make it very thin
- Bake for 20 minutes and add granola more and bake more for 15 minutes
- Spread granola once more and leave for 2 hours in the oven and turn it off
- Mix apricots and raisins with it and put in the airtight jar

8. Buttermilk Blueberry Pancake

Preparation Time: 25 minutes— Cook time: 20 minutes — Servings: 4

Ingredients
- Wholemeal spelt flour:1 cup or 125 gm
- White flour: 1 cup or 125 gm
- Baking powder: 2 tbsp
- Sugar: 2 tbsp
- Salt: ¾ tsp
- Chia eggs: 2 (water: 6 tbsp plus 2 tbsp ground chia seeds)
- Cider vinegar: 2 tbsp
- Nondairy milk: 500 ml
- Vanilla extract: 2 tsp
- Blueberries: 250 gm
- Vegetable oil: 3 tbsp and for frying
- Blueberries: 350 gm
- Lemon juice and zest: of one lemon
- Water: 2 tbsp
- Sugar: 150 gm
- Freshly grated nutmeg: ¼ tsp

Directions
- Mix milk and vinegar to make buttermilk and leave for 10 minutes
- In the meanwhile, make chia eggs by combining chia eggs ingredients and leave it for 10 minutes as well
- In a separate saucepan, combine all the coulis ingredients and cook on medium-low heat to get the texture like a jam
- In another bowl, combine all the dry pancake ingredients
- In next bowl, combine all the wet pancake ingredients
- Hand whisk wet and dry mixtures and fold in blueberries carefully
- Let the batter to sit for 5 minutes
- Take a large pancake pan and grease it
- On medium heat, pour the pancake batter
- Cook each side for three minutes till it turns golden and rise 1 cm
- Serve hot with coulis

9. Tropical Smoothie Green Bowl

Preparation Time: 10 minutes— Servings: 2

Ingredients
- Silken tofu: 300 gm
- Spinach leaves: half cup
- Coconut shavings: 2 tbsp
- Fresh pineapple: 100 gm
- Orange: 1
- Kiwi: 1
- Shelled hemp: 2 tbsp
- Dried figs: 3
- Chia seeds: 2 tbsp
- Almonds: a few

Directions
- Wash and drain spinach leaves and add leaves and tofu in the blender
- Mix them well in the blender and add pineapple, figs, and orange
- Blend to give the smooth texture
- You can place this in the fridge for many days in the airtight container
- Put it in the bowl when ready to eat
- Top the bowl with extra pineapple, chia seeds, kiwi, coconut shavings, and almonds

10. Coconut Chocolate Almond Butter

Preparation Time: 40 minutes— Yield: 1 Jar

Ingredients

- Desiccated coconut: 80gm
- Almonds: 300 gm (with skin)
- Melted coconut oil: 1 tbsp
- Cacao: 1 tbsp
- Vanilla extract: ½ tsp
- Salt: ½ tsp
- Maple syrup: 2 tbsp

Directions

- Preheat the oven 190C
- Roast almonds on the baking tray for 10 minutes
- Meanwhile, toast the coconut on medium flame in a pan till they turn light brown
- Now add almonds and coconut in the bled and blend for 30 minutes until they form a paste
- Stop the blender in between and scrape the sides
- Add rest of the ingredients and blend again to give a smooth co

11.Cranberry Oatmeal Cups

Preparation Time: 10 minutes— Cook time: 20 minutes — Servings: 12

Ingredients

- Rolled oats: 2 cups
- Chia egg: 1 (ground chia seeds 1 tbsp plus water 1 tbsp)
- Wholemeal spelt flour: 1 cup
- Cinnamon powder: 1 ½ tsp
- Overripe banana: 1
- Baking powder: 1 tsp
- Salt: ½ tsp
- Maple syrup: 125 ml
- Coconut oil: 125 ml
- Dried cranberries: 75 g dried (a bit more for toppings)
- Pumpkin seeds: 75 gm (a bit more for toppings)
- Sunflower seeds: 75 gm (a bit more for toppings)

Directions

- Preheat the oven 180C
- Prepare chia egg by combining 1 tbsp ground chia seeds with 3 tbsp water and keep aside
- Take a pan and melt coconut oil in it
- Take a big bowl and add all the dry ingredients
- In another bowl, mash bananas and add the cooled coconut oil along with the maple syrup, chia eggs, and vanilla extract and mix well
- Add this banana mixture to the dry ingredients and combine
- Take a muffin tray and grease it
- Place one scoop of oatmeal mixture in each muffin hole
- Tightly pack the mixture in the hole using a spoon
- Add toppings over the mixture and press
- Cook the oatmeal mixture in the oven for around 25 minutes
- When done, let them cool and then remove for the tray
- Make as many as your mixture allows
- Keep them in an airtight container and consume within 5 days

12. Keto granola cereal

Serves: 3 — Preparation time: 30 minutes — Meal Type: Breakfast

NUTRITIONAL VALUE PER SERVING: Calories 441 kcal — Fat 40g — Carbohydrates 4g — Protein 16g

Ingredients

- 1 cup of flaxseeds
- 1 large egg
- 1 cup Almonds
- 1 cup Hazelnuts
- 1 cup Pecans
- 1/3 cup Pumpkin seeds
- 1/3 cup Sunflower seeds
- 1/4 cup melted butter or coconut oil or ghee for dairy-free
- 1 tsp Vanilla extract

Directions

- Preheat oven to 370 degrees F, and line the baking drays with wax or parchment paper.
- Pulse almonds and hazelnuts in a food processor intermittently, until chopped into large pieces, then add pecans and chop again into large pieces. Pecans are added later since they are softer.
- Add the pumpkin seeds, sunflower seeds, and flaxseeds, and pulse just until everything is mixed well. Don't over-process; you should have most seeds in intact form.
- Whisk an egg white and pour it into the food processor.
- Then, whisk together the melted butter and vanilla extract in a small bowl, and evenly pour that in the food processor, too.
- Pulse again to mix well until it combines in the form of coarse meal and nut pieces, and everything should be a little moist from the egg white and butter.
- Transfer the mixture to the prepared baking tray, evenly pressing, bake for 15 to 18 minutes, or until slightly brown from the edges.
- Let it cool, then break it into pieces.

13. Keto Fruit Cereal

Serves: 3 — Preparation time: 20 minutes — Meal Type: Breakfast.

NUTRITIONAL VALUE PER SERVING: Calories 201 — Fat 44g — Carbohydrates 4g — Protein 19g

Ingredients

- 1 cup of coconut flakes
- ½ cup of sliced strawberries
- ¼ cup of sliced raspberries

Directions

- Preheat oven to 300 degrees F.
- Prepare a baking tray with parchment paper
- Slice the berries into small bits.
- Spread the coconut flakes on the tray, bake for 5 minutes until brown from the edges.
- Take out the baked coconut cereals, let it cool.
- Then, add in sliced raspberries and strawberries.
- Enjoy with almond milk.

14. Keto chicken and avocado

Serves: 1 — Preparation time: 20 minutes — Meal Type: Breakfast.
NUTRITIONAL VALUE PER SERVING: Calories 441 kcal — Fat 64g — Carbohydrates 9g — Protein 23g

Ingredients

- 6 medium-sized pieces of chicken Boneless.
- 1 avocado
- 2 eggs
- Keto Mayo
- Salt
- Pepper
- Ground Garlic
- 1/8 cup of olive oil

Directions

- Soft boil 2 eggs, and slice in half, so you have four pieces.
- Put the seasonings together in a bowl, and stir well.
- Sprinkle them generously on the chicken pieces, cover, and let it sit for 5 minutes.
- Heat olive oil in a pan, and fry the chicken until cooked, remove from the flame and set aside.
- Remove pit of the avocado, dice in half and set aside.
- Sprinkle a little salt on the avocados [optional].
- Spread mayo on the chicken [optional].
- On a place, set your eggs, meat, and avocados. Enjoy hot.

15. Egg Bagel

Preparation Time: 5 minutes— Cook Time: 15 minutes— Serving: 1

Ingredients

- Eggs: 2
- Blueberry bagel: ½
- Cream cheese: 1 tbsp
- Raspberry fruit spread: 1 tbsp
- Butter: 1 tbsp

Directions

- Toast the bagel
- Now add cream cheese to the bagel along with the fruit spread
- In a pan, fry two eggs in butter
- Take the serving plate and add bagel mixture
- Now place one egg with grated cheese and another egg on top

16. Golden Porridge Overnight

Preparation Time: 5 minutes— Cook Time: Overnight refrigeration — Servings: 2

Ingredients

- Porridge oats: 1 cup
- Ground turmeric: 1 tsp
- Ground cinnamon: ½ tsp
- Pepper: a pinch
- Ground ginger: ½ tsp
- Ground cardamom: ¼ tsp
- Coconut milk: 500 ml or 2 cups
- Vanilla: ½ tsp
- Shelled hemp: 2 tbsp
- Seasonal fruits
- Coconut flakes
- Raw honey
- Mint leaves
- Shelled hemp

Directions

- Except for the toppings, add all the ingredients to the container with the lid
- Close the lid tightly and shake
- Put it in the fridge for the whole night
- Divide the porridge into two bowls and serve with the toppings in the morning

17. Chia Seeds Porridge

Preparation Time: 5 minutes— Cook Time: 5 minutes — Servings: 2

Ingredients

- Rolled oats: 4 tbsp
- Chia seeds: 2 tbsp
- Almond: 250 ml
- Honey: as per your need
- Dry fruits: as per your need for topping
- Nuts: as per your need for topping

Directions

- Take a saucepan and add chia seeds, rolled oats, and almond milk
- Cook on a medium flame for over 5 minutes till the milk is absorbed
- Put in the bowl and serve
- Add your favorite sweetener, dry fruits, and nuts from the top

18. Lemon Blueberry Muffins

Preparation Time: 20 minutes— Cook Time: 25 minutes — Servings: 2

Ingredients

- Plain flour: 1 cup
- Organic egg: 1
- Golden caster sugar: 1 cup
- Ground nutmeg: 1 tsp
- Almond milk: ½ cup
- Wholemeal spelt flour: 1 cup
- Baking powder: 1 tsp
- Baking soda: 1 tsp
- Lemon juice and zest: 2 tbsp
- Fresh blueberry: 125 g
- Salt: ½ tsp
- Overripe banana: 2-3
- Vegetable oil: 60 ml

Directions

- Preheat the oven to 200C
- Take a muffin tin and place paper baking cases
- Take a large bowl and add flours, baking powder, sugar, salt, baking soda, ground nutmeg, and lemon zest
- Mash the banana in a separate bowl with a fork and pour lemon juice, almond milk, and vegetable oil
- Add all the wet and dry ingredients and combine well and mix in blueberries
- Scoop batter on the ready muffin tray
- Bake for 25 minutes and enjoy

19. Keto almond pancake

Serves: 1— Preparation time: 30 minutes — Meal Type: Breakfast.
NUTRITIONAL VALUE PER SERVING: Calories 430 kcal — Fat 19g — Carbohydrates 3g — Protein 21g

Ingredients
- 1 ½ cups of almond flour
- 3 teaspoons of baking powder
- 1 teaspoon of salt
- 1 tablespoon of stevia
- 1 ¼ cup of almond milk
- 1 egg
- 3 tablespoons of melted ghee
- 2 teaspoons of olive oil

Directions
- Put in dry ingredients and stir.
- In another bowl, mix egg, ghee, and milk together.
- Mix dry ingredients with wet ingredients, whisk well, until no lumps.
- Heat a frying pan, and pour in olive oil to the pan one teaspoon at a time for each pancake.
- Pour in the batter and brown each side equally.
- Serve warm.

20. Keto meatballs

Serves: 3 — Preparation time: 30 minutes — Meal Type: Breakfast.
NUTRITIONAL VALUE PER SERVING: Calories 632 kcal — Fat 43 — Carbohydrates 15g — Protein 49g

Ingredients
- 11 eggs
- 7 ounces of mozzarella cheese
- 4 ounces of chopped and cooked bacon
- 3 chopped scallions
- 1 ounce of ground beef
- Salt
- Pepper
- A teaspoon of olive oil

Directions
- Preheat oven to 350 degrees F, and grease the muffin tray with oil.
- Put the scallions evenly in the tin at the bottom.
- In a bowl, mix eggs and add a teaspoon of oil.
- Add in cheese, salt and pepper to taste. Mix well.
- In another bowl, mix bacon and chicken together.
- Add this meat mixture into cheese and stir well, until combined.
- Pour the mix into the muffin tray and bake for 17-20 minutes.
- Serve ho

21.Mango Chia Pudding

Preparation Time: 5 minutes— Servings: 4

Ingredients
- Chia seeds: 5 tbsp
- Banana: 1
- Mango can in syrup: 400 gm
- Mint leaves: 3 tbsp
- Lime juice: 1

Directions
- Take a blender and add lime juice and mango with syrup
- Blend to make a smooth mixture
- Pour the mixture into a bowl and add in chia seeds
- Shake the mixture well
- Leave the mixture in the fridge overnight
- Next morning, add the mixture in the serving bowls
- Top with mint and chopped banana

22. Keto scrambled eggs

Serves: 1 — Preparation time: 10 minutes — Meal Type: Breakfast.
NUTRITIONAL VALUE PER SERVING: Calories 148 kcal — Fat 15g — Carbohydrates 1.3g — Protein 12g

Ingredients
- 3 eggs
- 1 ounce of ghee
- Salt and pepper

Directions
- Whisk eggs, then add salt and pepper to taste. Mix well.
- Heat oil a skillet, and pour in the egg mixture and scramble until the eggs are cooked.
- Serve hot.

23. Keto flaxseed bread

Serves: 6 — Preparation time: 1-hour — Meal Type: Breakfast.
NUTRITIONAL VALUE PER SERVING: Calories: 199 kcal — Total Fat: 39g — Total Carbs: 8g — Protein: 15g

Ingredients
- 7 egg whites
- 2 egg yolks
- 6 tablespoons of coconut oil or olive oil
- 3 cups of flaxseed
- 3 sachets of Stevia
- 3 teaspoons of baking powder
- 1 teaspoon of salt
- ½ cups of water

Directions
- Preheat the oven to 350˚F.
- Pour in the egg whites, egg yolks, flaxseed, Stevia, oil, salt, water, and baking powder in a mixing bowl, and mix well with a wooden spoon.
- Put into a blender and blend for 2-3 minutes. You can use a hand mixer too.
- Grease a baking pan and line it with parchment paper.
- Pour in the batter in the pan, and bake for 30 minutes. Run the bread test.
- Take out from the oven and let it cool completely on a cake rack before slicing.

24. Keto Omelet

Serves: 1 — Preparation time: 10 minutes — Meal Type: Breakfast
NUTRITIONAL VALUE PER SERVING: Calories 550 kcal —Fat 37g — Carbohydrates 06.7g — Protein 24g

Ingredients
- 3 large eggs
- Salt and pepper
- ½ ounce of butter
- 4 sliced mushrooms
- ½ ounce for olive oil
- 1 ounce of shredded parmesan cheese
- 1 small chopped onion

Directions
- Whisk eggs, and season with salt and pepper, then mix well.
- Heat oil or butter in a frying pan.
- Add in mushrooms and onions and sauté until onions become soft.
- Pour in eggs mixture.
- When egg mixture is firm, then sprinkle cheese on top.
- When the bottom is cooked, flip with a spatula, cook from another side.
- Take out the omelette on a serving plate and enjoy.

25. Liquid cooked oats and skimmed milk

Preparation time: 30 minutes.

NUTRITIONAL VALUE PER SERVING: Calories: 230.9g Fat: 2g; Cholesterol: 18.0 mg; Sodium: 60.8 mg; Potassium: 1.8 mg; Total Carbohydrate: 32.5 g; Dietary Fiber: 7.0 g; Sugars: 6.5 g; Protein :9.1 g

Ingredients:
- ½ cup of Quaker oats
- ½ cup of water
- 1 cup of skimmed milk

Directions
- Pour in oats into a small bowl and put in water to the exact level of the oats
- Cover and leave for 20 minutes
- The oats should absorb the water
- Pour in the soaked oats in a sauce pan
- Put in the cup of skimmed milk
- Put it on a low heat and let it simmer till it becomes thick.
- Serve warm

26. Sugar free light yogurt

Preparation time: 30 minutes.

NUTRITIONAL VALUE PER SERVING: Calories: 50g Fat: 2g; Cholesterol: 11mg; Sodium: 36mg; Potassium: 1.8 mg; Total Carbohydrate: 10g; Sugars: 7g; Protein :3

Ingredients:
- 1 cup grapes
- ¼ cup of Silk Dairy-Free Almond yogurt

Directions
- Steam grapes in for five minutes in very little water
- Turn water and grapes in a cup and remove the skin
- Freeze grapes and complete water
- Blend the grapes until they are halfway smooth
- Put of blender and pour in yoghurt
- Blend well until smooth
- Freeze and enjoy cold

27. Coconut Creamy Acorn Soup

Preparation time: 1 ½ hours.

NUTRITIONAL VALUE PER SERVING. Calories: 250g; Fat: 10g; cholesterol: 1mg; pottasium:992mg; carbohydrates: 29g; 2.7 g fiber: 4g; sugar: 2g protein: 4g

Ingredients:
- 2 tablespoons of olive oil 1 large sliced onion
- 3 acorn squashes [cut and seeded]
- 2 tablespoons of olive oil
- 1 cup of chicken broth
- ½ cup of coconut milk
- 1 tablespoon of ground curry
- 1 basil leaf
- Pinch of salt

Directions
- Cut each acorn squash in half and seed
- Preheat oven to 400 degrees F
- Line a baking sheet and placed it acorns face down on it
- Mix olive oil with a pinch salt
- Rub the olive oil on the acorns
- Bake for 45 minutes
- In a saucepan at medium heat, pour in olive oil and onions
- Stir till soft
- Pour in broth and leave to simmer on low heat for 15 minutes
- Boil for 15 minutes
- While it is boiling, put in milk in a bowl and put in baked acorn squashes
- After 15 minutes, place them in blender and blend till smooth
- Take off fire and let cool
- Serve warm

28. Keto bacon and eggs

Serves: 1 — Preparation time: 10 minutes — Meal Type: Breakfast.

NUTRITIONAL VALUE Per Serving: Calories 212 kcal — Fat 20.3g — Carbohydrates 5g — Protein 19g

Ingredients
- 3 eggs
- Salt and pepper
- 3 spoons of shredded cheese
- 5 ounces of sliced bacon
- 3 spoons of olive oil
- 3 spoons of ghee
- Cherry tomatoes
- Fresh parsley

Directions
- Whisk the eggs, and season with salt and pepper.
- Heat ghee and oil in a pan.
- Put in bacon and sauté for 1 to 2 minutes and take it out and set aside.
- Pour in the eggs in the same pan to cook in the drippings.
- Turn off the heat and toss in the cheese to melt.
- Add bacon, and stir.
- Serve warm.

29.Keto Cream of wheat hot cereal

Servings: 1— Preparation time: 10 minutes.

NUTRITIONAL VALUE PER SERVING: Carbs: 78; Calories: 369; Total Fat: 0.5g; Protein: 11g; Sugar: 0

Ingredients:
- 2 tablespoons of cream of wheat cereal
- 1 cup of skimmed milk
- Pinch of salt

Directions
- In a small bowl, pour in your cream of wheat
- Next, pour in your milk and stir well.
- Pour the mix in a saucepan and bring to boil on a low heat for 5 minutes.
- Turn the fire off and add a pinch of salt.
- Stir thoroughly and serve warm.

30. Chicken breast fillets and peppers

Servings: 1— Preparation time: 10 minutes.
NUTRITIONAL VALUE PER SERVING: Carbs: 10.6; Calories: 211; Total Fat: 3.3g; Protein: 28.1g; Sugar: 0g

Ingredients:
- 1 skinless and boneless chicken
- ½ tablespoon of olive oil
- 1 small sliced onions
- Pinch of salt
- Pinch of thyme
- 1 small red pepper, diced
- 1 small tomato, diced
- ¼ teaspoon of grounded pepper
- 1 teaspoon of chopped parsley
- ¼ teaspoon of chopped oregano
- Low fat cooking spray

Directions
- Pour oil in skillet and heat at medium
- Stir fry till soft
- Pour in red peppers and stir fry

- When they are soft, put in tomatoes
- Add seasonings such as salt, thyme, grounded pepper, oregano, and parsley
- Stir fry for 5 minutes and take off heat and cover
- Spray cooking oil generously in dry pan
- Place chicken in pan and cook on medium heat
- Cook for three minutes on each side
- Take out the fried chicken and place in covered pan with tomatoes and pepper
- Place on fire and cook for three minutes
- Serve hot or warm

31.Keto Open-Faced Bagel Breakfast Sandwich

Preparation time: 5 minutes — Required cooking time: 5 minutes — Servings available: 2.
Nutrition Information (g): Calories (154), Fat (4), Fiber (3.5), Carbs (22.5), Protein (5.1)

Ingredients:
- 1 multigrain bagel, halved
- 2 slices tomato
- 1 cup microgreens
- Freshly ground black pepper
- 2 tablespoons cream cheese, divided
- 1 slice red onion

Directions
- Lightly toast the halved bagel, and then spread a spoonful of cheese cream on toasted bagels.
- Top both halves with tomatoes, greens and onion rings and sprinkle with black pepper.
- Serve and have fun with your breakfast!

32.Avocado Egg Bake

Preparation time: 15 minutes— Required cooking time: 5 minutes — Servings available: 2
Nutrition Information (g): Calories (245), Fat (4.1), Fiber (7.2), Carbs (9.3), Protein (9.1)

Ingredients:
- 1 avocado, halved
- 1 tablespoon chopped parsley
- 2 large eggs
- Freshly ground black pepper

Directions
- Carefully break an egg with the yolk unbroken, meanwhile preheat an oven to 420F.

- With a place baking sheet, line out halved avocado with cut sides down on the sheet, then pour the egg into one half and bake for 17 minutes till egg cooks.
- Once ready, garnish with sprinkled parsley and serve

33.Peach Berry Parfait

Preparation time: 6 minutes— Servings available: 2.
Nutrition Information (g): Calories (190), Fat (10.2), Fiber (14.2), Carbs (13), Protein (12.3)

Ingredients:
- 1 cup plain, unsweetened yogurt, divided
- 1 small peach, diced
- 1 teaspoon vanilla extract
- ½ cup blueberries
- 2 tablespoons walnut pieces

Directions
- In a mixing bowl, prepare a mix of yogurt with vanilla, share into two cups.
- Share the diced peach into each cup and garnish with walnut pieces to serve

34.Green Breakfast Soup

Preparation time: 6 minutes— Preparation cooking time: 5 minutes— Servings available: 2
Nutrition Information (g): Calories (220), Fat (18.2), Fiber (11.2), Carbs (13), Protein (5.3)

Ingredients:
- 2 cups spinach
- 1 avocado, halved
- Freshly ground black pepper
- 2 cups low-sodium vegetable or chicken broth (see Lower sodium tip)
- 1 teaspoon ground turmeric
- 1 teaspoon ground coriander
- 1 teaspoon ground cumin

Directions
- Using a blender, blend the combination of spinach, cumin, broth, coriander, and turmeric to a smooth paste.
- Heat mixture using medium heat for 3 minutes and serve.

35.Bean Sprout Salad

Preparation time: 10 - 15 minutes— Required cooking time: 5 minutes — Servings available: 2
Nutrition Information (g): Calories (170), Fat (5), Fiber (9), Carbs (18), Protein (7)

Ingredients:
- Lemon juice (1 tablespoon)
- Salt & Black pepper (A pinch)
- Chaat masala (1 tablespoon)
- Olive oil (1 tablespoon)
- 10 Minted leaves (Chopped)
- ½ Cup Yellow onions (Chopped)
- 1 Cucumber (Sliced)
- 1/3 cup Carrot (Grated)
- 1/3 Cup Tomato (Cubed)
- 1 ½ Cups of Bean sprouts (Soaked and drained after 12 hours)

Directions:
- Heat up a pan with medium heat and add the Olive oil.
- After a minute of heating, pour in the drained Bean sprouts, toss a bit and cook for a minute.
- Pour in other ingredients (sliced cucumber, cubed tomato, grated carrot, chaat masala, chopped onions & minted leaves, lemon juice, salt and pepper).
- Toss and cook for a minute.

36.Grilled Vegetables

Preparation time: 6 - 7 minutes— Required cooking time: 18 minutes — Servings available: 4
Nutrition Information (g): Calories (48), Fat (5), Fiber (10), Carbs (7), Protein (9)

Ingredients:
- 1/4 red bell pepper (diced)
- 1/4 yellow bell pepper (diced)
- 1/4 green bell pepper (diced)
- 1/4 zucchini (diced)
- 1/4 red onion (diced)
- 1 teaspoon thyme, fresh or dried
- 1 teaspoon oregano
- 1 teaspoon extra virgin olive oil

Directions:
- Heat up the broiler to medium-high temperature.
- Soak diced vegetables in warm water before use.
- Mix up vegetables with oil and herbs in an oven dish and toss mixture.
- Cook under the broiler for about 12 minutes till vegetables are a bit grilled.

37.Winter Berry Smoothie

Preparation time: 7 - 8 minutes— Required cooking time: 130 minutes — Servings available: 4
Nutrition Information (g): Calories (21), Fat (2), Fiber (8), Carbs (6), Protein (5)

Ingredients:
- 2 cups of water
- 1/4 cup cranberries
- 1/4 cup cherries (pitted)
- 1/4 cup blackberries

Directions:
- Add all cups of berries into a blender/smoothie maker.
- Blend to a smooth texture.
- Voila! Enjoy your rich breakfast.

38.Kidney friendly Porridge

Preparation time: 7 - 8 minutes— Required cooking time: 12 minutes — Servings available: 2
Nutrition Information (g): Calories (215), Fat (3), Fiber (8), Carbs (45), Protein (6)

Ingredients:
- ½ cup cream wheat farina
- ½ cup canned pears (Sliced and drained)
- 1cup water

Directions:
- Add a pinch of ground nutmeg to boiling water in a saucepan.
- Stop heating and gently add the cream wheat, while stirring till you have a good mix.
- Heat up the mixture and allow to boil.
- Reduce the heat and allow to cook for 4 minutes till it forms a thick texture.
- Add up canned pears and stir through.

39.Apple Chips

Preparation Time: 10 minutes— Cook Time: 1 hour— Servings: 4

Ingredients
- Apple: 2
- Cinnamon powder: as per your need

Directions
- Preheat the oven to 110C
- Use an apple corer to core the apples
- Make ¼ inch slices of apple in a slicer
- Take a baking sheet and line with parchment paper
- Add the apple slices to the sheet and sprinkle cinnamon powder
- Bake them for over one hour and make them crispy
- Cool them down after removing from the oven and place in the airtight container
- They can be consumed for over three days

40.Pan

Preparation time: 7 - 8 minutes— Required cooking time: 20 minutes — Servings available: 4
Nutrition Information (g): Calories (91), Fat (3), Fiber (8), Carbs (4), Protein (13)

Ingredients
- 2 egg whites
- 1/2 cup spinach leaves (washed)
- 1 tablespoon coconut oil
- 1 red bell pepper (diced)
- 4 oz skinless turkey breast (cooked)
- 1 teaspoon oregano
- 1/4 cup scallions

Directions
- Heat up the broiler to medium-high temperature.
- Add coconut oil into an oven with skillet proof and allow to heat till melted.
- Add the turkey, pepper, sauté and allow to heat for 14 minutes till it gets a soft texture.
- Pour in the spinach, egg whites, oregano and scallions, and mix for 5 minutes.
- Enjoy your meal!

41.Zucchini and Egg Bowl

Preparation time: 8 - 9 minutes— Required cooking time: 125 minutes — Servings available: 4
Nutrition Information (g): Calories (212), Fat (4), Fiber (8), Carbs (18), Protein (7)

Ingredients
- Salt and black pepper (a pinch)
- 4 tablespoons olive oil
- 2 tablespoons water
- 1 small avocado (pitted, peeled and chopped)
- 2 zucchinis (cut with a spiralizer)
- 2 eggs (whisked)
- 2 tablespoons green onions (chopped)
- 2 garlic cloves (minced)
- 2 sweet potatoes (Peeled and cubed)

Directions
- Heat up a pan with olive oil added using medium heat.
- Pour in the chopped green onions, a pinch of salt and black pepper then stir and allow to cook for 5 minutes.
- Reduce heat.
- Add whisked eggs, water, cubed potatoes, cut zucchinis then toss and cook covered on high heat for 120 minutes.
- To serve, share mix into bowls and add avocado pieces to each, breakfast is served!

42.Veggies Mix of Colors

Preparation time: 10 - 11 minutes— Required cooking time: 2 minutes — Servings available: 4
Nutrition Information (g): Calories (185), Fat (4), Fiber (8), Carbs (18), Protein (7)

Ingredients
- 1½ cups coconut cream
- 2 tablespoons olive oil
- 1 garlic clove (minced)
- ¼ cup parsley (chopped)
- 1 jalapeno (chopped)
- 1 cup beans sprouts (soaked for 12 hours and drained)
- 1½ cups cucumbers (sliced)
- Handful basil (chopped)
- Salt and black pepper (a pinch)
- ½ cup of coconut milk
- 2 teaspoons white vinegar
- 1 teaspoon dill (chopped)
- 1 handful chives (chopped)
- 1 cup quinoa (cooked)
- 2 cups cherry tomatoes (halved)
- 1 tablespoon almonds (crushed)
- 2 avocados (peeled, pitted and cubed)

Directions
- In a salad bowl, mix the quinoa with tomatoes, cucumbers, bean sprouts, basil, avocados, salt and pepper.
- In another bowl, whisk the oil with jalapeno, chives, parsley, dill, garlic, vinegar, coconut milk and cream.
- Add your mix into the salad mix and toss.
- Your breakfast is served!

43.Chilli Veggie and Quinoa Bowl

Preparation time: 10 - 11 minutes— Required cooking time: 2 minutes — Servings available: 2
Nutrition Information (g): Calories (175), Fat (4), Fiber (7), Carbs (11), Protein (7)

Ingredients
- 1 teaspoon sesame oil
- 1 teaspoon chilli paste
- ½ cup quinoa (cooked)
- 1 sweet potato (peeled, cooked and cubed)
- 1 bunch broccolini (steamed)
- 2 tablespoons orange juice
- 2 carrots (shredded)
- ¼ cup pomegranate seeds
- A handful bean sprouts (soaked for 12 hours, drained)
- 1 teaspoon sesame seeds
- 1 tablespoon olive oil
- 1 teaspoon white vinegar
- 1 scallion (chopped)

Directions
- Take a salad bowl and add the scallion with the sweet potato, broccolini, carrots, bean sprouts, pomegranate seeds, quinoa, oil and sesame seeds.
- In another bowl, whisk the sesame oil with chili paste, orange juice and vinegar.
- Add the chilli mix with salad and toss together.
- Breakfast is served!

44.Swiss Chard Bowls

Preparation time: 10 - 11 minutes— Required cooking time: 6 minutes — Servings available: 4
Nutrition Information (g): Calories (203), Fat (4), Fiber (6), Carbs (14), Protein (7)

Ingredients
- 1 garlic clove (minced)
- 1 cup quinoa (cooked)
- 1 carrot (shredded)
- 1 roasted red pepper (cubed)
- 2 teaspoons lemon juice
- 4 eggs (fried)
- 1 bunch Swiss chard (chopped)
- 2 teaspoons of olive oil
- ½ cup cherry tomatoes (halved)
- 1 green onion (chopped)
- Salt and black pepper (A pinch)

Directions
- Heat up a pan with olive oil added using medium heat.
- Add up the chard and allow to cook for 3 minutes.
- Pour in the onions, garlic, red pepper, tomatoes, carrot with a pinch of salt and pepper.
- Toss a bot and allow to cook for 3-4 minutes more.
- Pour in the lemon juice and quinoa then cook for 60 seconds.
- Divide into bowls and top each with a fried egg.
- Enjoy your dish!

45.Rosemary Oats

Preparation time: 9 - 10 minutes— Required cooking time: 18 minutes — Servings available: 2
Nutrition Information (g): Calories (203), Fat (4), Fiber (6), Carbs (14), Protein (7)

Ingredients:
- Salt and black pepper (A pinch)
- ½ cup oats
- ½ cup of water
- ½ teaspoon coconut oil (melted)
- ½ cup almond milk (unsweetened)
- ½ cup chopped onion
- ½ cup chopped collard greens
- ½ cup chopped tomato
- ½ cup sliced white mushrooms
- ½ tablespoon chopped rosemary

Directions
- Heat up a pan with coconut oil added using medium heat.
- Add the chopped onions, stir and cook for 60 seconds.
- Pour in the collard greens, tomato, rosemary, mushrooms with a pinch of salt and pepper, stir and cook for 5 minutes before turning off the heat.
- Take another pot mediumly heated, and heat up continuously with almond milk and water.
- Pour the collard green mix into the pan with the oats, stir and cook for 5 minutes more.
- Serve as desired

46.Fruit and Veggie Mix

Preparation time: 9 - 10 minutes— Required cooking time: 2 minutes — Servings available: 3.
Nutrition Information (g): Calories (140), Fat (4), Fiber (6), Carbs (27), Protein (7)

Ingredients
- 6 lettuce leaves (torn)
- 1 mango (cubed)
- 1 cucumber (sliced)
- 1 tablespoon hemp seeds
- 1 tablespoon lime juice
- 1 teaspoon dates (chopped)
- ½ teaspoon spirulina powder
- 1 cup baby spinach (torn)
- 1 peach (chopped)
- 10 strawberries (halved)
- 1 tablespoon tahini paste
- 1 tablespoon coconut water

Directions
- A simple fresh mix is required with no cooking.
- Startup a mix of tahini paste with water, lime juice, dates and spirulina into a bowl and stir.
- Take another bowl and prepare a mix with spinach, lettuce, mango, peach, cucumber, hemp seeds, peach and strawberries.
- Mix the salad by tossing, add the salad dressing to it and mix again by tossing gently.
- You have your dish!

47.Healthy Salad

Preparation time: 10 - 11 minutes— Required cooking time: 1 minute— Servings available: 2.
Nutrition Information (g): Calories (178), Fat (4), Fiber (6), Carbs (15), Protein (7)

Ingredients
- 1 cucumber (sliced)
- Salt and black pepper (A pinch)
- 2 handfuls cherry tomatoes (halved)
- 1 red bell pepper (cubed)
- Handful parsley (chopped)
- 1 tablespoon olive oil
- 1 avocado (peeled, pitted and cubed)
- Handful basil (torn)
- ¼ cup pine nuts (toasted)

Directions
- In order, add up all needed ingredients into a large bowl, and mix well.
- The dish is ready to be served!

48.Cinnamon Apple Salads

Required cooking time: 11 minutes— Servings available: 2
Nutrition Information (g): Calories (129), Fat (4), Fiber (8), Carbs (13), Protein (5)

Ingredients
- ½ cup chopped apple
- ½ cup chopped mango
- 2 tablespoons raisins
- ¼ cup fat-free plain yogurt
- 1-teaspoon cinnamon
- ½ cup cherry tomatoes
- 6 boiled quail eggs
- ¼ cup fat-free plain yogurt

Directions
- Prepare a mix containing the boiled quail eggs, chopped mango, cherry tomatoes, chopped tomatoes and raisins, then add to the ingredients plain yogurt and mix evenly.
- To serve, sprinkle on the top with cinnamon

49.Almond Pancake Rolls with Apple Syrup

Required cooking time: 15 minutes— Servings available: 2.
Nutrition Information (g): Calories (270), Fat (21), Fiber (2), Carbs (20), Protein (6)

Ingredients
- ¼ cup almond flour
- 3 tablespoons water
- 1 tablespoon granulated sugar
- 2 organic eggs
- 2 tablespoons unsalted butter
- 2 tablespoons maple syrup

Directions
- Prepare a mix containing eggs with water, sugar and flour in a bowl and mix well.
- Using medium heat, heat up a saucepan with butter.
- Pour in 2 full tablespoons of the mixture into the greased saucepan and spread to make a thin omelet. Repeat till the mixture finished.
- Rub the omelets with maple syrup and then roll each omelet.
- Serve once do

50.Mixed Fruit Salads

Required cooking time: 7 minutes— Servings available: 2.
Nutrition Information (g): Calories (280), Fat (2), Fiber (12), Carbs (74), Protein (5)

Ingredients
- 1 fresh apple (diced)
- 1 cup chopped pineapple
- 2 tablespoons lemon juice
- 2 oranges (peeled and chopped)
- 1 ripe mango (peeled and diced)

Directions
- Drizzle diced apples with lemon juice and toss to mix till apple turn brown.
- Add in the chopped orange, diced mango and chopped pineapple into the bowl with the apple, then toss to mix.
- Enjoy.

51.The Beach Boy Omelet

Required cooking time: 15 minutes— Servings available: 1

Ingredients
- 1 teaspoon canola oil
- 2 tablespoon green bell pepper (diced)
- 1 whole egg
- 1 tablespoon soy milk
- 2 sprigs parsley
- 2 tablespoon onion (diced)
- 2 tablespoon shredded frozen hash browns
- 2 egg whites

Directions
- Using medium heat, heat canola oil in a pan and add the diced pepper and onions, cook for 3 minutes, then add the shredded browns and saute for 4 minutes more.
- Whisk the eggs with the soy milk, and pour the mixture into a pan and heat.
- Pour the shredded brown mixture at the center of the cooking omelet and roll up in a solid form.
- Serve by garnishing with sprigs parsley.

52.Blueberry Smoothie Bowl

Servings available: 1

Ingredients:
- 1 cup blueberries, frozen
- 2 tbsp. whey protein powder
- ¼ cup plain fat-free Greek yogurt
- 1/3 cup vanilla almond milk, unsweetened
- 5 raspberries
- 2 strawberries (sliced)
- 1 tbsp. fiber cereal (sliced)
- 2 tsp coconut (shredded)

Directions
- Prepare a blending mix of yogurt, milk, protein powder and blueberries smooth.
- Nicely scoop into a serving bowl and garnish at the top with sliced strawberries, cereal and shredded coconut with toppings of raspberries.

53.Baked Egg Cups

Servings available: 1 egg cup (Giving 12 serves)

Ingredients
- 6 slices of bacon, low sodium
- 1/3 cup bell pepper
- ¼ teaspoon black pepper
- 12 eggs
- 1/3 cup of onion
- 1/3 cup mushrooms

Directions
- Bring the temperature of an oven to 349F and line it with baking sheets.
- Dice the veggies and crumble cooked bacon into the veggies, pour the mix into 12 cups.
- Whisk the eggs with pepper and add into each cup.
- Heat the muffin cups in the oven for 22 minutes till the muffins rise and solidify.
- Enjoy while hot.

54.Keto Coconut Porridge

Serves: 2 / Preparation time: 10 minutes / Cooking time: 5 minutes

Ingredients
- ½ cup unsweetened coconut flakes
- ¼ cup hemp seeds
- 1 tablespoon coconut flour
- ½ cup water
- 1/3 cup unsweetened coconut milk
- 1 teaspoon organic vanilla extract
- 1-2 teaspoons monk fruit sweetener

Directions
- In a pan, add the coconut, hemp seeds, water and coconut milk over medium heat and bring to boil, stirring frequently.
- Simmer for about 2 minutes, stirring continuously.
- Stir in vanilla extract and sweetener and remove from the heat.
- Serve with your desired topping.

- One Serving: Net Carbs: 3.6g; Calories: 198; Total Fat: 15.9g; Sat. Fat: 8g; Protein: 6.7g; Carbs: 8.6g; Fiber: 5g; Sugar: 2g

55.Keto Savory Cheese Muffins

Serves: 12 / Preparation time: 15 minutes / Cooking time: 25 minutes

Ingredients
- 2 cups almond flour
- ½ teaspoon baking soda
- ½ teaspoon dried thyme
- ¼ teaspoon salt
- 1 cup sour cream
- 2 tablespoons unsalted butter, melted
- 2 organic eggs
- 1 cup cheddar cheese, shredded
- ½ cup Muenster cheese, shredded

Directions
- Preheat the oven to 400 degrees F (200 C). Line 12 cups of a muffin tin with paper liners.
- In a bowl, add the flour, baking soda, thyme and salt and mix well.
- In another bowl, add the sour cream, butter and eggs and beat until well combined.
- Add the flour mixture and mix until just combined.
- Add the cheeses and mix until well combined.
- Place the mixture into the prepared muffin cups evenly.
- Bake for about 5 minutes.
- Now, reduce the temperature of oven to 350 degrees F (180 C).
- Bake for about 20 minutes or until top becomes golden brown.
- Remove the muffin tin from oven and place onto a wire rack to cool for about 10 minutes.
- Carefully invert the muffins onto the wire rack and serve warm.

One Serving: Net Carbs: 3.1g; Calories: 231; Total Fat: 20.5g; Sat. Fat: 7.5g;Protein: 9g; Carbs: 5.1g; Fiber: 2g; Sugar: 0.9g
One Serving: Net Carbs: 4g; Calories: 380; Total Fat: 30.3g; Sat. Fat: 11.8g; Protein: 20.7g; Carbs: 6.4g; Fiber: 2.4g; Sugar: 2.3g - Fat 72% / Protein 24% / Carbs 4

56.Keto Cheddar Scramble

Serves: 6 / Preparation time: 10 minutes / Cooking time: 8 minutes

Ingredients
- 2 tablespoons olive oil
- 1 jalapeño pepper, chopped
- 1 small yellow onion, chopped
- 12 large organic eggs, beaten lightly
- Salt and ground black pepper, as required
- 3 tablespoons fresh chives, chopped finely
- 4 ounces cheddar cheese, shredded

Directions
- Heat oil in a large skillet over medium heat and sauté the jalapeño pepper and onion for about 4-5 minutes.
- Add the eggs, salt and black pepper and cook for about 3 minutes, stirring continuously.
- Remove from the heat and immediately stir in the chives and cheese.
- Serve immediately.

One Serving: Net Carbs: 1.9g; Calories: 265; Total Fat: 20.9g; Sat. Fat: 7.8g; Protein: 17.5g; Carbs: 2.3g; Fiber: 0.4g; Sugar: 1.5g

57.Keto Fresh Strawberry Juice

Ingredients
- 2 cups fresh strawberries, hulled and sliced
- 2 cups chilled water
- 1 teaspoon fresh lime juice

Directions
- Add all ingredients in a blender and pulse until pureed finely.

Sugar: 4g

- Through a strainer strain the juice and transfer into glasses.
- Serve immediately.

One Serving: Net Carbs: 5.1g; Calories: 31; Total Fat: 0.3g; Sat. Fat: 0g; Protein: 0.6g; Carbs: 7g; Fiber: 1.9g;

58.Keto Tomato Scramble

Ingredients
- 1/3 cup heavy cream
- 4 large organic eggs
- 2 tablespoons fresh cilantro, chopped finely
- Salt and ground black pepper, as required
- 3 tablespoons butter
- 1 small tomato, chopped
- 1 Serrano pepper, chopped
- 2 tablespoons scallions, sliced thinly

Directions
- In a bowl, add the cream, eggs, cilantro, salt and pepper and beat until well combined.

- In a large nonstick frying pan, melt the butter over medium heat and sauté tomato and Serrano for about 2 minutes.
- Add the egg mixture and cook for about 3-4 minutes, stirring continuously.
- Garnish with the scallions and serve.
- Meal Prep Tip: Transfer the cooled scramble into an airtight container and refrigerate for up to 3 days. Reheat in microwave before serving.

One Serving: Net Carbs: 1.9gg; Calories: 251; Total Fat: 23.2g; Sat. Fat: 12.4g; Protein: 9.2g; Carbs: 2.5g; Fiber: 0.6g; Sugar: 1.5g

59.Keto Greens Smoothie

Ingredients
- 2 cups romaine lettuce, chopped
- 1 cup fresh baby spinach
- 1 cup fresh baby kale
- ¼ cup fresh mint leaves
- 2 tablespoons fresh lemon juice
- 8-10 drops liquid stevia
- 1½ cups water
- ½ cup ice cubes

Directions
- In a blender, place all the ingredients and pulse until smooth.
- Place the smoothie into glasses and serve immediately

One Serving: Net Carbs: 5g; Calories: 36; Total Fat: 0.4g; Sat. Fat: 0.2g; Protein: 2.2g; Carbs: 7g; Fiber: 2g; Sugar: 0.9g

60.Keto Pumpkin Smoothie

Ingredients
- 1/3 cup homemade pumpkin puree
- 1 teaspoon pumpkin pie spice
- 1 teaspoon ground cinnamon
- 8 drops liquid stevia
- 1 teaspoon organic vanilla extract
- 4 ounces cream cheese, softened
- ¼ cup heavy cream
- 1 cup unsweetened almond milk

Directions
- In a blender, place all the ingredients and pulse until smooth.
- Place the smoothie into glasses and serve immediately
- Meal Prep Tip: In 2 mason jars, divide the smoothie. Seal the jars and freeze for 1-2 days. Before serving, thaw the smoothie. Just before serving, in each jar, add a splash of almond milk and stir well.

One Serving: Net Carbs: 4.4g; Calories: 295; Total Fat: 27.3g; Sat. Fat: 16.2g; Protein: 5.6g; Carbs: 7g; Fiber: 2.6g; Sugar: 1.8g

61.Keto Creamy Porridge

Ingredients
- 1½ cups filtered water
- 1/3 cup almond flour
- 2 tablespoons golden flax meal
- Pinch of sea salt
- 2 organic eggs, beaten
- 2 tablespoons heavy cream
- 2 tablespoons Erythritol
- 4 teaspoons butter

Directions
- In a pan, mix together water, almond flour, ground flax and salt over medium-high heat and bring to a boil.
- Reduce the heat to medium and cook for about 2-3 minutes, beating continuously.

- Remove from the heat and slowly, add the eggs, beating eggs continuously.
- Return the pan over medium heat and cook for about 2-3 minutes or until mixture becomes thick.
- Remove from the heat and beat for at least 30 seconds.
- Add the heavy cream, Erythritol and butter and beat until well combined.
- Serve hot.
- Meal Prep Tip: Transfer the porridge in an airtight container and preserve in the refrigerator for up to 3days.

One Serving: Net Carbs: 1g; Calories: 106; Total Fat: 9.8g; Sat. Fat: 3.4g; Protein: 3.8g; Carbs: 2.3g; Fiber: 1.3g; Sugar: 0.3g

62.Keto Coconut Plain Waffle

Serves: 4 / Preparation time: 5 minutes / Cooking time: 15 minutes

Ingredients
- ¾ cup coconut flour
- ½ teaspoon baking powder
- ½ teaspoon baking soda
- 1 pastured egg
- 2 tablespoons butter
- ¾ cup coconut milk

Directions
- Place butter in a microwave-safe bowl then microwave until melted. Let the butter cool for a few minutes.
- Next, combine coconut flour with baking powder and baking soda then stir well.
- Pour coconut milk over the dry mixture then add an egg to the mixture. Beat until incorporated.
- After that, pour melted butter into the mixture then mix well. Let the batter rest for about 5 minutes.
- Preheat a waffle maker then make the waffles according to the machine's instructions.
- Once it is done, remove the waffles from the waffle maker and arrange on a serving dish. Repeat with the remaining batter.
- Serve and enjoy warm.

One Serving: Net Carbs: 2.7g: Calories: 184; Total Fat: 18g; Sat. Fat: 13.9g; Protein: 3g; Carbs: 4.6g; Fiber: 1.9g; Sugar: 1.7g - Fat 88% / Protein 6% / Carbs 6%

Keto Chaffles

63.Rich and Creamy Mini Chaffle

Servings: 2— Preparation Time: 5 minutes— Total Time: 10 minutes

Ingredients
- Eggs: 2
- Shredded mozzarella: 1 cup
- Cream cheese: 2 tbsp
- Almond flour: 2 tbsp
- Baking powder: ¾ tbsp
- Water: 2 tbsp (optional)

Directions
- Preheat your mini waffle iron if needed
- Mix all the above-mentioned ingredients in a bowl
- Grease your waffle iron lightly
- Cook in your mini waffle iron for at least 4 minutes or till the desired crisp is achieved
- Serve hot
- Make as many chaffles as your mixture and waffle maker allow

64.Jalapeno Cheddar Chaffle

Servings: 2— Preparation Time: 4 minutes— Total Time: 10 minutes

Ingredients
- Egg: 2
- Cheddar cheese: 1½ cup
- Deli Jalapeno: 16 slices

Directions
- Preheat a mini waffle maker if needed
- In a mixing bowl, beat eggs and add half cheddar cheese to them
- Mix them all well
- Shred some of the remaining cheddar cheese to the lower plate of the waffle maker
- Now pour the mixture to the shredded cheese
- Add the cheese again on the top with around 4 slices of jalapeno and close the lid
- Cook for at least 4 minutes to get the desired crunch
- Serve hot
- Make as many chaffles as your mixture allows

65.Crispy Zucchini Chaffles

Servings: 2— Preparation Time: 10 minutes— Total Time: 15 minutes

Ingredients
- Zucchini: 1 (small)
- Egg: 1
- Shredded mozzarella: half cup
- Parmesan: 1 tbsp
- Pepper: As per your taste
- Basil: 1 tsp

Directions
- Preheat your waffle iron
- Grate zucchini finely
- Add all the ingredients to zucchini in a bowl and mix well
- Grease your waffle iron lightly
- Pour the mixture into a full-size waffle maker and spread evenly
- Cook till it turns crispy
- Make as many chaffles as your mixture and waffle maker allow
- Serve crispy and hot

66.Simple and Crispy Chaffle

Servings: 2— Preparation Time: 5 minutes— Total Time: 10 minutes

Ingredients
- Cheddar cheese: 1/3 cup
- Egg: 1
- Baking powder: 1/4 teaspoon
- Flaxseed: 1 tsp (ground)
- Parmesan cheese: 1/3 cup

Directions
- Mix cheddar cheese, egg, baking powder, and flaxseed in a bowl
- In your mini waffle iron, shred half of the parmesan cheese
- Grease your waffle iron lightly
- Add the mixture from the step one to your mini waffle iron
- Again shred the remaining cheddar cheese on the mixtures
- Cook till the desired crisp is achieved
- Make as many chaffles as your mixture and waffle maker allow

67.Bacon Cheddar Chaffle

Servings: 2— Preparation Time: 5 minutes— Total Time: 10 minutes

Ingredients
- Bacon bite: As per your taste
- Egg: 1
- Cheddar cheese: 1½ cup

Directions
- Preheat your waffle iron if needed

- Mix all the above-mentioned ingredients in a bowl
- Grease your waffle iron lightly
- Cook in the waffle iron for about 5 minutes or till the desired crisp is achieved

- Serve hot
- Make as many chaffles as your mixture and waffle maker allow

68.EggPlant Cheddar Chaffle

Servings: 2— Preparation Time: 10 minutes— Total Time: 30 minutes

Ingredients
- Eggplant: 1 medium sized
- Egg: 1
- Cheddar cheese: 1½ cup

Directions
- Boil eggplant in water for 15 minutes
- Remove from water and blend to make a mixture
- Preheat your waffle iron if needed

- Mix all the above-mentioned ingredients in a bowl of eggplants
- Grease your waffle iron lightly
- Cook in the waffle iron for about 5 minutes or till the desired crisp is achieved
- Serve hot
- Make as many chaffles as your mixture and waffle maker allow

69.Jalapeno Bacon Swiss Chaffle

Servings: 2— Preparation Time: 10 minutes— Total Time: 15 minutes

Ingredients
- Shredded Swiss cheese: ½ cup
- Bacon piece: 2 tbsp
- Fresh jalapenos: 1 tbsp
- Egg: 1

Directions
- Preheat your waffle iron if needed
- Grease your waffle iron lightly
- Cook the bacon pieces separately in the pan

- Remove from heat and add shredded Swiss cheese and an egg
- Dice fresh jalapenos and add them too
- Mix them all well
- Cook in your waffle iron till you get the desired crisp
- Make as many chaffles as your mixture and waffle maker allow

70.Crispy Bacon Chaffle

Servings: 2— Preparation Time: 5 minutes— Total Time: 10 minutes

Ingredients
- Cheddar cheese: 1/3 cup
- Egg: 1
- Baking powder: 1/4 teaspoon
- Flaxseed: 1 tsp (ground)
- Parmesan cheese: 1/3 cup
- Bacon piece: 2 tbsp

Directions
- Cook the bacon pieces separately in the pan
- Mix cheddar cheese, egg, baking powder, and flaxseed to it

- In your mini waffle iron, shred half of the parmesan cheese
- Grease your waffle iron lightly
- Add the mixture from the step one to your mini waffle iron
- Again shred the remaining cheddar cheese on the mixtures
- Cook till the desired crisp is achieved
- Make as many chaffles as your mixture and waffle maker allow

71.Fried Pickle Chaffle

Servings: 2— Preparation Time: 5 minutes— Total Time: 10 minutes

Ingredients
- Egg: 1
- Mozzarella Cheese: ½ cup (shredded)
- Pork panko: ½ cup
- Pickle slices: 6-8 thin
- Pickle juice: 1 tbsp

Directions
- Mix all the ingredients well together

- Pour a thin layer on a preheated waffle iron
- Remove any excess juice from pickles
- Add pickle slices and pour again more mixture over the top
- Cook the chaffle for around 5 minutes
- Make as many chaffles as your mixture and waffle maker allow
- Serve hot!

72.Crunchy Olive Chaffle

Servings: 2— Preparation Time: 5 minutes— Total Time: 10 minutes

Ingredients
- Cheddar cheese: 1/3 cup
- Egg: 1
- Baking powder: 1/4 teaspoon
- Flaxseed: 1 tsp (ground)
- Parmesan cheese: 1/3 cup
- Olive: 6-8 sliced

Directions
- Mix cheddar cheese, egg, baking powder, and flaxseed together

- In your mini waffle iron, shred half of the parmesan cheese
- Grease your waffle iron lightly
- Add the mixture from the step one to your mini waffle iron
- Add the sliced olives
- Again shred the remaining cheddar cheese on the mixtures
- Cook till the desired crisp is achieved
- Make as many chaffles as your mixture and waffle maker allow

73.Bread Sandwich Chaffle

Servings: 2— Preparation Time: 10 minutes— Total Time: 15 minutes

Ingredients
- Almond flour: 1 tbsp
- Egg: 2
- Mayo: 2 tbsp
- Water: 2 tsp
- Garlic powder: ½ tsp
- Baking powder: 1/8 tsp

Directions
- Put all the ingredients together in a bowl and mix them well
- Preheat your waffle iron if needed
- Grease your waffle iron lightly
- Add the mixture to the waffle iron and spread thoroughly and heat
- Cook till the desired crisp is attained
- Make as many chaffles as your mixture and waffle maker allow

74.Copy Chickfila Sandwich Chaffle

Servings: 2— Preparation Time: 20 minutes— Total Time: 1 hour 30 minutes

Ingredients
- For chicken:
- Chicken Breast: 1
- Parmesan cheese: 4 tbsp
- Dill pickle juice: 4 tbsp
- Pork rinds: 2 tbsp
- Flax seed: 1 tsp (grounded)
- Butter: 1 tsp
- Salt: ¼ tsp or as per your taste
- Black pepper: ¼ tsp or as per your taste
- For Sandwich Bun:
- Egg: 1
- Mozzarella Cheese: 1 cup (shredded)
- Stevia glycerite: 4 drops
- Butter extract: ¼ tsp

Directions:
- Cut chicken into half-inch pieces and add in a ziplock bag with pickle juice
- Keep them together for an hour to overnight
- Preheat the air fryer for five minutes
- In a mixing bowl add all the chicken ingredients and mix well
- Now add the chicken and discard the pickle juice
- Cook the chicken in the air fryer at 400 degrees for 6 minutes from each side and set aside
- Mix all the sandwich bun ingredients in a bowl
- Put the mixture to the mini waffle maker and cook for 4 minutes
- Remove from heat
- Make the chaffle sandwich by adding the prepared chicken in between

75.Chaffle Sandwich with Eggs and Bacon

Servings: 2— Preparation Time: 5 minutes— Total Time: 10 minutes

Ingredients
- For Chaffles:
- Egg: 2
- Cheddar cheese: 1 cup (shredded)
- For Sandwich:
- Bacon strips: 4
- American cheese: 2 slices
- Egg: 2

Directions
- Preheat a mini waffle maker if needed and grease it
- In a mixing bowl, beat eggs and add shredded cheddar cheese to them
- Mix them all well and pour the mixture to the lower plate of the waffle maker
- Close the lid
- Cook for at least 4 minutes to get the desired crunch
- In the meanwhile, cook slices on bacon on medium flame in a large non-stick pan till they turn crispy and pat dry with a paper towel after removing them
- In the same pan, fry eggs
- Remove the chaffle from the heat
- Make as many chaffles as your mixture and waffle maker allow
- Assemble slices of bacon, egg and cheese slice in between the two chaffles and enjoy!

76.Keto Sandwich Chaffle

Servings: 2— Preparation Time: 5 minutes— Total Time: 10 minutes

Ingredients
- Egg: 2
- Cheddar cheese: 1 cup shredded
- Almond flour: 2 tbsp

Directions:
- Preheat a mini waffle iron if needed
- In a mixing bowl, beat eggs and add cheddar cheese to them
- To enhance the texture, add almond flour to it
- Mix them all well and pour to the greasy mini waffle iron
- Cook for at least 4 minutes to get the desired crunch
- Remove the chaffle from the heat and keep aside for around one minute
- Take two chaffles and place your favorite garnishing in between to make a sandwich
- Make as many chaffles as your mixture and waffle maker allow

77.BLT Chaffle

Servings: 2— Preparation Time: 5 minutes— Total Time: 10 minutes

Ingredients
- Egg: 2
- Mozzarella cheese: 1 cup (shredded)
- Green onion: 1 tbsp (diced)
- Italian seasoning: ½ tsp
- Bacon strips: 4
- Lettuce leaves: 2
- Tomato: 1 sliced
- Mayo: 2 tbs

Directions
- Preheat a mini waffle maker if needed and grease it
- In a mixing bowl, beat eggs and add all the ingredients to it
- Mix them all well
- Pour the mixture to the lower plate of the waffle maker and spread it evenly to cover the plate properly
- Close the lid
- Cook for at least 4 minutes to get the desired crunch
- Remove the chaffle from the heat and keep aside for around one minute
- Make as many chaffles as your mixture and waffle maker allow
- Serve with bacon, lettuce, mayo, and tomato in between two chaffles

78.Katsu Chaffle Sandwich

Servings: 2— Preparation Time: 20 minutes— Total Time: 1 hour 30 minutes

Ingredients
- Egg: 2
- Mozzarella cheese: 1 cup (shredded)
- Green leaf lettuce: 2 leaves (optional)
- Ketchup: 2 tbsp (sugar-free)
- Oyster Sauce: 1 tbsp
- Worcestershire Sauce: 2 tbsp
- Swerve/Monkfruit: 1 tsp
- Chicken thigh: 2 pieces boneless or ¼ lb boneless
- Almond flour: 1 cup
- Egg: 1
- Salt: ¼ tsp or as per your taste
- Black pepper: ¼ tsp or as per your taste
- Pork Rinds: 3 oz. unflavored
- Vegetable oil: 2 cups for deep frying
- Brine:
- Water: 2 cups
- Salt: 1 tbsp

Directions
- In a pot, cook the chicken by adding two cups of water to it with salt and bring to boil
- Close the lid of the pot and cook for 30 minutes
- Pat dry the chicken by using a kitchen towel and add salt and black pepper to both sides
- In a mixing bowl, add sugar-free ketchup, oyster sauce, Swerve/Monkfruit, and Worcestershire sauce; combine them well and set aside to put it in the sandwich later
- Grind unflavored pork rinds in a food processor and turn into very fine crumbs
- Take three mixing bowls and add almond flour in 1 bowl, beaten eggs in 1 bowl, and crushed pork rinds to the last one

79.Sausage Biscuits and Gravy Breakfast Chaffle

Servings: 4— Preparation Time: 10 minutes— Total Time: 20 minutes

Ingredients
- Egg: 2
- Mozzarella cheese: 1 cup
- Onion: ¼ tbsp (granulated)
- Garlic: ¼ tbsp (granulated)
- Butter: 2 tbsp
- Garlic: 1 tbsp (finely minced)
- Almond flour: 1 tbsp
- Cornbread starch: 10 drops
- Baking powder: 1 tsp
- Dried parsley: 1 tsp
- Keto sausage biscuit and gravy: 1 batch

Directions
- Preheat a mini waffle maker if needed and grease it
- In a mixing bowl, beat eggs and add all the chaffle ingredients except the last one
- Mix them all well
- Pour the mixture to the lower plate of the waffle maker and spread it evenly to cover the plate properly
- Close the lid
- Cook for at least 4 minutes to get the desired crunch
- Remove the chaffle from the heat and keep aside
- Make as many chaffles as your mixture and waffle maker allow
- Prepare Sausage Gravy recipe and serve with yummy chaffles

80.Mushroom Stuffed Chaffles

Servings: 2— Preparation Time: 15 minutes— Total Time: 40 minutes

Ingredients
- Egg: 2
- Mozzarella Cheese: ½ cup (shredded)
- Onion powder: ½ tsp
- Garlic powder: ¼ tsp
- Salt: ¼ tsp or as per your taste
- Black pepper: ¼ tsp or as per your taste
- Dried poultry seasoning: ½ tsp
- Onion: 1 small diced
- Mushrooms: 4 oz.
- Celery stalks: 3
- Butter: 4 tbsp
- Eggs: 3

Directions
- Preheat a mini waffle maker if needed and grease it
- In a mixing bowl, add all the chaffle ingredients
- Mix them all well
- Pour the mixture to the lower plate of the waffle maker and spread it evenly to cover the plate properly and close the lid
- Cook for at least 4 minutes to get the desired crunch
- Remove the chaffle from the heat and keep aside
- Make as many chaffles as your mixture and waffle maker allow
- Take a small frying pan and melt butter in it on medium-low heat
- Sauté celery, onion, and mushrooms to make them soft
- Take another bowl and tear chaffles down into minute pieces
- Add the eggs and the veggies to it
- Take a casserole dish, and add this new stuffing mixture to it
- Bake it at 350 degrees for around 30 minutes and serve hot

81.Jalapeno Grilled Cheese Bacon Chaffle

Servings: 2— Preparation Time: 15 minutes— Total Time: 20 minutes

Ingredients
- Egg: 2
- Mozzarella Cheese: 1 cup (shredded)
- Jalapenos: 2 sliced with seeds removed along with the skin
- Cream cheese: ½ cup
- Monterey jack: 2 slices
- Cheddar cheese: 2 slices
- Bacon: 4 slices cooked

Directions
- Add over two tablespoons of cream cheese to the half-cut jalapenos
- Bake them for around 10 minutes and set aside
- Preheat a mini waffle maker if needed and grease it
- In a mixing bowl, beat eggs and add mozzarella cheese to them
- Mix them all well
- Pour the mixture to the lower plate of the waffle maker and spread it evenly to cover the plate properly
- Close the lid
- Cook for at least 4 minutes to get the desired crunch
- Remove the chaffle from the heat and keep aside for around one minute
- Make as many chaffles as your mixture and waffle maker allow
- Make a sandwich by placing a slice of Monterey jack, a cheese slice, 2 bacon slice in between two chaffles and enjoy!

21

82.Japanese styled Breakfast Chaffle

Servings: 2— Preparation Time: 5 minutes— Total Time: 10 minutes

Ingredients

- Egg: 1
- Mozzarella Cheese: 1/2 cup (shredded)
- Bacon: 1 slice
- Kewpie Mayo: 2 tbsp
- Green onion: 1 stalk

Directions

- Preheat a mini waffle maker if needed and grease it
- In a mixing bowl, beat an egg and put 1 tbsp of Kewpie Mayo
- Chop green onion and put half of it in the mixing bowl and half aside
- Cut bacon into pieces of ¼ inches and add in the mixing bowl
- Mix them all well

- Sprinkle around 1/8 cup of shredded mozzarella cheese to the lower plate of the waffle maker and pour the mixture over it
- Again sprinkle 1/8 cup of shredded mozzarella cheese to the top of the mixture
- Close the lid
- Cook for at least 4 minutes to get the desired crunch
- Remove the chaffle from the heat and drizzle Kewpie mayo
- Serve by sprinkling the remaining green onions
- Make as many chaffles as your mixture and waffle maker allow

83.Monte Cristo Chaffle:

Servings: 2— Preparation Time: 5 minutes— Total Time: 10 minutes

Ingredients

- Egg: 2
- Cream cheese: 2 tbsp
- Vanilla extract: 1 tbsp
- Almond flour: 2 tbsp
- Heavy cream: 1 tsp
- Cinnamon powder: 1 tsp
- Swerve sweetener: 1 tbsp
- Cheese: 2 slices
- Ham: 2 slices
- Turkey: 2 slices

Directions:

- Preheat a mini waffle maker if needed and grease it
- In a mixing bowl, add all the chaffle ingredients
- Mix them all well

- Pour the mixture to the lower plate of the waffle maker and spread it evenly to cover the plate properly
- Close the lid
- Cook for at least 4 minutes to get the desired crunch
- Remove the chaffle from the heat and keep aside for around one minute
- Make as many chaffles as your mixture and waffle maker allow
- Serve with a cheese slice, a turkey, and a ham
- You can also serve with any of your favorite low carb raspberry jam on top

84.Zucchini Nut Bread Chaffle

Servings: 2— Preparation Time: 5 minutes— Total Time: 10 minutes

Ingredients

- Egg: 1
- Zucchini: 1 cup (shredded)
- Cream Cheese: 2 tbsp softened
- Cinnamon: 1/2 tsp
- Erythritol blend: 1 tsp
- Nutmeg: 1 tbsp (grounded)
- Butter: 2 tsp
- Baking powder: ½ tsp
- Walnuts: 3 tbsp
- Coconut flour: 2 tsp
- Cream cheese: 4 tbsp
- Cinnamon: ¼ tsp
- Butter: 2 tbsp
- Caramel: 2 tbsp (sugar-free)
- Walnuts: 1 tbsp (chopped)

Directions:

- Grate zucchini and leave it in a colander for 10 minutes

- Squeeze with your hands as well to drain much water
- Preheat a mini waffle maker if needed and grease it
- In a mixing bowl, beat an egg, zucchini, and other chaffle ingredients
- Pour the mixture to the lower plate of the waffle maker and spread it evenly to cover the plate properly and close the lid
- Cook for at least 4 minutes to get the desired crunch
- Remove the chaffle from the heat
- Make as many chaffles as your mixture and waffle maker allow
- Whisk all the frosting ingredients together except for walnuts and give a uniform consistency
- Serve the chaffles with frosting on top and chopped nuts

85.Garlic Bread Chaffle

Servings: 2— Preparation Time: 15 minutes— Total Time: 20 minutes

Ingredients

- Egg: 2
- Mozzarella Cheese: 1 cup (shredded)
- Garlic powder: ½ tsp
- Italian seasoning: 1 tsp
- Cream cheese: 1 tsp
- For the Garlic Butter Topping:
- Garlic powder: ½ tsp
- Italian seasoning: 1/2 tsp
- Butter: 1 tbsp
- Mozzarella Cheese: 2 tbsp (shredded)
- Parsley: 1 tbsp

Directions

- Preheat a mini waffle maker if needed and grease it
- In a mixing bowl, add all the ingredients of the chaffle and mix well

- Pour the mixture to the lower plate of the waffle maker and spread it evenly to cover the plate properly and close the lid
- Cook for at least 4 minutes to get the desired crunch
- In the meanwhile, melt butter and add the garlic butter ingredients
- Remove the chaffle from the heat and apply the garlic butter immediately
- Make as many chaffles as your mixture and waffle maker allow
- Put the chaffles on the baking tray and sprinkle the mozzarella cheese on the chaffles
- Bake for 5 minutes in an oven at 350 degrees to melt the cheese
- Serve hot and enjoy

86.Peanut Butter & Jelly Sammich Chaffle

Servings: 2— Preparation Time: 20 minutes— Total Time: 30 minutes

Ingredients
- Egg: 2
- Mozzarella: ¼ cup
- Vanilla extract: 1 tbsp
- Coconut flour: 2 tbsp
- Baking powder: ¼ tsp
- Cinnamon powder: 1 tsp
- Swerve sweetener: 1 tbsp
- Blueberries: 1 cup
- Lemon zest: ½ tsp
- Lemon juice: 1 tsp
- Xanthan gum: 1/8 tsp
- Water: 2 tbsp
- Swerve sweetener: 1 tbsp

Directions
- For the blueberry compote, add all the ingredients except xanthan gum to a small pan
- Mix them all and boil
- Lower the heat and simmer for 8-10 minutes; the sauce will initiate to thicken
- Add xanthan gum now and stir
- Now remove the pan from the stove and allow the mixture to cool down
- Put in refrigerator
- Preheat a mini waffle maker if needed and grease it
- In a mixing bowl, add all the chaffle ingredients and mix well
- Pour the mixture to the lower plate of the waffle maker and spread it evenly to cover the plate properly
- Close the lid
- Cook for at least 4 minutes to get the desired crunch
- Remove the chaffle from the heat and keep aside
- Make as many chaffles as your mixture and waffle maker allow
- Serve with the blueberry compote you prepared and enjoy!

87.Avocado Toast Chaffle

Servings: 2— Preparation Time: 5 minutes— Total Time: 10 minutes

Ingredients
- Egg: 2
- Cheddar cheese: 1 cup
- Whole avocado: 1 whole
- Lemon juice: 1 tsp
- Salt: ¼ tsp or as per your taste
- Black pepper: ¼ tsp or as per your taste

Directions
- Peel avocados, cut and put them in a bowl
- Add salt, black pepper, and lemon juice to them
- Mash them all together with the fork
- Preheat a mini waffle maker if needed and grease it
- In a mixing bowl, beat eggs and add cheddar cheese to them
- Mix them all well and pour the mixture to the lower plate of the waffle maker
- Close the lid
- Cook for at least 4 minutes to get the desired crunch
- Remove the chaffle from the heat and keep aside for around one minute
- Apply the avocado spread to the chaffles and serve
- Make as many chaffles as your mixture and waffle maker allow

88.Cinnamon Chaffle

Servings: 2— Preparation Time: 10 minutes— Total Time: 15 minutes

Ingredients
- Egg: 1
- Mozzarella: ½ cup
- Vanilla extract: 1 tbsp
- Almond flour: 1 tbsp
- Baking powder: ½ tsp
- Cinnamon powder: ½ tsp

Directions
- Preheat your waffle iron if needed
- Mix all the above-mentioned ingredients in a bowl
- Grease your waffle iron lightly
- Cook in the waffle iron for about 5 minutes or till the desired crisp is achieved
- Make as many chaffles as your mixture and waffle maker allow
- Serve hot with your favorite toppings

89.Mc Griddle Chaffle

Servings: 2— Preparation Time: 5 minutes— Total Time: 10 minutes

Ingredients
- Egg: 2
- Mozzarella Cheese: 1½ cup (shredded)
- Maple Syrup: 2 tbsp (sugar-free)
- Sausage patty: 2
- American cheese: 2 slices
- Swerve/Monkfruit: 2 tbsp

Directions
- Preheat a mini waffle maker if needed and grease it
- In a mixing bowl, beat eggs and add shredded mozzarella cheese, Swerve/Monkfruit, and maple syrup
- Mix them all well and pour the mixture to the lower plate of the waffle maker
- Close the lid
- Cook for at least 4 minutes to get the desired crunch
- Remove the chaffle from the heat
- Prepare sausage patty by following the instruction given on the packaging
- Place a cheese slice on the patty immediately when removing from heat
- Take two chaffles and put sausage patty and cheese in between
- Make as many chaffles as your mixture and waffle maker allow
- Serve hot and enjoy!

90.Cinnamon Swirl Chaffle

Ingredients

- Egg: 2
- Cream Cheese: 2 oz softened
- Almond flour: 2 tbsp
- Vanilla Extract: 2 tsp
- Cinnamon: 2 tsp
- Vanilla extract: 2 tsp
- Splenda: 2 tbsp
- Cream cheese: 2 oz softened
- Splenda: 2 tbsp
- Vanilla: 1 tsp
- Butter: 2 tbsp unsalted butter
- For Cinnamon Drizzle:
- Splenda: 2 tbsp
- Butter: 1 tbsp
- Cinnamon: 2 tsp

Directions

- Preheat the waffle maker
- Grease it lightly
- Mix all the chaffle ingredients together
- Pour the mixture to the waffle maker
- Cook for around 4 minutes or till chaffles become crispy
- Keep them aside when done
- In a small bowl, mix the ingredients of icing and cinnamon drizzle
- Heat it in a microwave for about 10 seconds to gain a soft uniformity
- Whirl on cooled chaffles and enjoy!

91.Chicken Mozzarella Chaffle

Ingredients

- Chicken: 1 cup
- Egg: 2
- Mozzarella cheese: 1 cup and 4 tbsp
- Tomato sauce: 6 tbsp
- Basil: ½ tsp
- Garlic: ½ tbsp
- Butter: 1 tsp

Directions

- In a pan, add butter and include small pieces of chicken to it
- Stir for two minutes and then add garlic and basil
- Set aside the cooked chicken
- Preheat the mini waffle maker if needed
- Mix cooked chicken, eggs, and 1 cup mozzarella cheese properly
- Spread it to the mini waffle maker thoroughly
- Cook for 4 minutes or till it turns crispy and then remove it from the waffle maker
- Make as many mini chaffles as you can
- Now in a baking tray, line these mini chaffles and top with the tomato sauce and grated mozzarella cheese
- Put the tray in the oven at 400 degrees until the cheese melts
- Serve hot

92.Chicken Jamaican Jerk Chicken Chaffle

Ingredients

- Egg: 2
- Mozzarella Cheese: 1 cup (shredded)
- Butter: 1 tbsp
- Almond flour: 2 tbsp
- Turmeric: ¼ tsp
- Baking powder: ¼ tsp
- Xanthan gum: a pinch
- Onion powder: a pinch
- Garlic powder: a pinch
- Salt: a pinch
- Organic ground chicken: 1 pound
- Dried thyme: 1 tsp
- Garlic: 1 tsp (granulated)
- Butter: 2 tbsp
- Dried parsley: 2 tsp
- Black pepper: 1/8 tsp
- Salt: 1 tsp
- Chicken broth: ½ cup
- Jerk seasoning: 2 tbsp
- Onion: ½ medium chopped

Directions

- In a pan, melt butter and sauté onion
- Add all the remaining ingredients of chicken Jamaican jerk and sauté
- Now add chicken and chicken broth and stir
- Cook on medium-low heat for 10 minutes
- Then cook on high heat and dry all the liquid
- For chaffles, preheat a mini waffle maker if needed and grease it
- In a mixing bowl, beat all the chaffle ingredients
- Pour the mixture to the lower plate of the waffle maker and spread it evenly to cover the plate properly and close the lid
- Cook for at least 4 minutes to get the desired crunch
- Remove the chaffle from the heat and keep aside for around one minute
- Make as many chaffles as your mixture and waffle maker allow
- Add the chicken in between of a chaffle and fold and enjoy

93.Chicken Green Chaffles

Ingredients

- Chicken: 1/3 cup boiled and shredded
- Cabbage: 1/3 cup
- Broccoli: 1/3 cup
- Zucchini: 1/3 cup
- Egg: 2
- Mozzarella Cheese: 1 cup (shredded)
- Butter: 1 tbsp
- Almond flour: 2 tbsp
- Baking powder: ¼ tsp
- Onion powder: a pinch
- Garlic powder: a pinch
- Salt: a pinch

Directions

- In a deep saucepan, boil cabbage, broccoli, and zucchini for five minutes or till it tenders, strain, and blend
- Mix all the remaining ingredients well together
- Pour a thin layer on a preheated waffle iron
- Add a layer of the blended vegetables on the mixture
- Again add more mixture over the top
- Cook the chaffle for around 5 minutes
- Serve with your favorite sauce

94.Buffalo Chicken Chaffle

Servings: 2— Preparation Time: 5 minutes— Total Time: 10 minutes

Ingredients

- Egg: 2
- Cheddar Cheese: 1 cup
- Buffalo sauce: 4 tbsp or as per your taste
- Softened cream cheese: ¼ cup
- Chicken: 1 cup
- Butter: 1 tsp

Directions

- Heat the butter in the pan and add shredded chicken to it
- Now remove from heat and add buffalo sauce as per your taste
- In a bowl, add cooked chicken, cheddar cheese, softened cream cheese, and eggs
- Mix all the ingredients well
- Preheat the waffle maker and grease it
- Now sprinkle a little cheddar cheese at the lower plate of the waffle maker
- Spread your prepared batter evenly on the waffle maker
- Now add a bit of cheese on the top as well and close the lid
- Heat the chaffle for over 4 minutes or until it turns crispy
- Make as many chaffles as your mixture and waffle maker allow
- Serve hot with extra buffalo sauce

95.Artichoke and Spinach Chicken Chaffle

Servings: 2— Preparation Time: 10 minutes— Total Time: 25 minutes

Ingredients

- Chicken: 1/3 cup cooked and diced
- Spinach: 1/2 cup cooked and chopped
- Artichokes: 1/3 cup chopped
- Egg: 1
- Mozzarella Cheese: 1/3 cup (shredded)
- Cream cheese: 1 ounce
- Garlic powder: ¼ tsp

Directions

- Preheat a mini waffle maker if needed and grease it
- In a mixing bowl, add all the ingredients
- Mix them all well
- Pour the mixture to the lower plate of the waffle maker and spread it evenly to cover the plate properly
- Close the lid
- Cook for at least 4 minutes to get the desired crunch
- Remove the chaffle from the heat and keep aside for around one minute
- Make as many chaffles as your mixture and waffle maker allow
- Serve hot and enjoy!

96.Garlic Chicken Chaffle

Servings: 2— Preparation Time: 10 minutes— Total Time: 25 minutes

Ingredients

- Chicken: 3-4 pieces
- Lemon juice: ½ tbsp
- Garlic: 1 clove
- Kewpie mayo: 2 tbsp
- Egg: 1
- Mozzarella cheese: ½ cup
- Salt: As per your taste

Directions

- In a pot, cook the chicken by adding one cup of water to it with salt and bring to boil
- Close the lid of the pot and cook for 15-20 minutes
- When done, remove from stove and shred the chicken pieces leaving the bones behind; discard the bones
- Grate garlic finely into pieces
- Beat the egg in the mixing bowl, add garlic, lemon juice, Kewpie mayo, and 1/8 cup of cheese
- Preheat the waffle maker if needed and grease it
- Add the mixture to the waffle maker and cook for 4-5 minutes or until it is done
- Remove the chaffles from the pan and preheat the oven
- In the meanwhile, set the chaffles on a baking tray and spread the chicken on them
- After that, sprinkle the remaining cheese on the chaffles
- Put the tray in the oven and heat till the cheese melts
- Serve hot
- Make as many chaffles as you like

97.Chicken Cauli Chaffle

Servings: 2— Preparation Time: 12 minutes— Total Time: 25 minutes

Ingredients

- Chicken: 3-4 pieces or ½ cup when done
- Soy Sauce: 1 tbsp
- Garlic: 2 clove
- Cauliflower Rice: 1 cup
- Egg: 2
- Mozzarella cheese: 1 cup
- Salt: As per your taste
- Black pepper: ¼ tsp or as per your taste
- White pepper: ¼ tsp or as per your taste
- Green onion: 1 stalk

Directions

- Melt butter in oven or stove and set aside
- In a pot, cook the chicken by adding one cup of water to it with salt and bring to boil
- Close the lid of the pot and cook for 15-20 minutes
- When done, remove from stove and shred the chicken pieces leaving the bones behind; discard the bones
- Grate garlic finely into pieces
- In a small bowl, beat egg and mix chicken, garlic, cauliflower rice, soy sauce, black pepper, and white pepper
- Mix all the ingredients well
- Preheat the waffle maker if needed and grease it
- Place around 1/8 cup of shredded mozzarella cheese to the waffle maker
- Pour the mixture over the cheese on the waffle maker and add 1/8 cup shredded cheese on top as well
- Cook for 4-5 minutes or until it is done
- Repeat and make as many chaffles as the batter can
- Sprinkle chopped green onion on top and serve hot!

98.Easy Chicken Halloumi Burger Chaffle

Servings: 2— Preparation Time: 15 minutes— Total Time: 20 minutes

Ingredients
- Egg: 2
- Mozzarella Cheese: 1 cup (shredded)
- Butter: 1 tbsp
- Almond flour: 2 tbsp
- Baking powder: ¼ tsp
- Onion powder: a pinch
- Garlic powder: a pinch
- Salt: a pinch
- Ground chicken: 1 lb
- Onion powder: ½ tbsp
- Garlic powder: ½ tbsp
- Halloumi cheese: 1 cup
- Salt: ¼ tsp or as per your taste
- Black pepper: ¼ tsp or as per your taste
- Lettuce leaves: 2
- American cheese: 2 slices

Directions
- Mix all the chicken patty ingredient in a bowl
- Make equal-sized patties; either grill them or fry them
- Preheat a mini waffle maker if needed and grease it
- In a mixing bowl, add all the chaffle ingredients and mix well
- Pour the mixture to the lower plate of the waffle maker and spread it evenly to cover the plate properly and close the lid
- Cook for at least 4 minutes to get the desired crunch
- Remove the chaffle from the heat and keep aside for around one minute
- Make as many chaffles as your mixture and waffle maker allow
- Serve with the chicken patties, lettuce, and a cheese slice in between of two chaffles

99.Chicken Eggplant Chaffle

Servings: 2— Preparation Time: 15 minutes— Total Time: 25 minutes

Ingredients
- Eggs: 2
- Cheddar cheese: ½ cup
- Parmesan cheese: 2 tbsp
- Italian season: ¼ tsp
- Chicken: 1 cup
- Eggplant: 1 big
- Salt: 1 pinch
- Black pepper: 1 pinch

Directions
- Boil the chicken in water for 15 minutes and strain
- Shred the chicken into small pieces and set aside
- Cut the eggplant in slices and boil in water and strain
- Add a pinch of salt and pepper

- Add all the chaffle ingredients in a bowl and mix well to make a mixture
- Add the boiled chicken as well
- Preheat a mini waffle maker if needed and grease it
- Pour the mixture to the lower plate of the waffle maker and spread it evenly to cover the plate properly
- Add the eggplant over two slices on the mixture and cover the lid
- Cook for at least 4 minutes to get the desired crunch
- Remove the chaffle from the heat and keep aside for around one minute
- Make as many chaffles as your mixture and waffle maker allow
- Serve hot with your favorite sauce

100.Chicken Garlic Chaffle Roll

Servings: 2— Preparation Time: 20 minutes— Total Time: 30 minutes

Ingredients
- Chicken mince: 1 cup
- Salt: ¼ tsp or as per your taste
- Black pepper: ¼ tsp or as per your taste
- Egg: 2
- Lemon juice: 1 tbsp
- Mozzarella Cheese: 1 cup (shredded)
- Butter: 2 tbsp
- Garlic powder: 1½ tsp
- Bay seasoning: ½ tsp
- Parsley: for garnishing

Directions
- In a frying pan, melt butter and add chicken mince
- When done, add salt, pepper, 1 tbsp garlic powder, and lemon juice and set aside

- In a mixing bowl, beat eggs and add mozzarella cheese to them with ½ garlic powder and bay seasoning
- Mix them all well and pour to the greasy mini waffle maker
- Cook for at least 4 minutes to get the desired crunch
- Remove the chaffle from the heat, add the chicken mixture in between and fold
- Make as many chaffles as your mixture and waffle maker allow
- Top with parsley
- Serve hot and enjoy!

101.Halloumi Cheese Chaffle

Servings: 2— Preparation Time: 5 minutes— Total Time: 10 minutes

Ingredients
- Halloumi cheese: 3 oz.
- Pasta sauce: 2 tbsp

Directions
- Make ½ inch thick slices of Halloumi cheese
- Put the cheese in the unheated waffle maker and turn it on

- Cook the cheese for over 4-6 minutes till it turns golden brown
- Remove from heat and allow it to cool for a minute
- Spread the sauce on the chaffle and eat instantly

102.Ginger Chicken Cucumber Chaffle Roll

Servings: 2— Preparation Time: 20 minutes— Total Time: 30 minutes

Ingredients
- Chicken mince: 1 cup
- Salt: ¼ tsp or as per your taste
- Black pepper: ¼ tsp or as per your taste
- Lemon juice: 1 tbsp
- Butter: 2 tbsp
- Garlic juvenile: 2 tbsp
- Garlic powder: 1 tsp
- Soy sauce: 1 tbsp
- Egg: 2
- Mozzarella cheese: 1 cup (shredded)
- Garlic powder: 1 tsp
- Egg: 2
- Mozzarella Cheese: 1 cup (shredded)
- Butter: 1 tbsp
- Almond flour: 2 tbsp
- Baking powder: ¼ tsp
- Salt: a pinch
- Chicken pieces: 2-4
- Ginger powder: ½ tbsp
- Salt: ¼ tsp or as per your taste
- Black pepper: ¼ tsp or as per your taste
- Soy sauce: 1 tbsp
- Spring onion: 1 stalk

Directions
- Boil the chicken in saucepan, when done remove from water and pat dry
- Shred the chicken into small pieces and add all the seasoning and spices
- Finely chop the spring onion and mix with the chicken and set aside
- Preheat a mini waffle maker if needed and grease it
- In a mixing bowl, add all the chaffle ingredients and mix well
- Pour a little amount of mixture to the lower plate of the waffle maker and spread it evenly to cover the plate properly
- Add the chicken mixture on top and again spread the thin layer of mixture and close the lid
- Cook for at least 4 minutes to get the desired crunch
- Remove the chaffle from the heat
- Make as many chaffles as your mixture and waffle maker allow
- Serve hot and enjoy

103.Chicken Jalapeno Chaffle

Servings: 2— Preparation Time: 15 minutes— Total Time: 25 minutes

Ingredients
- Egg: 2
- Cheddar cheese: 1½ cup
- Deli Jalapeno: 16 slices
- Boiled chicken: 1 cup (shredded)

Directions
- Preheat a mini waffle maker if needed
- In a mixing bowl, beat eggs and add chicken and half cheddar cheese to them
- Mix them all well
- Shred some of the remaining cheddar cheese to the lower plate of the waffle maker
- Now pour the mixture to the shredded cheese
- Add the cheese again on the top with around 4 slices of jalapeno and close the lid
- Cook for at least 4 minutes to get the desired crunch
- Serve hot
- Make as many chaffles as your mixture allows

104.Chicken Stuffed Chaffles

Servings: 2— Preparation Time: 15 minutes— Total Time: 40 minutes

Ingredients
- Egg: 2
- Mozzarella Cheese: ½ cup (shredded)
- Garlic powder: ¼ tsp
- Salt: ¼ tsp or as per your taste
- Black pepper: ¼ tsp or as per your taste
- Onion: 1 small diced
- Chicken: 1 cup
- Butter: 4 tbsp
- Salt: ¼ tsp or as per your taste
- Black pepper: ¼ tsp or as per your taste

Directions
- Preheat a mini waffle maker if needed and grease it
- In a mixing bowl, add all the chaffle ingredients
- Mix them all well
- Pour the mixture to the lower plate of the waffle maker and spread it evenly to cover the plate properly and close the lid
- Cook for at least 4 minutes to get the desired crunch
- Remove the chaffle from the heat and keep aside
- Make as many chaffles as your mixture and waffle maker allow
- Take a small frying pan and melt butter in it on medium-low heat
- Sauté chicken and onion and add salt and pepper
- Take another bowl and tear chaffles down into minute pieces
- Add chicken and onion to it
- Take a casserole dish, and add this new stuffing mixture to it
- Bake it at 350 degrees for around 30 minutes and serve hot

105. Easy Chicken Vegetable Chaffles

Servings: 2 Preparation Time: 15 minutes— Total Time: 40 minutes

Ingredients
- Egg: 2
- Mozzarella Cheese: 1 cup (shredded)
- Salt: a pinch
- Chicken pieces: 2-4
- Ginger powder: ½ tbsp
- Salt: ¼ tsp or as per your taste
- Black pepper: ¼ tsp or as per your taste
- Cauliflower: 3 tbsp
- Cabbage: 3 tbsp
- Green pepper: 1 tbsp
- Spring onion: 1 stalk

Directions
- Boil the chicken, green pepper, cauliflower, and cabbage in saucepan, when done strain the water
- Shred the chicken into small pieces and blend all the vegetables and mix them together
- Finely chop the spring onion and mix with the chicken and set aside
- Preheat a mini waffle maker if needed and grease it
- In a mixing bowl, add all the chaffle ingredients and mix well
- Pour a little amount of mixture to the lower plate of the waffle maker and spread it evenly to cover the plate properly
- Add the chicken mixture on top and again spread the thin layer of mixture and close the lid
- Cook for at least 4 minutes to get the desired crunch
- Remove the chaffle from the heat
- Make as many chaffles as your mixture and waffle maker allow
- Serve hot and enjoy

106. Cabbage Chicken Chaffle:

Servings: 2 Preparation Time: 15 minutes— Total Time: 40 minutes

Ingredients:
- Chicken: 3-4 pieces or ½ cup when done
- Soy Sauce: 1 tbsp
- Garlic: 2 clove
- Cabbage: 1 cup
- Egg: 2
- Mozzarella cheese: 1 cup
- Salt: As per your taste
- Black pepper: ¼ tsp or as per your taste
- White pepper: ¼ tsp or as per your taste

Directions:
- Melt butter in oven or stove and set aside
- In a pot, cook the chicken and cabbage by adding one cup of water to it with salt and bring to boil
- Close the lid of the pot and cook for 15-20 minutes
- When done, remove from stove and shred the chicken pieces leaving the bones behind; discard the bones
- Strain water from cabbage and blend
- Grate garlic finely into pieces
- In a small bowl, beat egg and mix chicken, cabbage, garlic, soy sauce, black pepper, and white pepper
- Mix all the ingredients well
- Preheat the waffle maker if needed and grease it
- Place around 1/8 cup of shredded mozzarella cheese to the waffle maker
- Pour the mixture over the cheese on the waffle maker and add 1/8 cup shredded cheese on top as well
- Cook for 4-5 minutes or until it is done
- Make as many chaffles as your mixture and waffle maker allow
- Serve hot!

107. Chicken Zucchini Chaffle

Servings: 2 Preparation Time: 15 minutes— Total Time: 40 minutes

Ingredients
- Chicken: 1 cup boneless pieces
- Zucchini: 1 (small)
- Egg: 2
- Salt: as per your taste
- Shredded mozzarella: 1 cup
- Parmesan: 2 tbsp
- Pepper: as per your taste
- Basil: 1 tsp
- Water: ½ cup

Directions
- In a small saucepan, add chicken with a half cup of water and boil till chicken tenders
- Preheat your waffle iron
- Grate zucchini finely
- Add all the ingredients to zucchini in a bowl and mix well
- Shred chicken finely and add it as well
- Grease your waffle iron lightly
- Pour the mixture into a full-size waffle maker and spread evenly
- Cook till it turns crispy
- Make as many chaffles as your mixture and waffle maker allow
- Serve crispy and hot

108. Chicken Spinach Chaffle

Servings: 2 Preparation Time: 15 minutes— Total Time: 40 minutes

Ingredients
- Spinach: ½ cup
- Chicken: ½ cup boneless
- Egg: 1
- Shredded mozzarella: half cup
- Pepper: As per your taste
- Garlic powder: 1 tbsp
- Onion powder: 1 tbsp
- Salt: As per your taste
- Basil: 1 tsp

Directions
- Boil chicken in water to make it tender
- Shred-it into small pieces and set aside
- Boil spinach in a saucepan for 10 minutes and strain
- Preheat your waffle iron
- Add all the ingredients to boiled spinach in a bowl and mix well
- Now add the shredded chicken
- Grease your waffle iron lightly
- Pour the mixture into a full-size waffle maker and spread evenly
- Cook till it turns crispy
- Make as many chaffles as your mixture and waffle maker allow
- Serve crispy and with your favorite keto sauce

109.Beef Teriyaki Avocado Chaffle Burger

Servings: 2 Preparation Time: 15 minutes— Total Time: 40 minutes

Ingredients

- Egg: 2
- Mozzarella cheese: 1 cup (shredded)
- Avocado: half
- Green Leaf Lettuce: 2 leaves optional
- Ground Beef: ½ lb
- Pork Panko: 1 tbsp
- Salt: ¼ tsp
- Egg: 1
- Salt: ¼ tsp or as per your taste
- Black pepper: ¼ tsp or as per your taste
- Japanese Sake: 2 tbsp
- Soy Sauce: 1 tbsp
- Xanthan Gum: 1/8 tsp
- Swerve/Monkfruit: 1 tbsp

Directions:

- In a saucepan, add Japanese Sake, Soy Sauce, Xanthan Gum, and Swerve/Monkfruit and bring to boil on high heat
- Then lower the heat and cook the mixture for a minute or two and mix continuously
- When Xanthan Gum dissolves, remove from heat and let it cool
- Take a mixing bowl and add ground beef, pork panko, egg, salt, and pepper, and mix with your hands
- When the mixture becomes smooth, turn it into a ball and press it on a plate and make it a patty

- A patty should be over ¼ inch thick and make sure to put your thumb in between the patty so that it doesn't expand upward and retains its shape
- Preheat the grill to 350 degrees and cook the patties from both sides on medium to low heat for 4-5 minutes till patties turn brown
- You can also use a frying pan to fry the patties
- Preheat a mini waffle maker if needed
- In a mixing bowl, beat eggs and add mozzarella cheese to them
- Mix them all well and pour to the greasy mini waffle maker
- Cook for at least 4 minutes to get the desired crunch
- Remove the chaffle from the heat and keep aside
- Make as many chaffles as your mixture and waffle maker allow
- Cut avocado in slices
- Wash green leaf lettuce and dry
- Take two chaffles and arrange a beef patty with the slices of avocado, green lettuce, and teriyaki sauce in between to make a burger
- Serve hot and enjoy

110.Sloppy Joe Chaffle

Servings: 2Preparation Time: 15 minutes— Total Time: 40 minutes

Ingredients

- Ground beef: 1 lb
- Onion powder: 1 tsp
- Tomato paste: 3 tbsp
- Garlic: 1 tsp (minced)
- Chili powder: 1 tbsp
- Cocoa powder: 1 tbsp
- Bone broth: ½ cup
- Coconut aminos: 1 tsp (soy sauce could be used instead)
- Mustard powder: 1 tbsp
- Paprika: ½ tsp
- Swerve brown: 1 tsp
- Salt: ¼ tsp or as per your taste
- Black pepper: ¼ tsp or as per your taste
- Egg: 1
- Cheddar cheese: ½ cup
- Jalapeno: 5 slices (diced)
- Corn extract: ¼ tsp
- Salt: ¼ tsp or as per your taste
- Franks red hot sauce: 1 tsp

Directions

- In a saucepan, add ground beef and sprinkle salt and pepper first
- Now add all the other ingredients and let it simmer
- Preheat a mini waffle maker if needed and grease it
- In a mixing bowl, beat eggs and add cheddar cheese to them with the remaining ingredients
- Pour the mixture to the lower plate of the waffle maker and spread it evenly to cover the plate properly and close the lid
- Cook for at least 4 minutes to get the desired crunch
- Remove the chaffle from the heat
- Make as many chaffles as your mixture and waffle maker allow
- Add the warm Sloppy Joe on top
- Serve hot and enjoy!

111.Beef Strips Chaffle

Servings: 2Preparation Time: 15 minutes— Total Time: 40 minutes

Ingredients

- Egg: 1
- Mozzarella Cheese: ½ cup (shredded)
- Salt: ¼ tsp or as per your taste
- Black pepper: ¼ tsp or as per your taste
- Ginger powder: 1 tbsp
- Beef strips: 8 pieces
- Butter: 2 tbsp
- Salt: ¼ tsp or as per your taste
- Black pepper: ¼ tsp or as per your taste
- Red chili flakes: ½ tsp

Directions

- In a frying pan, melt butter and fry beef strips on medium-low heat

- Add water to make them tender and boil for 30 minutes
- Add the spices at the end and set aside
- Mix all the chaffle ingredients well together
- Pour a thin layer on a preheated waffle iron
- Add beef strips and pour again more mixture over the top
- Cook the chaffle for around 5 minutes
- Make as many chaffles as your mixture and waffle maker allow
- Serve hot with your favorite sauce

112.Beef BBQ Chaffle

Ingredients
- Beef mince: 1/2 cup
- Butter: 1 tbsp
- BBQ sauce: 1 tbsp (sugar-free)
- Almond flour: 2 tbsp
- Egg: 1
- Cheddar cheese: ½ cup

Directions
- Cook the beef mince in the butter and half cup water on a low-medium heat for 20 minutes
- Then increase the flame to reduce water
- Preheat your waffle iron

- In mixing bowl, add all the chaffle ingredients including beef mince and mix well
- Grease your waffle iron lightly
- Pour the mixture to the bottom plate evenly; also spread it out to get better results and close the upper plate and heat
- Cook for 6 minutes or until the chaffle is done
- Make as many chaffles as your mixture and waffle maker allow

113.Beef Eggplant Chaffle

Ingredients:
- Eggs: 2
- Cheddar cheese: ½ cup
- Parmesan cheese: 2 tbsp
- Italian season: ¼ tsp
- Beef mince: 1 cup
- Eggplant: 1 big
- Salt: 1 pinch
- Black pepper: 1 pinch
- Red chili flakes: 1/2 tsp

Directions
- Cook the beef mince with half cup water on medium-low flame for 20 minutes
- Increase the flame afterward to remove excess water
- Cut the eggplant in slices and boil in water and strain
- Add a pinch of salt and pepper with red chili flakes

- Add all the chaffle ingredients in a bowl and mix well to make a mixture
- Add the boiled beef
- Preheat a mini waffle maker if needed and grease it
- Pour the mixture to the lower plate of the waffle maker and spread it evenly to cover the plate properly
- Add the eggplant about two slices on the mixture and cover the lid
- Cook for at least 4 minutes to get the desired crunch
- Remove the chaffle from the heat
- Make as many chaffles as your mixture and waffle maker allow
- Serve hot with your favorite sauce

114.Beef Stuffed Chaffles

Ingredients:
- Egg: 2
- Mozzarella Cheese: ½ cup (shredded)
- Garlic powder: ¼ tsp
- Salt: ¼ tsp or as per your taste
- Black pepper: ¼ tsp or as per your taste
- Onion: 1 small diced
- Beef mince: 1 cup
- Butter: 4 tbsp
- Salt: ¼ tsp or as per your taste
- Black pepper: ¼ tsp or as per your taste

Directions
- Preheat a mini waffle maker if needed and grease it
- In a mixing bowl, add all the chaffle ingredients
- Mix them all well
- Pour the mixture to the lower plate of the waffle maker and spread it evenly to cover the plate properly and close the lid

- Cook for at least 4 minutes to get the desired crunch
- Remove the chaffle from the heat and keep aside
- Make as many chaffles as your mixture and waffle maker allow
- Take a small frying pan and melt butter in it on medium-low heat
- Sauté beef mince and onion and add salt and pepper
- Cook for over 20 minutes
- Take another bowl and tear chaffles down into minute pieces
- Add beef and onion to it
- Take a casserole dish, and add this new stuffing mixture to it
- Bake it at 350 degrees for around 30 minutes and serve hot

115.Jalapeno Beef Chaffle

Ingredients:
- Boiled Beef: ½ cup shredded
- Onion powder: 1/8 tsp
- Garlic powder: 1/8 tsp
- Eggs: 1
- Cheddar cheese: 1/4 cup
- Jalapeno: 1 diced
- Cream cheese: 1 tbsp
- Parmesan cheese: 1/8 tbsp

Directions
- Preheat a mini waffle maker if needed and grease it
- In a mixing bowl, beat an egg and add all the ingredients

- Mix them all well
- Pour the mixture to the lower plate of the waffle maker and spread it evenly to cover the plate properly
- Close the lid
- Cook for at least 4 minutes to get the desired crunch
- Remove the chaffle from the heat and keep aside for around one minute
- Make as many chaffles as your mixture and waffle maker allow
- Serve hot and enjoy!

116.Beef Pickled Sandwich Chaffle
Servings: 2 Preparation Time: 15 minutes— Total Time: 40 minutes

Ingredients
- Chicken Breast: 1
- Parmesan cheese: 4 tbsp
- Dill pickle juice: 4 tbsp
- Pork rinds: 2 tbsp
- Flaxseed: 1 tsp (grounded)
- Butter: 1 tsp
- Salt: ¼ tsp or as per your taste
- Black pepper: ¼ tsp or as per your taste
- Egg: 1
- Mozzarella Cheese: 1 cup (shredded)
- Stevia glycerite: 4 drops
- Butter extract: ¼ tsp

Directions:
- Cut the beef into half-inch pieces and add in a ziplock bag with pickle juice
- Keep them together for an hour to overnight
- In a mixing bowl add all the beef ingredients and mix well
- Now add the beef and discard the pickle juice
- Cook the beef on the frying pan for 6 minutes from each side at low flame and set aside
- Mix all the sandwich bun ingredients in a bowl
- Put the mixture to the mini waffle maker and cook for 4 minutes
- Remove from heat
- Make the chaffle sandwich by adding the prepared beef in between

117.Ginger Beef Chaffle:
Servings: 2 Preparation Time: 15 minutes— Total Time: 40 minutes

Ingredients
- Beef mince: 1 cup
- Salt: ¼ tsp or as per your taste
- Black pepper: ¼ tsp or as per your taste
- Butter: 2 tbsp
- Garlic juvenile: 2 tbsp
- Garlic powder: 1 tsp
- Soy sauce: 1 tbsp
- Water: ½ cup
- Egg: 2
- Mozzarella cheese: 1 cup (shredded)
- Garlic powder: 1 tsp

Directions
- In a frying pan, melt butter and add juvenile garlic and sauté for 1 minute
- Now add beef mince and cook by adding water till it tenders
- Let the water to dry out, when done, add rest of the ingredients and set aside
- In a mixing bowl, beat eggs and add mozzarella cheese to them with garlic powder
- Mix them all well and pour to the greasy mini waffle maker
- Cook for at least 4 minutes to get the desired crunch
- Remove the chaffle from the heat and top with garlic beef
- Make as many chaffles as your mixture and waffle maker allow
- Serve hot and enjoy

118.Easy Beef Burger Chaffle
Servings: 2 Preparation Time: 15 minutes— Total Time: 40 minutes

Ingredients
- Egg: 2
- Mozzarella Cheese: 1 cup (shredded)
- Butter: 1 tbsp
- Almond flour: 2 tbsp
- Baking powder: ¼ tsp
- Salt: a pinch
- Ground beef: 1 lb
- Onion powder: ½ tbsp
- Garlic powder: ½ tbsp
- Red chili flakes: ½ tbsp
- Cheddar cheese: 1 cup
- Salt: ¼ tsp or as per your taste
- Black pepper: ¼ tsp or as per your taste
- Lettuce leaves: 2
- American cheese: 2 slices

Directions
- Mix all the beef patty ingredient in a bowl
- Make equal-sized patties; either grill them or fry them on a medium-low heat
- Preheat a mini waffle maker if needed and grease it
- In a mixing bowl, add all the chaffle ingredients and mix well
- Pour the mixture to the lower plate of the waffle maker and spread it evenly to cover the plate properly and close the lid
- Cook for at least 4 minutes to get the desired crunch
- Remove the chaffle from the heat and keep aside for around one minute
- Make as many chaffles as your mixture and waffle maker allow
- Serve with the beef patties, lettuce, and a cheese slice in between of two chaffles

119.Beef Garlic Chaffle Roll:
Servings: 2 Preparation Time: 15 minutes— Total Time: 40 minutes

Ingredients
- Beef mince: 1 cup
- Salt: ¼ tsp or as per your taste
- Black pepper: ¼ tsp or as per your taste
- Egg: 2
- Lemon juice: 1 tbsp
- Water: 1/2 cup
- Mozzarella Cheese: 1 cup (shredded)
- Butter: 2 tbsp
- Garlic powder: 1½ tsp
- Bay seasoning: ½ tsp
- Parsley: for garnishing
- Cabbage: ½ cup

Directions
- In a frying pan, melt butter and add the beef mince
- Add ½ cup water for the mince to tender
- When done, add salt, pepper, 1 tbsp garlic powder, and lemon juice and set aside
- In a mixing bowl, beat eggs and add mozzarella cheese to them with ½ garlic powder and bay seasoning
- Mix them all well and pour to the greasy mini waffle maker
- Cook for at least 4 minutes to get the desired crunch
- Remove the chaffle from the heat, add the beef mixture in between and fold
- Make as many chaffles as your mixture and waffle maker allow
- Top with parsley and add cabbage in between
- Serve hot and enjoy!

120.Cauli Beef Chaffle:

Servings: 2 Preparation Time: 15 minutes— Total Time: 40 minutes

Ingredients
- Beef fine mince: 1 cup
- Soy Sauce: 1 tbsp
- Garlic: 2 clove
- Cauliflower rice: 1 cup
- Egg: 2
- Mozzarella cheese: 1 cup
- Salt: As per your taste
- Black pepper: ¼ tsp or as per your taste
- White pepper: ¼ tsp or as per your taste
- Green onion: 1 stalk

Directions
- Melt butter in oven or stove and set aside
- In a pot, cook the beef mince by adding one cup of water to it with salt and bring to boil
- Close the lid of the pot and cook for 15-20 minutes
- When done, cook on high flame till the water dries
- Grate garlic finely into pieces
- In a small bowl, beat egg and mix the beef mince, garlic, cauliflower rice, soy sauce, black pepper, and white pepper
- Mix all the ingredients well
- Preheat the waffle maker if needed and grease it
- Place around 1/8 cup of shredded mozzarella cheese to the waffle maker
- Pour the mixture over the cheese on the waffle maker and add 1/8 cup shredded cheese on top as well
- Cook for 4-5 minutes or until it is done
- Repeat and make as many chaffles as the batter can
- Sprinkle chopped green onion on top and serve hot!

121.Beef Zucchini Chaffle

Servings: 2 Preparation Time: 15 minutes— Total Time: 40 minutes

Ingredients
- Zucchini: 1 (small)
- Beef: ½ cup boneless
- Egg: 1
- Shredded mozzarella: half cup
- Pepper: As per your taste
- Salt: As per your taste
- Basil: 1 tsp

Directions:
- Boil beef in water to make it tender
- Shred it into small pieces and set aside
- Preheat your waffle iron
- Grate zucchini finely
- Add all the ingredients to zucchini in a bowl and mix well
- Now add the shredded beef
- Grease your waffle iron lightly
- Pour the mixture into a full size waffle maker and spread evenly
- Cook till it turns crispy
- Make as many chaffles as your mixture and waffle maker allow
- Serve crispy and with your favorite keto sauce

122.Spinach Beef Chaffle

Servings: 2 Preparation Time: 15 minutes— Total Time: 40 minutes

Ingredients
- Spinach: ½ cup
- Beef: ½ cup boneless
- Egg: 1
- Shredded mozzarella: half cup
- Pepper: As per your taste
- Garlic powder: 1 tbsp
- Salt: As per your taste
- Basil: 1 tsp

Directions:
- Boil beef in water to make it tender
- Shred it into small pieces and set aside
- Boil spinach in a saucepan for 10 minutes and strain
- Preheat your waffle iron
- Add all the ingredients to boiled spinach in a bowl and mix well
- Now add the shredded beef
- Grease your waffle iron lightly
- Pour the mixture into a full-size waffle maker and spread evenly
- Cook till it turns crispy
- Make as many chaffles as your mixture and waffle maker allow
- Serve crispy and with your favorite keto sauce

123.Crab Chaffle Roll

Servings: 2 Preparation Time: 15 minutes— Total Time: 40 minutes

Ingredients:
- Crab Meat: 1 ½ cup
- Egg: 2
- Mozzarella Cheese: 1 cup (shredded)
- Lemon juice: 2 tsp
- Kewpie Mayo: 2 tbsp
- Garlic powder: ½ tsp
- Bay seasoning: ½ tsp

Directions
- Cook crab meat if needed
- In a small mixing bowl, mix crab meat with lemon juice and Kewpie mayo and keep aside
- In a mixing bowl, beat eggs and add mozzarella cheese to them with garlic powder and bay seasoning
- Mix them all well and pour to the greasy mini waffle maker
- Cook for at least 4 minutes to get the desired crunch
- Remove the chaffle from the heat, add the crab mixture in between and fold
- Make as many chaffles as your mixture and waffle maker allow
- Serve hot and enjoy!

124.Garlic Lobster Chaffle Roll

Servings: 2 Preparation Time: 15 minutes— Total Time: 40 minutes

Ingredients
- Egg: 2
- Mozzarella Cheese: 1 cup (shredded)
- Bay seasoning: ½ tsp
- Garlic powder: ¼ tsp
- Langostino Tails: 1 cup
- Kewpie Mayo: 2 tbsp
- Garlic powder: ½ tsp
- Lemon juice: 2 tsp
- Parsley: 1 tsp (chopped) for garnishing

Directions:
- Defrost langostino tails
- In a small mixing bowl, mix langostino tails with lemon juice, garlic powder, and Kewpie mayo; mix properly and keep aside
- In another mixing bowl, beat eggs and add mozzarella cheese to them with garlic powder and bay seasoning
- Mix them all well and pour to the greasy mini waffle maker
- Cook for at least 4 minutes to get the desired crunch
- Remove the chaffle from the heat, add the lobster mixture in between and fold
- Make as many chaffles as your mixture and waffle maker allow
- Serve hot and enjoy!

125.Fried Fish Chaffles

Servings: 2 Preparation Time: 15 minutes— Total Time: 40 minutes

Ingredients
- Egg: 2
- Mozzarella Cheese: 1 cup (shredded)
- Bay seasoning: ½ tsp
- Garlic powder: ¼ tsp
- Fish boneless: 1 cup
- Garlic powder: 1 tbsp
- Onion powder: 1 tbsp
- Salt: ¼ tsp or as per your taste
- Black pepper: ¼ tsp or as per your taste
- Turmeric: ¼ tsp
- Red chili flakes: ½ tbsp
- Butter: 2 tbsp

Directions
- Marinate the fish with all the ingredients of the fried fish except for butter
- Melt butter in a medium-size frying pan and add the marinated fish
- Fry from both sides for at least 5 minutes and set aside
- Preheat a mini waffle maker if needed and grease it
- In a mixing bowl, beat eggs and add all the chaffle ingredients
- Mix them all well
- Pour the mixture to the lower plate of the waffle maker and spread it evenly to cover the plate properly
- Close the lid
- Cook for at least 4 minutes to get the desired crunch
- Remove the chaffle from the heat and keep aside for around one minute
- Make as many chaffles as your mixture and waffle maker allow
- Serve hot with the prepared fish

126.Tuna Melt Chaffle

Servings: 2 Preparation Time: 15 minutes— Total Time: 40 minutes

Ingredients
- Egg: 1
- Mozzarella Cheese: 1/2 cup (shredded)
- Tuna: 3 oz without water
- Salt: a pinch

Directions
- Preheat a mini waffle maker if needed and grease it
- In a mixing bowl, mix all the ingredients well
- Pour the mixture to the lower plate of the waffle maker and spread it evenly to cover the plate properly
- Close the lid
- Cook for at least 4 minutes to get the desired crunch
- Remove the chaffle from the heat and keep aside for around one minute
- Make as many chaffles as your mixture and waffle maker allow
- Serve hot and enjoy!

127.Crispy Crab Chaffle

Servings: 2 Preparation Time: 15 minutes— Total Time: 40 minutes

Ingredients
- Egg: 1
- Mozzarella Cheese: ½ cup (shredded)
- Salt: ¼ tsp or as per your taste
- Black pepper: ¼ tsp or as per your taste
- Ginger powder: 1 tbsp
- Crab meat: 1 cup
- Butter: 2 tbsp
- Salt: ¼ tsp or as per your taste
- Black pepper: ¼ tsp or as per your taste
- Red chili flakes: ½ tsp

Directions
- In a frying pan, melt butter and fry crab meat for two minutes
- Add the spices at the end and set aside
- Mix all the chaffle ingredients well together
- Pour a thin layer on a preheated waffle iron
- Add prepared crab and pour again more mixture over the top
- Cook the chaffle for around 5 minutes
- Make as many chaffles as your mixture and waffle maker allow
- Serve hot with your favorite sauce

128.Keto Icecream Chaffle

Servings: 2 Preparation Time: 15 minutes— Total Time: 40 minutes

Ingredients
- Egg: 1
- Swerve/Monkfruit: 2 tbsp
- Baking powder: 1 tbsp
- Heavy whipping cream: 1 tbsp
- Keto ice cream: as per your choice

Directions
- Take a small bowl and whisk the egg and add all the ingredients
- Beat until the mixture becomes creamy
- Pour the mixture to the lower plate of the waffle maker and spread it evenly to cover the plate properly
- Close the lid
- Cook for at least 4 minutes to get the desired crunch
- Remove the chaffle from the heat and keep aside for a few minutes
- Make as many chaffles as your mixture and waffle maker allow
- Top with your favorite ice cream and enjoy!

129.Double Chocolate Chaffle

Servings: 2 Preparation Time: 15 minutes— Total Time: 40 minutes

Ingredients
- Egg: 2
- Coconut flour: 4 tbsp
- Cocoa powder: 2 tbsp
- Cream cheese: 2 oz
- Baking powder: ½ tsp
- Chocolate chips: 2 tbsp (unsweetened)
- Vanilla extract: 1 tsp
- Swerve/Monkfruit: 4 tbsp

Directions
- Preheat a mini waffle maker if needed and grease it
- In a mixing bowl, beat eggs
- In a separate mixing bowl, add coconut flour, cocoa powder, Swerve/Monkfruit, and baking powder, when combine pour into eggs with cream cheese and vanilla extracts
- Mix them all well to give them uniform consistency and pour the mixture to the lower plate of the waffle maker
- On top of the mixture, sprinkle around half tsp of unsweetened chocolate chips and close the lid
- Cook for at least 4 minutes to get the desired crunch
- Remove the chaffle from the heat and keep aside for around one minute
- Make as many chaffles as your mixture and waffle maker allow
- Serve with your favorite whipped cream or berries

130.Cream Cheese Mini Chaffle

Servings: 2 Preparation Time: 15 minutes— Total Time: 40 minutes

Ingredients:
- Egg: 1
- Coconut flour: 2 tbsp
- Cream cheese: 1 oz
- Baking powder: ¼ tsp
- Vanilla extract: ½ tsp
- Swerve/Monkfruit: 4 tsp

Directions:
- Preheat a waffle maker if needed and grease it
- In a mixing bowl, mix coconut flour, Swerve/Monkfruit, and baking powder
- Now add an egg to the mixture with cream cheese and vanilla extract
- Mix them all well and pour the mixture to the lower plate of the waffle maker
- Close the lid
- Cook for at least 4 minutes to get the desired crunch
- Remove the chaffle from the heat
- Make as many chaffles as your mixture and waffle maker allow
- Eat the chaffles with your favorite toppings

131.Choco Chip Cannoli Chaffle

Servings: 4 Preparation Time: 15 minutes— Total Time: 40 minutes

Ingredients:
- Egg yolk: 1
- Swerve/Monkfruit: 1 tbsp
- Baking powder: 1/8 tsp
- Vanilla extract: 1/8 tsp
- Almond flour: 3 tbsp
- Chocolate chips: 1 tbsp
- Cream cheese: 4 tbsp
- Ricotta: 6 tbsp
- Sweetener: 2 tbsp
- Vanilla extract: 1/4 tsp
- Lemon extract: 5 drops

Directions
- Preheat a mini waffle maker if needed and grease it
- In a mixing bowl, add all the chaffle ingredients and mix well
- Pour the mixture to the lower plate of the waffle maker and spread it evenly to cover the plate properly and close the lid
- Cook for at least 4 minutes to get the desired crunch
- In the meanwhile, prepare cannoli topping by adding all the ingredients in the blender to give the creamy texture
- Remove the chaffle from the heat and keep aside to cool them down
- Make as many chaffles as your mixture and waffle maker allow
- Serve with the cannoli toppings and enjoy

132.Cream Cheese Pumpkin Chaffle

Servings: 2Preparation Time: 15 minutes— Total Time: 40 minutes

Ingredients
- Egg: 2
- Cream cheese: 2 oz
- Coconut flour: 2 tsp
- Swerve/Monkfruit: 4 tsp
- Baking powder: ½ tsp
- Vanilla extract: 1 tsp
- Canned pumpkin: 2 tbsp
- Pumpkin spice: ½ tsp

Directions
- Take a small mixing bowl and add Swerve/Monkfruit, coconut flour, and baking powder and mix them all well
- Now add egg, vanilla extract, pumpkin, and cream cheese, and beat them all together till uniform consistency is achieved
- Preheat a mini waffle maker if needed
- Pour the mixture to the greasy waffle maker
- Cook for at least 4 minutes to get the desired crunch
- Remove the chaffle from the heat
- Make as many chaffles as your mixture and waffle maker allow
- Serve with butter or whipped cream that you like!

133.Easy Blueberry Chaffle

Servings: 2 Preparation Time: 15 minutes— Total Time: 40 minutes

Ingredients:
- Egg: 2
- Cream cheese: 2 oz
- Coconut flour: 2 tbsp
- Swerve/Monkfruit: 4 tsp
- Baking powder: ½ tsp
- Vanilla extract: 1 tsp
- Blueberries: ½ cup

Directions
- Take a small mixing bowl and add Swerve/Monkfruit, baking powder, and coconut flour and mix them all well
- Now add eggs, vanilla extract, and cream cheese, and beat them all together till uniform consistency is achieved
- Preheat a mini waffle maker if needed and grease it
- Pour the mixture to the lower plate of the waffle maker
- Add 3-4 fresh blueberries above the mixture and close the lid
- Cook for at least 4 minutes to get the desired crunch
- Remove the chaffle from the heat
- Make as many chaffles as your mixture and waffle maker allow
- Serve with butter or whipped cream that you like!

134.Apple Pie Chayote Tacos Chaffle

Servings: 2 Preparation Time: 15 minutes— Total Time: 40 minutes

Ingredients:
- Egg: 2
- Cream cheese: ½ cup
- Baking powder: 1 tsp
- Vanilla extract: ½ tsp
- Powdered sweetener: 2 tbsp
- Chayote squash: 1
- Butter: 1 tbsp
- Swerve: ¼ cup
- Cinnamon powder: 2 tsp
- Lemon: 2 tbsp
- Cream of tartar: 1/8 tsp
- Nutmeg: 1/8 tsp
- Ginger powder: 1/8 tsp

Directions
- For around 25 minutes, boil the whole chayote; when it cools, peel it and slice
- Add all the remaining filling ingredients to it

- Bake the chayote for 20 minutes covered with foil
- Pour ¼ of the mixtures to the blender to make it a sauce
- Add to chayote slices and mix
- For the chaffles, preheat a mini waffle maker if needed and grease it
- In a mixing bowl, add all the chaffle ingredients and mix well
- Pour the mixture to the lower plate of the waffle maker and spread it evenly to cover the plate properly and close the lid
- Cook for at least 4 minutes to get the desired crunch
- Make as many chaffles as your mixture and waffle maker allow
- Fold the chaffles and serve with the chayote sauce in between

135.Rice Krispie Treat Copycat Chaffle:

Servings: 2 Preparation Time: 15 minutes— Total Time: 40 minutes

Ingredients
- Egg: 1
- Cream cheese: 4 tbsp
- Baking powder: 1 tsp
- Vanilla extract: ½ tsp
- Powdered sweetener: 2 tbsp
- Pork rinds: 4 tbsp (crushed)
- Heavy whipping cream: ¼ cup
- Xanthan gum: ½ tsp
- Powdered sweetener: 1 tbsp
- Vanilla extract: ¼ tsp

Directions
- Preheat a mini waffle maker if needed and grease it
- In a mixing bowl, add all the chaffle ingredients
- Mix them all well

- Pour the mixture to the lower plate of the waffle maker and spread it evenly to cover the plate properly and close the lid
- Cook for at least 4 minutes to get the desired crunch
- Remove the chaffle from the heat and keep aside for around one minute
- Make as many chaffles as your mixture and waffle maker allow
- For the marshmallow frosting, add all the frosting ingredients except xanthan gum and whip to form a thick consistency
- Add xanthan gum at the end and fold
- Serve frosting with chaffles and enjoy!

136.Smores Keto Chaffle:

Servings: 2 Preparation Time: 15 minutes— Total Time: 40 minutes

Ingredients
- Egg: 1
- Mozzarella Cheese: ½ cup (shredded)
- Baking powder: ¼ tsp
- Vanilla extract: ½ tsp
- Swerve: 2 tbsp
- Pink salt: a pinch
- Psyllium husk powder: ½ tbsp
- Dark chocolate bar: ¼
- Keto Marshmallow crème fluff: 2 tbsp

Directions
- Create the keto marshmallow crème fluff
- Beat the egg that much that it will become creamy and further add Swerve brown and vanilla to it and mix well
- Now add cheese to the mixture with Psyllium husk powder, salt, and baking powder and leave chocolate and marshmallow

- Mix them all well and allow the batter to set for 3-4 minutes
- Preheat a mini waffle maker if needed and grease it
- Pour the mixture to the lower plate of the waffle maker and spread it evenly to cover the plate properly
- Close the lid
- Cook for at least 4 minutes to get the desired crunch
- Remove the chaffle from the heat and keep aside for around one minute
- Make as many chaffles as your mixture and waffle maker allow
- Now serve the chaffle with 2 tbsp marshmallow and chocolate bar

137.Maple Iced Soft Cookies Chaffles

Servings: 4 Preparation Time: 15 minutes— Total Time: 40 minutes

Ingredients
- Egg yolk: 1
- Cake batter extract: 1/8 tsp
- Almond flour: 3 tbsp
- Baking powder: 1/8 tsp
- Vanilla extract: 1/8 tsp
- Sweetener: 1 tbsp
- Butter: 1 tbsp
- Nutmeg: for garnishing
- Cinnamon powder: 1 tbsp
- Powdered sweetener: 1 tbsp
- Heavy cream: ½ tsp
- Maple extract: 1/8 tsp
- Water: ½ tsp

Directions
- Preheat a mini waffle maker if needed and grease it

- In a mixing bowl, add all the chaffle ingredients and mix well
- Pour the mixture to the lower plate of the waffle maker and spread it evenly to cover the plate properly and cover the lid
- Cook for at least 4 minutes to get the desired crunch
- Remove the chaffle from the heat and keep aside so it cools down
- Make as many chaffles as your mixture and waffle maker allow
- For the maple icing, add all the icing ingredient and whisk well
- Spread the icing on the chaffle and sprinkle nutmeg and cinnamon on top

138.Pumpkin Cookies Chaffle:

Servings: 4 Preparation Time: 15 minutes— Total Time: 40 minutes

Ingredients
- Egg yolk: 1
- Cake batter extract: 1/8 tsp
- Almond flour: 3 tbsp
- Baking powder: 1/8 tsp
- Vanilla extract: 1/8 tsp
- Sweetener: 1 tbsp
- Butter: 1 tbsp
- Powdered sweetener: 1 tbsp
- Vanilla extract: ¼ tsp
- Water: ½ tsp
- Granular sweetener: 1 tbsp
- Food coloring: 1 drop

Directions
- Preheat a pumpkin waffle maker if needed and grease it
- In a mixing bowl, combine all the chaffle ingredients and mix well
- Pour the mixture to the lower plate of the pumpkin waffle maker and spread it evenly to cover the plate properly
- Close the lid
- Cook for at least 4 minutes to get the desired crunch
- Remove the chaffle from the heat and keep aside so it cools down
- Make as many chaffles as your mixture and waffle maker allow
- For the icing, whisk all the ingredient
- Do the same as above for sprinkles
- Add these toppings to the chaffles and enjoy

139.Pecan Pie Cake Chaffle:

Servings: 2 Preparation Time: 15 minutes— Total Time: 40 minutes

Ingredients
- Egg: 1
- Cream cheese: 2 tbsp
- Maple extract: ½ tbsp
- Almond flour: 4 tbsp
- Sukrin Gold: 1 tbsp
- Baking powder: ½ tbsp
- Pecan: 2 tbsp chopped
- Heavy whipping cream: 1 tbsp
- Butter: 2 tbsp
- Sukrin Gold: 1 tbsp
- Pecan: 2 tbsp chopped
- Heavy whipping cream: 2 tbsp
- Maple syrup: 2 tbsp
- Egg yolk: 2 large
- Salt: a pinch

Directions
- In a small saucepan, add sweetener, butter, syrups, and heavy whipping cream and use a low flame to heat
- Mix all the ingredients well together
- Remove from heat and add egg yolks and mix
- Now put it on heat again and stir
- Add pecan and salt to the mixture and let it simmer
- It will thicken then remove from heat and let it rest
- For the chaffles, add all the ingredients except pecans and blend
- Now add pecan with a spoon
- Preheat a mini waffle maker if needed and grease it
- Pour the mixture to the lower plate of the waffle maker and spread it evenly to cover the plate properly and close the lid
- Cook for at least 4 minutes to get the desired crunch
- Remove the chaffle from the heat and keep aside for around one minute
- Make as many chaffles as your mixture and waffle maker allow
- Add 1/3 the previously prepared pecan pie filling to the chaffle and arrange like a cake

140.German Chocolate Chaffle Cake:

Servings: 2 Preparation Time: 15 minutes— Total Time: 40 minutes

Ingredients
- Egg: 1
- Cream cheese: 2 tbsp
- Powdered sweetener: 1 tbsp
- Vanilla extract: ½ tbsp
- Instant coffee powder: ¼ tsp
- Almond flour: 1 tbsp
- Cocoa powder: 1 tbsp (unsweetened)
- Egg Yolk: 1
- Heavy cream: ¼ cup
- Butter: 1 tbsp
- Powdered sweetener: 2 tbsp
- Caramel: ½ tsp
- Coconut flakes: ¼ cup
- Coconut flour: 1 tsp
- Pecans: ¼ cups chopped

Directions
- Preheat a mini waffle maker if needed and grease it
- In a mixing bowl, beat eggs and add the remaining chaffle ingredients
- Mix them all well
- Pour the mixture to the lower plate of the waffle maker and spread it evenly to cover the plate properly and close the lid
- Cook for at least 4 minutes to get the desired crunch
- Remove the chaffle from the heat and let them cool completely
- Make as many chaffles as your mixture and waffle maker allow
- In a small pan, mix heavy cream, egg yolk, sweetener, and butter at low heat for around 5 minutes
- Remove from heat and add the remaining ingredients to make the filling
- Stack chaffles on one another and add filling in between to enjoy the cake

141.Almond Chocolate Chaffle Cake:

Ingredients
- Egg: 1
- Cream cheese: 2 tbsp
- Powdered sweetener: 1 tbsp
- Vanilla extract: ½ tbsp
- Instant coffee powder: ¼ tsp
- Almond flour: 1 tbsp
- Cocoa powder: 1 tbsp (unsweetened)
- Melted Coconut Oil: 1 ½ tbsp
- Heavy cream: 1 tbsp
- Cream cheese: 4 tbsp
- Powdered sweetener: 1 tbsp
- Vanilla extract: ½ tbsp
- Coconut: ¼ cup finely shredded
- Whole almonds: 14

Directions:

- Preheat a mini waffle maker if needed and grease it
- In a mixing bowl, add all the chaffle ingredients
- Mix them all well
- Pour the mixture to the lower plate of the waffle maker and spread it evenly to cover the plate properly
- Close the lid
- Cook for at least 4 minutes to get the desired crunch
- Remove the chaffle from the heat and keep aside for around one minute
- Make as many chaffles as your mixture and waffle maker allow
- Except for almond, add all the filling ingredients in a bowl and mix well
- Spread the filling on the chaffle and spread almonds on top with another chaffle at almonds – stack the chaffles and fillings like a cake and enjoy

142.Carrot Cake Chaffle

Ingredients
- Carrot: ½ cup (shredded)
- Egg: 1
- Heavy whipping cream: 2 tbsp
- Butter: 2 tbsp (melted)
- Powdered sweetener: 2 tbsp
- Walnuts: 1 tbsp (chopped)
- Almond flour: ¾ cup
- Cinnamon powder: 2 tsp
- Baking powder: 1 tsp
- Pumpkin sauce: 1 tsp
- Cream cheese: ½ cup
- Heavy whipping cream: 2 tbsp
- Vanilla extract: 1 tsp
- Powdered sweetener: ¼ cup

Directions
- Mix all the ingredients together one by one until they form a uniform consistency
- Preheat a mini waffle maker if needed and grease it
- Pour the mixture to the lower plate of the waffle maker
- Close the lid
- Cook for at least 4 minutes to get the desired crunch
- Prepare frosting by combining all the ingredients of the cream cheese frosting using a hand mixer
- Remove the chaffle from the heat and keep aside for around a few minutes
- Make as many chaffles as your mixture and waffle maker allow
- Stack the chaffles with frosting in between in such a way that it gives the look of a cake

143.Peanut Butter Keto Chaffle Cake

Ingredients:
- Egg: 1
- Peanut Butter:: 2 tbsp (sugar-free)
- Monkfruit: 2 tbsp
- Baking powder: ¼ tsp
- Peanut butter extract: ¼ tsp
- Heavy whipping cream: 1 tsp
- Monkfruit: 2 tsp
- Cream cheese: 2 tbsp
- Butter: 1 tbsp
- Peanut butter: 1 tbsp (sugar-free)
- Vanilla: ¼ tsp

Directions
- Preheat a mini waffle maker if needed and grease it
- In a mixing bowl, beat eggs and add all the chaffle ingredients
- Mix them all well and pour the mixture to the lower plate of the waffle maker
- Close the lid
- Cook for at least 4 minutes to get the desired crunch
- Remove the chaffle from the heat and keep aside for around a few minutes
- Make as many chaffles as your mixture and waffle maker allow
- In a separate bowl, add all the frosting ingredients and whisk well to give it a uniform consistency
- Assemble chaffles in a way that in between two chaffles you put the frosting and make the cake

144.Strawberry Shortcake Chaffle

Ingredients
- Egg: 1
- Heavy Whipping Cream: 1 tbsp
- Any non-sugar sweetener: 2 tbsp
- Coconut Flour: 1 tsp
- Cake batter extract: ½ tsp
- Baking powder: ¼ tsp
- Strawberry: 4 or as per your taste

Directions
- Preheat a mini waffle maker if needed and grease it
- In a mixing bowl, beat eggs and add non-sugar sweetener, coconut flour, baking powder, and cake batter extract
- Mix them all well and pour the mixture to the lower plate of the waffle maker
- Close the lid
- Cook for at least 4 minutes to get the desired crunch
- Remove the chaffle from the heat and keep aside for around two minutes
- Make as many chaffles as your mixture and waffle maker allow
- Serve with whipped cream and strawberries on top

145.Italian Cream Chaffle Cake

Servings: 3 Preparation Time: 15 minutes— Total Time: 40 minutes

Ingredients:

- Egg: 4
- Mozzarella Cheese: ½ cup
- Almond flour: 1 tbsp
- Coconut flour: 4 tbsp
- Monkfruit sweetener: 1 tbsp
- Vanilla extract: 1 tsp
- Baking powder: 1 ½ tsp
- Cinnamon powder: ½ tsp
- Butter: 1 tbsp (melted)
- Coconut: 1 tsp (shredded)
- Walnuts: 1 tsp (chopped)
- Cream cheese: 4 tbsp
- Butter: 2 tbsp
- Vanilla: ⅓ tsp
- Monkfruit sweetener: 2 tbs

Directions

- Blend eggs, cream cheese, sweetener, vanilla, coconut flour, melted butter, almond flour, and baking powder
- Make the mixture creamy
- Preheat a mini waffle maker if needed and grease it
- Pour the mixture to the lower plate of the waffle maker
- Close the lid
- Cook for at least 4 minutes to get the desired crunch
- Remove the chaffle from the heat and keep aside to cool it
- Make as many chaffles as your mixture and waffle maker allow
- Garnish with shredded coconut and chopped walnuts

146.Banana Cake Pudding Chaffle

Servings: 2 Preparation Time: 15 minutes— Total Time: 40 minutes

Ingredients

- Cream cheese: 2 tbsp
- Banana extract: 1 tsp
- Mozzarella cheese: ¼ cup
- Egg: 1
- Sweetener: 2 tbsp
- Almond flour: 4 tbsp
- Baking powder: 1 tsp
- Egg yolk: 1 large
- Powdered sweetener: 3 tbsp
- Xanthan gum: ½ tsp
- Heavy whipping cream: 1/2 cup
- Banana extract: ½ tsp
- Salt: a pinch

Directions

- In a pan, add powdered sweetener, heavy cream, and egg yolk and whisk continuously so the mixture thickens
- Simmer for a minute only

- Add xanthan gum to the mixture and whisk again
- Remove the pan from heat and add banana extract and salt and mix them all well
- Shift the mixture to a glass dish and refrigerate the pudding
- Preheat a mini waffle maker if needed and grease it
- In a mixing bowl, add all the chaffle ingredients
- Mix them all well and pour the mixture to the lower plate of the waffle maker
- Close the lid
- Cook for at least 5 minutes to get the desired crunch
- Remove the chaffle from the heat and keep aside for around a few minutes
- Stack chaffles and pudding one by one to form a cake

38

Appetizers

147. Tacos With Bacon And Guacamole

Serves: 2 — Preparation time: 15 minutes — Meal Type: Appetizers.
NUTRITIONAL VALUE PER SERVING: Calories 387 kcal — Protein 11g — Carbs 9g — Fiber 5g — Fat: 35g

Ingredients
- 3 tablespoons diced cooked sweet potatoes
- 2 slices cooked uncured all-natural bacon
- 2 eggs
- 1 tablespoon Brain Octane Oil
- 1 tablespoon grass-fed ghee
- 1 medium organic avocado
- ¼ cup chopped romaine lettuce
- ¼ teaspoon Himalayan pink salt
- Micro cilantro

Directions
- Crack an egg without piercing the yolk, and set aside.
- Heat a small skillet at medium heat level, then add a tablespoon of ghee.
- Pour in your egg and pierce the yolk, and cook from both sides for a minute or two.

It should be solid, but not overcooked. Take out on a paper towel
- Repeat the process with the second egg. You'll now have two yolks that will serve as the cages for your taco.
- Mash avocado in a bowl with light hands. When half done, add Brain Octane oil and Himalayan pink salt.
- Spread the avocado mix evenly on each part of the eggs, then place chopped romaine lettuce evenly on both tacos.
- Spread the diced sweet potatoes evenly on both sides, then put a strip of bacon on each side.
- Place your micro cilantro evenly, then sprinkle some Himalayan pink salt, and fold in half. Enjoy!

148. Chicken Avocado Salad

Serves: 4 — Preparation time: 40 minutes — Meal Type: Appetizer.
NUTRITIONAL VALUE PER SERVING: Calories 256g — Total Fat 49g — Total Carbs 8g — Protein: 19

Ingredients
- 1 pound of boneless chicken thighs
- 4 tablespoons of extra virgin olive oil
- 3 tablespoons of chopped celeries
- 2 tablespoons of cilantro
- 1 large ripe avocado
- 1 ½ teaspoon of oregano
- 1 tablespoon of lemon juice
- ½ cup almond milk ½ cup diced onion
- ½ teaspoon pepper

Directions
- Pour in almond milk in a bowl, add in the oregano, then stir well.

- Slice up the boneless chicken thighs, and rub the slices with the almond milk mixture. Let it sit for 13 to 15 minutes.
- Preheat an oven to 300°F, and line the baking tray with a foil sheet.
- Place the coated chicken slices on the baking tray and bake for 30 to 40 minutes.
- Meanwhile, slice the avocado into cubes, then drizzles some olive oil and lemon juice, and set aside.
- In a salad bowl, mix in the cilantro, chopped celeries, and onion, and sprinkle some pepper, mix well.
- Take out the chicken and garnish with the avocado mix and salad. Serve warm.

149. Keto Philly cheesesteak pockets

Serves: 4 — Preparation time: 40 minutes — Meal Type: Appetizer.
NUTRITIONAL VALUE PER SERVING: Carbs 7.5g — Calories: 439 — Total Fat: 52.2g — Protein: 12.7g

Ingredients
- 4 ounces of cream cheese cut into chunks
- 3 sliced red baby bell peppers
- 3 tablespoons of onion salt
- 2 cups shredded mozzarella cheese low moisture
- 2 tablespoons of grass-fed butter or other healthy fat
- 2 eggs
- 2 tablespoon of no sugar added ketchup
- 2 tablespoons Keto mayo
- 1 sliced yellow onion
- 1 teaspoon of garlic powder
- 1 teaspoon of Italian seasoning
- 1 tablespoon of onion salt
- 1 teaspoon of sea salt
- 1 ½ cups of almond flour
- 1 sliced jalapeno
- 1 teaspoon of sea salt
- 1 teaspoon of ground parsley
- 1 teaspoon of black pepper
- I pound of shaved steak
- 1 tablespoon of Lime Juice
- 1 tablespoon of Sriracha
- Mayo Sauce

`Directions
- Whisk the eggs and set aside.
- Pour mozzarella and cream cheese to a microwave-safe bowl, and place in a microwave for half a minute. Use a spoon or spatula to mix the mozzarella and cream cheese well.

- Add garlic powder, Italian seasoning, and onion salt to the bowl, then the beaten egg, almond flour, and mix thoroughly, until firm like yellowish dough. Set aside.
- Thinly slice your shaved meat.
- Melt butter in a preheated skillet on medium heat.
- Add in the onions, and peppers, and sauté until tender.
- Add shaved meat, and sauté until brown.
- Take off the skillet, and immediately pour in the American cheese and cover. The heat will melt it. After 4 to 5 minutes, stir the contents of the skillet thoroughly.
- Take out the dough and divide into 10 to 12 balls., or depending on your desired size. Flatten each ball with the help of a rolling pin.
- Spread the meat mixture on each flattened ball evenly, ensuring enough space to seal.
- Fold the flattened dough in half, and use a fork to seal the edges.
- Heat the frying oil. When hot enough, carefully place the pockets inside, and fry until golden brown from each side.
- In another bowl, mix the lime juice, No-Sugar-Added Ketchup, sriracha, and mayo. Use a fork to mix well.
- Spread on pockets before serving.

150. Low carb Caesar salad

Serves: 4 — Preparation time: 20 minutes — Meal Type: Appetizer.
NUTRITIONAL VALUE PER SERVING: Calories: 112 — Total Fat: 32g — Total Carbs: 5.0g — Protein: 14.3g

Ingredients
- 1 head of romaine lettuce
- 6 slices of cooked and diced bacon
- ½ cup shredded parmesan cheese
- 5 tablespoons grated parmesan cheese
- 3 teaspoons Worcestershire sauce
- 2 teaspoons fresh lemon juice
- 2 minced anchovy fillets, or anchovy sauce
- 2/3 cup Keto mayonnaise
- ¼ cup sour cream
- 1 minced garlic clove
- 1 teaspoon mustard powder
- Black pepper

Directions
- Slice the lettuce, and mix with cheese and bacon like a normal salad.
- For the dressing, put all the ingredients in a single bowl and mix well.
- Set down your salad and top with as much dressing as you want. Enjoy!

151. Keto Cauliflower And Eggs

Serves: 4 — Preparation time: 20 minutes — Meal Type: Appetizer.
Nutritional Value Per Serving: Calories: 224 kcal — Total Fat: 22g — Total Carbs: 8.2g — Protein: 23.5 g

Ingredients
- 5 hard-boiled eggs
- 2 stalks celery
- 1 ½ cups of Greek yoghurt
- ¼ teaspoon of pepper
- 1 head of cauliflower
- 1 tablespoon of white vinegar
- 1 tablespoon of yellow mustard
- 1 teaspoon of salt
- 1 cup of water
- ¾ of a white onion, diced

Directions
- Chop cauliflower in bite-size pieces, and place it in a pot with a cup of water.
- Drain the cauliflower and set aside
- Dice up the boiled eggs, mix into the cauliflower.
- Dice the celery and onion, then add in the cauliflower and egg mixture.
- Add the Greek yoghurt, pepper, white vinegar, yellow mustard salt, and diced white onion to the mixture, and mix well with a wooden spoon.
- Dish with salt and serve.

152. Zucchini pizza bites

Serves: 4 — Preparation time: 30 minutes — Meal Type: Appetizer.
NUTRITIONAL VALUE PER SERVING: Calories 231 kcal — Protein: 26.7g — Carbs: 4.8g — Fat 74g

Ingredients
- 4 large zucchinis
- 1 cup of tomato sauce
- 2 teaspoon oregano
- 4 cups mozzarella cheese
- ½ cup parmesan cheese
- Low carb pizza toppings of your choice

Directions
- Slice your zucchinis into small pieces, in a quarter of an inch or less.
- Preheat oven to 450°F.
- Line a baking pan or tray with foil set it aside.
- Place zucchini pieces on the pan. Top them with tomato sauce, cheese, oregano, and other low carb toppings you like.
- Bake for five minutes, then broil for five minutes more.
- Serve warm.

153. Egg on avocado

Serves: 3 — Preparation time: 20 minutes — Meal Type: Appetizer
NUTRITIONAL VALUE PER SERVING: Calories: 364 kcal — Total Carbs: 2.5g — Total Fat: 55.5g — Protein: 13.5g

Ingredients
- 1 ½ teaspoon of garlic powder
- ¾ teaspoons of sea salt
- 1/3 cup of Parmesan cheese
- ¼ teaspoon of black pepper
- 4 avocados
- 6 small eggs

Directions
- Preheat muffin tins to 350°F.
- Slice the avocado into half, and take the seed out.
- Mix pepper, salt, and garlic well.
- Generously season your avocado with the above seasoning mix.
- Place the seasoned avocado in the muffin tin; side with the empty hollow facing up.
- Whisk the egg and gently pour in each avocado. If you doubt that avocado has enough space, scrape the inside lightly.
- Finally, sprinkle cheese on top of the avocado.
- Repeat the process for all, then bake for 15 minutes.
- Serve hot.

154. Grilled cauliflower and cheese

Serves: 2 — Preparation time: 30 minutes — Meal Type: Appetizer.
NUTRITIONAL VALUE PER SERVING: Calories: 224 kcal — Total Fat: 22g — Total Carbs: 8.2g — Protein: 23.5 g

Ingredients:
- 65 grams of parmesan cheese
- 13 grams of basil
- 1 cauliflower head
- 1 pinch of salt
- 2 large eggs
- ½ teaspoon of red pepper flakes
- 1 teaspoon of oregano
- 1 teaspoon of garlic
- Keto-friendly toppings

Directions
- Grate cauliflower or process for 5 seconds or less to give the grated effect in a food processor.
- Sprinkle salt and cover for 15 minutes.
- Then, wring out the moisture from the cauliflower. You can do this with a clean towel or light cloth. Simply place it in and squeeze.
- Preheat a skillet on low heat.
- Place cauliflower in a bowl, then add basil, eggs, red pepper flakes, oregano, and garlic, and mix well.
- Mould a spoonful of the mixture into a flat form on the skillet, and let it cook for 7 to 10 minutes from each side.
- Sprinkle the cheese and toppings, and let it melt.
- Serve hot.

155. Coconut Cookies

Serves: 2 — Preparation time: 30 minutes — Meal Type: Appetizer,

NUTRITIONAL VALUE PER SERVING: Calories: 287 kcal — Total Fat: 19g — Total Carbs: 6.5g — Protein: 6.8g

Ingredients:
- 150 grams of peanut butter
- 2 tablespoons of coconut oil
- 13 grams of basil
- 1 teaspoon of vanilla extract
- ½ teaspoon of coconut extract
- 80 grams of unsweetened coconut flake

Directions:
- Preheat oven to 325˚.
- Mix the peanut butter, and oil in a microwave-safe bowl, and microwave for 20-40 seconds to melt it. Mix well.
- Mix in coconut flakes, and cover for ten minutes.
- Roll out the mixture into cookie sizes and place on a cookie sheet.
- Bake for 10-12 minutes, then serve.

156. Italian chicken soup

NUTRITIONAL VALUE PER SERVING: Calories: 202.5kal; protein 15.8g; Carbohydrate: 20.6g; Fat 7g. Preparation time: 40 minutes.

Ingredients:
- 1 pound ground chicken
- Italian seasoned canned stewed tomatoes
- 1 can of rinsed and drained black beans
- ½ teaspoon fresh ground pepper
- 1 packet of Tofu
- 1 can of 99% fat free chicken
- ½ white onion
- ½ bay leaf
- 1 teaspoon salt
- 1 can of un-drained mixed vegetables
- 1 can of un-drained gold and white corn

Directions
- Mix bay leaf, broth and all the vegetables and season with salt and pepper
- Bring to a boil over low heat
- In a non-stick skillet, sauté onions until they become clear
- Add ground chicken, cook well and squeeze in a paper towel to remove all trace of fat
- Take chicken and Tofu and add to the cooking vegetables for about 10 minutes
- Garnish the meal with fresh Basil and baby spinach
- Boil for 30 minutes on low heat
- Strain to remove pieces of meat and vegetables

157. British clam broth

NUTRITIONAL VALUE PER SERVING: Calories: 97.2kal; protein 7.8g; Carbohydrate: 16.2g; Fat 7g Preparation time: 30 minutes

Ingredients:
- ¼ teaspoon liquid smoke
- ¼ teaspoon pepper
- ¼ teaspoon salt
- 1 15 ounce can of evaporated milk (fat free)
- 1 15 ounce can of chicken broth (fat free)
- 1 medium sized fresh potato
- 1, 6 ounce can of undrained clams
- 1 bottle of clam juice (optional)

Directions
- Microwave your potato and chop it into smaller bits
- Mix it pepper, clam juice, milk, chicken broth, liquid smoke and season with salt
- Boil the mixture
- Dice the clams and add to the mixture
- Take off the fire immediately to prevent overcooking of the clams
- Season to taste with salt and pepper
- Boil on low heat for an hour
- Strain out to remove pieces of meat and vegetables

158. Green pea chicken

NUTRITIONAL VALUE PER SERVING: Calories: 120 kal; protein 13.4g; Carbohydrate: 14.4g; Fat 7g.

Ingredients:
- 2 jars of baby green peas
- 4 tablespoons of sour cream (fat free)
- 2 spoons of chicken unjury
- 1/8 teaspoon of nutmeg
- 1/8 teaspoon of salt
- 1 cup half and half (fat free)

Directions
- Wash the fresh green baby peas
- Blend the peas , half and half, and nutmeg to a smooth consistency
- Pour into a cup and microwave for one minute.
- Allow to cool before pouring into blender with unjury chicken protein powder.
- Blend till veru smooth
- Place 2 spoonful's of fat free sour cream on the top before consumption
- Refrigerate to store

159. Baked potato soup

NUTRITIONAL VALUE PER SERVING: 328 calories; 14.8 g total fat; 6.1 g saturated fat; 29 mg cholesterol; 400 mg sodium. 1023 mg potassium; 37.5 g carbohydrates; 2.7 g fiber; 2 g sugar; 14.1 g protein; 422 Preparation time: 50 mins

Ingredients:
- 4 cups reduced-sodium chicken broth
- 2 tablespoons canola oil
- 1 large chopped onion
- ¼ teaspoon freshly ground pepper
- ½ cup reduced-fat sour cream
- ½ cup shredded extra-sharp Cheddar cheese
- 1 ½ pounds medium russet potatoes
- 2 slices bacon

Directions
- Cut each slice of bacon in two
- Pour canola oil in large saucepan and heat on medium heat
- Put in the slices of bacon and fry on medium heat. Turn around until it is crisp. When it is fried and crisp, pick it out and put in paper towel to drain out
- Put in the onions into the oil and stir fry till it is soft
- Pour in potatoes and broth and oil for 15 minutes
- Take potatoes out and blend them until they completely smooth. It should still have chunks
- Put the mashed potatoes back in the pot and pour in sour cream, cheese and pepper
- Boil for 3 minutes

160. Acorn Soup

NUTRITIONAL VALUE PER SERVING: Calories: 210g; Fat: 10g; Cholesterol: 1mg; Potassium:902mg; carbohydrates: 27g; 2.7 g fiber: 4g; sugar; 1.6g protein: 3.7g Preparation time: 1 ½ hours

Ingredients:
- 1 large sliced onion
- 2 tablespoons of canola oil
- 1 ¼ cup of chicken broth
- 1 tablespoon of ground curry
- ¼ teaspoon of black pepper
- 3 acorn squashes
- 2 tablespoons of olive oil

Directions
- Cut each acorn squash in half and seed
- Preheat oven to 400 degrees F
- Line a baking sheet and placed it acorns face down on it
- Mix olive oil with salt
- Rub the olive oil on the acorns
- Bake for 45 minutes
- In a saucepan at medium heat, pour in canola oil and onions
- Stir till light and soft
- Pour in broth and leave to simmer on low heat for 15 minutes
- Put in baked acorn, curry, and pepper
- Boil for 15 minutes
- Take off fire and let cool
- Place in blender and blend till smooth
- Serve warm

161. Tomato soup

NUTRITIONAL VALUE PER SERVING: Calories: 270g; Fat: 9g; carbohydrates: 40g; 2.7 g; sugar; 24g protein: 20.5g Preparation time: 45 minutes

Ingredients:
- 250g of fresh and firm tomatoes
- Salt to taste
- 1 large onion
- 1 tablespoon of curry
- 1 tablespoon turmeric powder
- 1 teaspoon red pepper
- 200 grams of chicken stock
- 3 teaspoons of canola oil

Directions
- Chop up tomatoes and blend alone. Add little water so it is thick and smooth
- Place large saucepan and heat at medium heat
- Pour in oil and then onions
- Stir fry till onions is soft
- Put in curry and pepper
- Pour in stock and close pot
- Allow to boil for 15 minutes
- When cool, blend again if your mixture is not fully smooth

162. Carrot chicken soup

NUTRITIONAL VALUE PER SERVING: Calories: 120g Fat: 10g ; carbohydrates: 15g; protein: 27g; potassium: 148mg Preparation time: 1 ½ hours.

Ingredients:
- 250g of raw and bone-free chicken, no skin
- ½ teaspoon
- 1 small onion, chopped
- 2 stock cubes
- 1 tablespoon of curry
- 1 tablespoon turmeric powder
- 1 teaspoon red pepper
- 1 bay leaf
- 3 carrots
- 4 cups of water

Directions
- Chop chicken in small pieces
- Next, chop the carrot in small pieces
- Place chicken, salt to, carrot, onions, stock cubes, curry, turmeric, pepper in large saucepan
- Pour in water and place on heat
- Let boil for 45 minutes
- When boiled take out chunks of carrot and meat and blend till roughly. Do not let it get smooth
- Put back in pot and boil let simmer on low heat for 3 hours
- Strain to take out all particles

163. Keto Broccoli Salad

Serves: 3 — Preparation time: 20 minutes — Meal Type: Appetizer.
NUTRITIONAL VALUE PER SERVING: Calories: 147 — Total Fat: 21g — Total Carbs: 3.5g — Protein: 6.8g

Ingredients:
- 5 thin slices of bacon
- 1 ½ head of broccoli, cut into bite-size pieces
- ½ of a small red onion
- ¼ cups of shredded Cheddar
- ¼ of toasted and thinly sliced almonds
- 1 teaspoon of chopped chives
- Kosher salt
- Six cups of fat water
- 8 small-sliced boneless and skinned chicken breasts
- 2 tablespoons of apple cider vinegar
- 1/3 cups of Keto mayonnaise
- 1 tablespoon of Keto mustard
- Black pepper
- Kosher salt

Directions:
- Cut the broccoli into tiny sizes
- Add fat water in a pot, add a teaspoon of salt, and let it boil.3
- Meanwhile, add iced water in a large pot.
- When the salted water boils, put in the broccoli florets, and cook for 1-2 minutes.
- Take out the broccoli florets and immerse in the ice water for 2 to 3 minutes, then drain.
- In another bowl, put in chicken breasts, apple cider vinegar, Keto mayonnaise, Keto mustard, black pepper, a pinch of salt, then toss, and put in a refrigerator.
- In another bowl, add in the bacon, broccoli, onions, shredded cheddar, almonds, chives, and a pinch of salt for the salad.
- Toss the refrigerated dressing over the salad before serving.

164. Tuna Stuffed Avocado

Serves: 2 — Preparation time: 15 minutes — Meal Type: Appetizer
NUTRITIONAL VALUE PER SERVING: Calories: 700 kcal — Total Fat: 40g — Total Carbs: 4g — Protein: 30g

Ingredients:
- 2 medium-sized Avocados
- ¼ cup of Keto Mayo
- ¼ cup of grated Parmesan cheese
- 1/3 teaspoons of Paprika
- 1/3 teaspoons of pepper
- ½ cup of cheddar cheese
- 1 tablespoon of Chives
- 1 can tuna
- 1 spoon of olive oil

Directions
- Cut the avocado in two and take out the pit. Set aside.

- Preheat the oven to 350˚.
- Mix the Keto mayo and Tuna, then add oil and stir well.
- Put the mixture in the avocados, and sprinkle with pepper.
- Bake at 300˚for 5 minutes.
- Meanwhile, melt the cheese in a microwave-safe bowl.
- Smear the cheese generously on the avocados.
- Toss chives and Paprika on them, and serve.

165. Keto Chicken-Cheese Salad

Serves: 4 — Preparation time: 30 minutes — Meal Type: Appetizer
NUTRITIONAL VALUE PER SERVING: Calories: 103 kcal — Total Fat: 30g — Total Carbs: 4.8g — Protein: 13.9g

Ingredients:
- ½ head of romaine lettuce
- 6 slices of cooked and diced chicken
- 2 slices of cooked and diced bacon
- ½ cup shredded parmesan cheese
- 5 tablespoons grated parmesan cheese
- 3 teaspoons Worcestershire sauce
- 2/3 cup Keto mayonnaise
- ¼ cup sour cream
- 1 minced garlic clove
- 1 teaspoon Keto mustard

Directions
- Slice the lettuce, and toss in the chicken and bacon.
- Melt cheese in the microwave, and add in the chicken, lettuce and bacon mixture. Toss well.
- For the dressing, put the cheese, sauce, and mayo in a bowl, mix well. Then, add the sour cream, garlic and mustard.
- Add the desired amount of dressing in the salad, and enjoy.

166. Keto Hamburger Salad

Serves: 3 — Preparation time: 25 minutes — Meal Type: Appetizer
NUTRITIONAL VALUE PER SERVING: Calories: 632 kcal — Total Fat: 43g — Total Carbs: 15g — Protein: 49g

Ingredients:
- 1 pound of ground beef
- 2 cloves of ground garlic
- 1 onion
- 3 tablespoons of grass-fed ghee
- 1 sliced avocado
- Arugula
- Basil leaf
- 1 teaspoon of brain octane oil
- 1 large chopped tomato
- 1 tablespoon of olive oil

Directions
- Mix in beef, seasoning, and a teaspoon of brain octane oil. Mix well.

- Dice onions, and put half of the onions in the meat mixture, mix again.
- Shape the meat into patties form.
- Heat oil or ghee in a pan on medium heat.
- Fry the patties, and let each side brown equally.
- Put another pot on the fire, and add olive oil.
- Put in your avocado slices, the remaining onions, arugula and basil leaf and sauté the salad for 1 minute.
- Place patties and salad in a bowl with chopped tomatoes, and serve.

167. Keto tomato and avocado salad

Serves: 3 — Preparation time: 15 minutes — Meal Type: Appetizer
NUTRITIONAL VALUE PER SERVING: Calories: 448 kcal — Total Fat: 40.3g — Total Carbs: 2.8g — Protein: 16.9g

Ingredients:
- 6 cherry tomatoes
- 1 small avocado
- 2 hardboiled eggs
- 2 cups of mixed green salad
- 2 pounds of shredded chicken breast
- 1 ounce of crumbled feta cheese
- ½ cup of cooked and crumbled bacon

Directions
- Dice tomatoes, avocadoes and eggs. Toss them in a bowl together.
- In another bowl, put the green salad mix, then add the cheese, bacon, and chicken, and mix thoroughly.
- Mix in the tomatoes, avocadoes, and egg well.
- Enjoy.

168. Purple Sweet Potato Salmon sushi Roll

Serves: 3 — Preparation time: 15 minutes — Meal Type: Appetizer
NUTRITIONAL VALUE PER SERVING: Calories: 391.25 kcal— Total Fat: 15.5g — Total Carbs: 43.4g— Protein: 11.4g

Ingredients:
- 4 ounces of wild-caught sashimi-grade salmon
- 2 purple sweet potatoes
- 2 Nori sheets
- Brain Octane Oil
- Sushi mat
- Pink Himalayan sea salt
- 1 red bell pepper
- 1 yellow bell pepper
- 1 avocado
- 1 cucumber

Directions
- Steam the potatoes so that the skins will come right off. Then, mash them carefully.
- Dice the peppers in small pieces.
- Thinly slice the salmon.

- Spread the sushi mat and spread a Nori sheet over it.
- With a spoon, spread the mashed sweet potatoes over the Nori sheet.
- Once cooled, spread out a sushi mat.
- Place your salmon and vegetables in the middle of the Nori sheet.
- Roll up the Nori sheet as much as you can. You are aiming for a sushi/burrito look.
- Place the sushi roll onto a cutting board, and with a very sharp knife, cut the roll into sushi pieces. Be mindful, a blunt knife can injure the rolls.
- Sprinkle salt and Brain Octane Oil, then serve.

Main Course and Vegetables

169. Baked Lamb Ribs Macadamia With Tomato Salsa

Serves: 2 — Preparation time: 40 minutes — Meal Type: Main Course or Lunch.
NUTRITIONAL VALUE PER SERVING: Calories: 241 kcal— Total Fat: 22.1g — Total Carbs: 1.5g— Protein: 10.1g

Ingredients:

- ½ pound of fresh lamb ribs
- ½ cup of cherry tomatoes
- ⅓ teaspoon pepper
- ½ cup of macadamia
- ½ tablespoon of macadamia oil
- ¼ cup fresh parsley
- 1 teaspoon of balsamic vinegar
- 1 teaspoon of minced garlic
- 2 tablespoons of extra virgin olive oil

Directions

- Cut lamb ribs into strips or pieces.
- Preheat oven to 210°C, and line baking tray with aluminium foil.
- Place the macadamia, garlic, parsley, pepper, and olive oil, in the food processor. Blend till the mixture is smooth and lump-free.
- Rub your processed mixture all over the lamb pieces, coat well enough.
- Arrange your strips nicely in the baking tray and bake for 20-25 minutes.
- Meanwhile, slice the cherry tomatoes into ¼ pieces, then place them in an aluminium cup.
- Pour macadamia oil on the tomatoes. Use a spoon to mix the oil and tomatoes without squishing it. The aim is to get the oil all over it.
- Take out the cooked lamb on a plate.
- Place your tomatoes in the oven for 4-5 minute, take out and drizzle with balsamic vinegar, stir well.
- Pour the tomatoes on the lamb and serve warm.

170. Grilled Garlic Butter Shrimp

Serves: 2-4 — Preparation time: 30 minutes — Meal Type: Main course or Lunch.
NUTRITIONAL VALUE PER SERVING: Cholesterol: 326mg— Total Fat: 16g — Total Carbs: 4g— Protein: 11.5g4g

Ingredients:

- 1 pound of large shrimps
- 1¼ tablespoon of minced garlic
- 1 teaspoon minced parsley, minced
- ½ cup of butter
- Salt and pepper
- Bamboo skewers

Directions

- Defreeze, peel, and devein the shrimp. Be careful not to take off the tails.
- Preheat the grill to medium heat at 360°F.
- Mix the melted butter with garlic, then add salt and pepper to your taste in a small bowl.
- Put your bamboo skewers through the shrimp.
- Place the shrimps on the preheated grill, and cook.
- Spread your garlic and butter mixture on the side facing you.
- After two minutes, turn it over and spread the garlic and butter mix on the other side, let it cook for 2 minutes more, ensuring both sides are evenly cooked.
- Remove the shrimp, garnish with parsley, and serve hot.

171. Tomato Chili Chicken Tender with Fresh Basils

Serves: 2-4 — Preparation time: 45 minutes — Meal Type: Main course/Lunch.
NUTRITIONAL VALUE PER SERVING: Calories: 410 kcal — Total Fat: 31.9g — Total Carbs: 43.4g— Protein: 11.4g

Ingredients:

- 2 pounds of boneless chicken thighs
- 4 tablespoons extra virgin olive oil
- 3 tablespoons lemongrass
- 3 tablespoons red chilli flakes
- 2½ tablespoons minced garlic
- 2 cups of water
- ¼ cup sliced red tomatoes
- ½ cup fresh basils
- Salt and pepper

Directions

- Cut the chicken into small to medium pieces, and place them in a skillet.
- Add some minced garlic, lemongrass, salt and pepper to taste. Then, pour water over the chicken. Let it boil until the water evaporates completely.
- Take out the chicken and set it aside.
- Heat a saucepan and add olive oil in it. Then, place the chicken and let it cook till it is brown.
- Place your tomatoes, basils, and chilli flakes on it. Remove from the stove and serve hot.

172. Lean Hamburgers

Servings: 1— Preparation time: 40 minutes
NUTRITIONAL VALUE PER SERVING: Potassium: 290mg Carbs: 8; Calories: 200; Total Fat: 9g; Protein: 25g; Sugar: 0g; Cholesterol: 60mg;

Ingredients:

- ¼ pound 95 percent of ground lean beef
- ½ chopped onion
- ½ tablespoon of Worcestershire sauce
- Pinch of salt
- ¼ teaspoon of grounded pepper
- 1 tablespoon of canola oil
- low carb hamburger bun

Directions

- Heat oil in skillet on medium heat
- Pour in onions and stir fry till soft
- Take off heat and allow cool
- When slightly cool, pour in ground beef, pinch of salt and pepper
- Stir and pour mixture in bowl
- From it, form a single patty. Make sure it is pressed together and firm
- Place the patty in a grill for 11 to 15 minutes on medium heat
- Place fried patty in low carb hamburger bun

173. Meatballs

Servings: 1 Servings: 1— Preparation time: 40 minutes.
NUTRITIONAL VALUE PER SERVING: Carbs: 8; Calories: 200; Total Fat: 10g; Protein: 22.1g; Sugar: 0g; Fibers: 2.1g

Ingredients:
- ¼ pound of ground lean beef
- 1/8 cup of fine, dry breadcrumbs
- 1/8 cup milk
- Freshly ground black pepper
- 1 small egg
- 1 tablespoon fresh parsley leaves
- ½ teaspoon of salt
- 1 small diced onion
- 1/8 teaspoon of minced garlic

Directions
- Rim baking sheet and preheat oven to 400°F
- Crack and mix egg
- In a bowl, pour in breadcrumbs and then milk. Stir and leave
- Mix pepper, parsley, and salt in another bowl. Pour in about half of the mixed egg
- Mix and pour in beef. Use your hands to mix very well
- Pour in the breadcrumbs mix
- Add onions and mix well
- Mold the mix into balls. You should have about 5
- Bake at 400°F for 20 to 25 minutes till very brown
- Serve hot

174. Shrimp ceviche

Servings: 5 ounces per person— Preparation time: 30 minutes.
NUTRITIONAL VALUE PER SERVING:Calories: 160 kals; Fat: 1 gram; Cholesterol: 0.022 grams; Sodium: 0.265 grams; Carbohydrates: 13 grams; Dietary Fiber: 2 grams; Sugar: 5 grams; Protein: 25 grams.

Ingredients:
- 1 cup of fresh lime juice
- 1 pound of medium raw shrimp
- 3 small minced chili peppers (Serrano)
- 1 small onion (red) finely chopped (approx. ¾ cup chopped)
- 1 bunch cilantro, stemmed, chopped finely.
- 5 medium sized tomatoes, diced

Directions
- Wash shrimps thoroughly in clean water. Make sure that the water is at room temperature.
- Put in the shrimp into a medium sized bowl and pour the fresh lime juice into bowl as well
- Leave the shrimp to marinate (soak) in the lime until the color changes to pink. (This should take about 10 minutes). The shrimp must be marinated properly to produce the distinctive flavor.
- Add in your finely chopped onions, minced chili peppers, and diced tomatoes and cilantro. Stir gently to let the flavor circulate.
- Add salt to taste.
- Refrigerate for at least one hour and serve cold

175. Baked Chicken With Vegetables

Servings: 5 ounces per person— Preparation time: 2 hours.
NUTRITIONAL VALUE PER SERVING: Calories grams: 240 kals; Sugar: 9.998 grams; Carbohydrate: 25 grams, Protein: 26 grams; Fat: 3.5; Fibre: 4 grams; Sodium: 0.130 grams.

Ingredients:
- 1½ cup water
- 3 finely sliced carrots,
- ½ of a large onion, (quartered)
- 2 potatoes,
- Raw chicken (cut into several pieces and remove all the top skin)
- 1 teaspoon of thyme
- ¼ teaspoon of pepper

Directions
- Wash, peel and Slice your potatoes
- Put the sliced potatoes, onions and carrots in a roasting pan
- Place pieces of raw chicken on top of the vegetables
- Then mix your teaspoon of thyme and quarter spoon of pepper together and mix with water.
- Pour this suspension over the chicken. It will sink to the vegetables below.
- Repeat this process once or twice during baking by spooning the suspension over the chicken and vegetables. This will enable the spices and seasoning to permeate the chicken adequately
- Leave to bake for 50 minutes at 425.

176.Mozzarella and Persimmon Bruschettas

Preparation Time: 15 minutes— Cook Time: 20 minutes— Servings: 12

Ingredients
- Persimmon: 1 large
- Sourdough baguette: ½
- Buffalo mozzarella: 300 gm
- Brown sugar: ¼ cup or 60 gm
- Coriander: a small bunch
- Balsamic vinegar: 1 cup or 250 ml
- Pomegranate: ½
- Salt & pepper: as per your taste
- Olive oil

Directions
- Take a small saucepan and add sugar and vinegar in it
- Cook on medium till the mixture remains half
- Slice baguette into one-inch pieces
- Brush them with olive oil and toast lightly
- Make small slices of persimmon as well
- On each baguette, put a mozzarella chunk, then persimmon slices
- Sprinkle chopped coriander, salt and pepper, and pomegranate on top
- Add balsamic glaze on top before serving

177.Goat Cheese Watermelon Salad

Preparation Time: 10 minutes— Cook Time: 10 minutes— Servings: 1

Ingredients
- Watermelon: ½ small
- Coriander: 1 large bunch
- Olive oil: 3 tbsp
- Goat cheese: 150 gm
- Lemon juice: 1 tbsp
- Garlic: 1 clove crushed
- Salt & pepper: as per your taste
- Sourdough bread: to make 3 handfuls of croutons of 3 cm

Directions:
- Preheat the grill
- Take the fresh coriander, wash and dry
- Remove leaves from the stalks and place in the salad bowl
- Now dice fresh watermelon and add to the salad bowl
- Combine crushed garlic and olive oil in a small bowl and combine well and add into the salad bowl and mix
- Make 3 cm pieces of sourdough bread and brush with olive oil and grill to make croutons
- Add them to the salad bowl and top with grated goat cheese
- Season with salt and pepper

178.Carrot Salad

Ingredients

- Carrots: 600 gm
- Dijon mustard:1 tsp
- Caster sugar: 1 tsp
- Lemon juice: 1 tbsp
- Olive oil: 3 tbsp
- Salt & pepper: as per your taste
- Fresh parsley leaves: 2 tbsp

Directions

- Take carrots, peel and grate them
- Chop parsley leaves using a knife
- Make the dressing using lemon juice, Dijon mustard, sugar, and olive oil
- Now add parsley and carrot in a large salad bowl
- Pour dressing on top of it and mix well
- Add salt and pepper as per your taste

179. Baked salmon

Servings: 5 ounces per person— Preparation time: 35 minutes.

NUTRITIONAL VALUE PER SERVING: Calories grams: 180 kals; Carbohydrate: 4 grams, Protein: 28 grams; Fat: 7; Fiber: 1 grams; Cholesterol: 60mg

Ingredients:

- 1 pound side of salmon without the skin
- 3 sprigs of rosemary
- 1/8 teaspoon of pepper
- 1 ½ tablespoon of olive oil
- 1 teaspoon of salt
- 1 small lemon thinly sliced
- 1 clove of chopped garlic

Directions

- Prepare baking sheet and line with aluminum foil and spray with baking spray

- Preheat oven to 375 degrees F
- Mix the oil, pepper, and salt
- Rub generously on salmon
- Place 1 ½ rosemary in the middle of the baking pan
- Place half of the lemon on the rosemary
- Place salmon on lemon and rosemary
- Place the garlic and remaining rosemary and lemon on it

180. Pork crack slaw

Serves: 4 — Preparation time: 25 minutes — Meal Type: Main course/Lunch

NUTRITIONAL VALUE PER SERVING: Calories: 445 kcal— Total Fat: 32g — Total Carbs: 9g— Protein: 21g

Ingredients:

- 1 pound of ground pork sausage
- 1 teaspoon of mixed garlic
- 1 Bags of ready-mix dry coleslaw
- 1 teaspoon of sesame oil
- 2 tablespoons of rice vinegar
- ¼ of a red onion
- ¼ tablespoons of ground ginger
- Salt and pepper to taste

Directions

- Place the sausage in a pot and cook till brown, then put in chopped red onions while cooking.

- When the sausage is ready, pour in the rice vinegar, sesame oil, minced garlic, coleslaw kits and salt and pepper to taste.
- Stir and thoroughly cook for 5 to 7 minutes.
- Add in the soy sauce and cover the pot.
- Let it simmer for 5 to ten minutes. Dice in half of the green onion, and slice the other half to serve with it.
- Take it out and serve warm.

181. Keto lasagna

Serves: 4 — Preparation time: 25 minutes — Meal Type: Main course/Lunch.

NUTRITIONAL VALUE PER SERVING: Calories: 546 kcal— Total Fat: 32g — Total Carbs: 50g— Protein: 32g

Ingredients:

- 16 ounces of ricotta
- 8 ounces block cream cheese
- 4 cups of shredded mozzarella
- 4 minced cloves of garlic
- 3 large eggs
- 2 cups of freshly grated Parmesan cheese
- 1 tablespoon of extra virgin olive oil
- 1 ½ tablespoon of tomato paste
- 1 ½ ground beef
- ¾ cups of marinara
- ½ white or yellow onion
- 1 tablespoon of dried oregano
- Cooking spray, butter, or oil
- Pinch crushed red pepper flakes
- Chopped parsley
- Black pepper
- Kosher salt
- Cooked Lasagna sheets/noodles

Directions

- Preheat the oven to about 350° F, and line a large baking tray with parchment paper or foil and grease with oil or butter.
- In another bowl, put in 2 ½ cups of mozzarella, 8 ounces of cheese, and 1 cup of parmesan cheese. Put in all the eggs and mix very well. Add salt and pepper to taste.

- Pour on the baking sheet and spread it out evenly, then bake for 15-20 minutes till its golden brown.
- Heat some oil in a large skillet, and sauté chopped onions until tender.
- Then, add garlic, and cook for a few more minutes.
- Poor in tomato paste, and heat the mixture, then add salt and pepper to taste.
- Mix in the ground beef, and cook until the meat loses its pink colour. Then, add marinara and red pepper flakes. Mix well.
- Pour in a small amount of the sauce into a baking pan.
- Then, lay 2 lasagna sheets at the base of a lasagna deep dish. Divide the ricotta into 3 parts. Spread one part of the ricotta over the lasagna noodles. Spread another part on the remaining meat and sauce which is on the top. Pour in the last part with the parmesan cheese. Make similar layers and pour cheese at the very top.
- Place the lasagna in the oven until the cheese melts and the sauce bubbles up.
- Take out and sprinkle parsley and cheese, if you desire.

182. Easy meal prep chicken soup

Serves: 4 — Preparation time: 40 minutes — Meal Type: Main course/Lunch.
NUTRITIONAL VALUE PER SERVING: Calories: 158 kcal— Total Fat: 64g — Total Carbs: 5g— Protein: 22g

Ingredients:
- 15 chicken breast tenderloins
- 2 tablespoons garlic powder
- 1 cup of chopped carrots
- 1 cup of chopped celery
- 1 tablespoon butter
- Salt
- Black pepper

Directions
- Place chicken breast tenderloins in 1 ½ cups of water.
- Add salt, black pepper, and 1 tablespoon of garlic in it.
- Let the chicken boil for 20-25 minutes till soft and almost cooked.
- Put in chopped carrots, chopped celery, and another tablespoon of garlic.
- Put in butter and cover for 5 to 10 minutes. Soup is ready.
- You can freeze it in the refrigerator until needed by simply reheating it.

183. Keto burger

Serves: 2-6 — Preparation time: 45 minutes — Meal Type: Main course/Lunch.
NUTRITIONAL VALUE PER SERVING: Calories: 687 kcal— Total Fat: 59g — Total Carbs: 2g— Protein: 39g

Ingredients:
- 4 pounds of ground hamburger meat
- 8 tablespoons of half-melted butter
- 5 cloves of garlic, minced
- 4 tablespoons Worcestershire sauce
- 1 teaspoon of ground black pepper
- 1 tablespoon of salt

Directions
- Mix in the meat, sauce, pepper, and garlic, and salt to taste in a mixing bowl. Mix well with a big spoon.
- Pour out the mixture on a clean board and mould into a patties form or shape.
- Put a tablespoon of butter in the centre of each patty, and mould the butter into the patties.
- Place on a grill, and cook each side for around seven minutes. Serve hot.
- You can try cooking these burgers in foil to prevent it from catching fire due to the increased fat levels.

184. Calamari mayo with cauliflower broccoli salad

Serves: 4-6 — Preparation time: 30 minutes — Meal Type: Main course/Lunch
NUTRITIONAL VALUE PER SERVING: Calories: 452 kcal— Total Fat: 39g — Total Carbs: 5g— Protein: 19.5g

Ingredients:
- 1 ½ pound of fresh squids
- 1 ½ tablespoon of lemon juice
- 2 eggs
- 2 cups of almond flour
- 2 cups of broccoli florets
- 2 cups of cauliflower florets
- 1 cup of extra virgin olive oil
- 1 diced onion
- ½ cup diced cheddar cheese
- ½ cup of mayonnaise
- ½ teaspoon of pepper
- ½ cup of sour cream

Directions
- Steam cauliflower and broccoli until they are soft and tender. Set it aside.
- Remove squid ink.
- Whisk the eggs, and add salt and pepper to taste.
- Cut the squid into rings, and put in the egg mixture.
- Pour in almond flour, and rub into the squid and egg mix well.
- Heat oil in a pan, and fry the squid until it is golden brown.
- Take out the squid and set it aside.
- In a separate bowl, mix in mayonnaise, lemon juice, and sour cream thoroughly.
- To serve, place the fried squid on a plate with the steam broccoli and cauliflower florets, then pour the mayonnaise, lemon juice, and sour cream on it.
- Sprinkle dry cheddar cheese on top for garnishing.

185. Keto strawberry rice

Serves: 3 — Preparation time: 15 minutes — Meal Type: Main course/Lunch.
NUTRITIONAL VALUE PER SERVING: Calories: 245 kcal— Total Fat: 32g — Total Carbs: 15g— Protein: 16g

Ingredients:
- 3 cups of sliced strawberries
- 2 cups of cooked rice
- 2 tablespoons of grass-fed butter
- 2 cup full-fat organic coconut milk
- 1 tablespoon of pure vanilla extract
- ½ cup birch xylitol
- Himalayan pink salt
- ¼ teaspoon ground cinnamon
- ¼ teaspoon vanilla extract

Directions
- Put your 2 ½ cups of sliced strawberries, cinnamon, cooked rice, grass-fed butter, full-fat organic coconut milk, pure vanilla extract, birch xylitol, and a pinch of salt in a saucepan.
- Cook for 2-30 minutes while stirring continuously, until creamy.
- Slice the remaining strawberries, put on the rice mixture. Serve warm.

186. Keto white rice

Serves: 3 — Preparation time: 60 minutes — Meal Type: Main course/Lunch.
NUTRITIONAL VALUE PER SERVING: Calories: 229 kcal— Total Fat: 49g — Total Carbs: 15g— Protein: 26g

Ingredients:
- 1 cup of rice
- 1 cup of diced tomatoes
- 1 ¼ cups of diced peppers
- Extra virgin olive oil ½ cup
- ½ cup of boiled ground beef
- 1/8 cup of diced green onions
- 1/8 cup of sliced spring onions
- Salt to taste
- Adobo seasoning

Directions
- Put 3 to 4 cups of water in a large saucepan and bring to boil, add rice and salt.
- After 16-20 minutes, the rice should be ready. If you aren't quite sure you can fish it for grain or three to test.
- Strain the water from rice. Straining the water drains out some of the starch, which means you reduce the carbs. You can use a strainer or colander with tiny holes.
- Place your strained rice in a pot and cover.
- Preheat your saucepan, add olive oil and heat it slightly.
- Sauté diced green onions for 15 seconds stirring continuously.
- Add in spring onions and fry for another 15 seconds stirring continuously.
- Mix in pepper and stir for half a minute, then add tomatoes and stir well for 5-7 minutes
- Add in boiled ground beef, a teaspoon of salt, and a teaspoon of Adobo seasoning.
- Mix well and cook for 5-8 minutes.
- Place your boiled rice in a serving dish, then spread your sauce over the rice.
- Enjoy hot.

187. Steamed Veggies And Prawn With Coconut Milk

Serves: 2 — Preparation time: 40 minutes — Meal Type: Main course/Lunch.
NUTRITIONAL VALUE PER SERVING: Calories: 243 kcal— Total Fat: 31g — Total Carbs: 4.5g — Protein: 17g

Ingredients:
- 1 pound of fresh shrimps
- 4 tablespoons of extra virgin olive oil
- 1 egg
- 1/8 cup of coconut milk
- ½ cup almond flour
- ¼ cup of water
- 1/8 of cup grated cheddar cheese
- 1/8 cup of diced carrot
- 1/8 of cup diced onion
- 1/8 of cup chopped leek

Directions
- Peel prawns, remove heads and set aside.
- Whisk an egg in a bowl.
- Mix water and almond flour together until no lumps are formed.
- Pour in half of the egg mixture in, mix well.
- Use the mixture to make omelettes.
- Take your peeled prawns and put them in a food processor, blend until smooth.
- Preheat a skillet, and pour in 1 ½ spoon of the olive oil.
- Sauté onion and sauté until golden brown.
- Add the leek and carrot, and stir for ten seconds more.
- Pour in coconut milk, keep stirring until the milk evaporates.
- Put the cooked veggies, prawns, and remaining half egg into the bowl, and mix well.
- Put an omelette on a plate, then a tablespoon of the prawn mix. Fold the omelette like an envelope.
- Repeat with the rest of the omelettes.
- Preheat a pan, and pour the remaining olive oil into it.
- When the oil is a bit hot, put the prawn envelopes in the pan.
- Cook for 2 minutes on each side till golden brown.
- Serve warm

188. Mediterranean Pork Chops

Serves: 8 — Preparation time: 640 minutes — Meal Type: Main course/Lunch
NUTRITIONAL VALUE PER SERVING: Calories: 297 kcal— Total Fat: 49g — Total Carbs: 9g— Protein: 30g

Ingredients:
- 8 boneless pork loin chops
- 1 teaspoon of black pepper
- 1 teaspoon of kosher salt
- 7 minced garlic cloves
- 2 tablespoons of chopped and fresh rosemary

Directions
- Mix garlic and rosemary in a bowl.
- Place pork chops in it, and sprinkle pepper and salt to taste. Coat the chops well.
- Place pork chops in a roasting pan at 425 degrees F for ten minutes.
- Reduce the temperature of the oven to 350 F degrees, and continue roasting for about 20-25 minutes.
- Serve warm.

189. Spicy turmeric goat satay

Serves: 2 — Preparation time: 40 minutes — Meal Type: Main course/Lunch.
NUTRITIONAL VALUE PER SERVING: Calories: 360 kcal— Total Fat: 28g — Total Carbs: 3.1g— Protein: 21g

Ingredients:
- 1 pound of ground goat meat
- 3 teaspoons of grated garlic
- 1 tablespoon red chilli flakes
- 1 teaspoon of turmeric
- 1 egg, whisked
- ½ cup of diced onion

Directions
- Combines diced onion, grated garlic, turmeric, and red chilli flakes, mix well.
- Rub the above mixture into ground goat meat, then add in the whisked egg.
- Preheat a steamer.
- Mould the meat mixture around a wooden skewer.
- Place the meat in the steamer for 20 minutes.
- Take the meat out and set aside for cooling.
- Meanwhile, preheat the grill, and place satay on it. Grill it for 2-3 minutes until each side is lightly brown.
- Serve warm.

190. Air Fried Cream Cheese Pumpkin Pockets

Serving: 8 Prep time: 25 minutes Total time: 55 minutes.
Nutritional Value: Energy: 221 cal, Carbs: 29 g, Protein: 2 g, Fat: 9.9 g, Sodium: 249 mg

Ingredients
- Granulated sugar: 1/3 cup
- Pumpkin pie cheese: 1 and ½ tsp.
- Cream cheese: 2 oz.
- Canned pumpkin: ¼ cup
- Pillsbury refrigerated crescent dinner rolls: 1 cam
- Melted butter: 1 tbsp.
- powdered sugar: ½ cup
- Milk: 2 tsp.
- Vanilla: ½ tsp.
- Chopped pecans: 2 tbsp.

Directions
- Combine pumpkin pie spice and granulated sugar in a container. In another container, blend 4 tbsp. pumpkin pie sugar mixture with cream cheese with food processor, then add pumpkin and beat more until fully combined.
- Separate crescent rolls into 4 parts and shape each into rectangle of 6*4 inches.
- Top the right side of rectangle with the cream cheese pumpkin mixture and fold the left side on right side pressing with a fork or finger tips. Brush the rectangles with melted butter slightly.
- Air fry the pumpkin pockets at 375 degree F for 10 minutes. Turn the sides using togs and again air fry until golden brown.
- Meanwhile mix drizzle ingredients in a medium sized bowl. Pour on the warm pumpkin pockets and sprinkle with pecans.

191. Air fried Avocado Chips

Serving: 2 Prep time: 4 minutes Total time: 8 minutes.
Nutritional Value: Energy: 320 g, Carbs: 40 g, Proteins: 9.2 g Fats: 18 g Sodium: 464 mg

Ingredients
- De-seeded, peeled, sliced avocado: 1
- Panko bread crumbs: ½ cup
- All purpose flour: ¼ cup
- Large beaten egg: 1
- Water: 1 tsp.
- Kosher salt: ¼ tsp.
- Ground Black pepper: ½ tsp.
- Cooking spray.

Directions
- Pre heat the air fryer to 400 degree F. spray basket with cooking spray
- Combine flour and salt in a container, egg and water in another and panko bread crumbs in the last container. Dredge avocado slices in each respectively.
- Air fry for 4 minutes, flip the sides and again fry until golden brown.

192. Air fried Parmesan Zucchini fries

Serving: 2 Prep time: 5 minutes Total time: 20 minutes.
Nutritional Value: Energy: 160 calories Carbs: 21 g Proteins: 10.9 g Fats: 6.5 g Sodium: 385 mg

Ingredients
- Thinly sliced Zucchini: 1
- Large beaten egg: 1
- Grated Parmesan cheese: ¾ cup
- Panko bread crumbs: 1 cup

Directions
- Pre heat the air fryer at 350 degree F.
- Mix panko bread crumbs and parmesan cheese. Dip zucchini in egg and then coat with panko bread crumbs mixture. Gently press to firm the coating.
- Air fry the zucchini fries for 10 minutes, shake the air fryer basket and again air fry for 5 minutes.
- Serve with coleslaw. Relish.

193. Air fried Falafel

Serving: 20 Prep time: 15 minutes Total time: 30 minutes.
Nutritional Value: 60 calories Carbs: 10 g Proteins: 3 g Fats: 1 g Sodium: 99 mg

Ingredients
- Dry garbanzo beans: 1 cup
- Stem removed Fresh cilantro, 1 and ½ cups
- Stem removed fresh flat leafed parsley: ¾ cup
- Small quartered red onion: 1
- Garlic: 1 clove
- Chickpea flour: 2 tbsp.
- Powdered coriander: 1 tbsp.
- Ground cumin: 1 tbsp.
- Sriracha sauce: 1 tbsp.
- Salt and black pepper: as needed
- Baking powder: ½ tsp
- Baking soda: ¼ tsp.

Directions
- Soak chickpeas in cold water overnight. Pat dry with paper towel.
- Beat together chickpeas, parsley, onion, cilantro and garlic in a blender. Then add chickpea flour, cumin, sriracha, kosher salt, coriander, and pepper and mix well.
- Pre heat the air fryer to 375 degree F.
- Add baking powder and baking soda to the chickpea mixture and combine manually. Shape them into patties.
- Transfer the falafel patties to air fryer and air fry for about 10 minutes. Shake and again fry for 5 minutes.

194. Air Fried Tofu With Peanut Dipping Sauce

Serving: 16 Prep time: 5 minutes Total time: 17 minutes.
Nutritional Value: Energy: 255 calories, Carbs: 21.1 g, Protein: 12.5 g Fats: 14 g Sodium: 455 mg

Ingredients
- Cubed Tofu: 16 oz.
- All purpose flour: 1 and ½ cup
- Kosher salt: ½ tsp.
- Freshly ground black pepper: ½ tsp.
- Olive oil spray
- For dipping sauce
- Low sodium peanut butter: ¼ cup
- Minced garlic: 1 tsp.
- Light soy sauce: 12 tbsp.
- Fresh lime juice: 1 tbsp.
- Brown sugar: 1 tsp.
- Water: 1/3 cup
- Chopped roasted peanuts: 2 tbsp.

Directions
- Combine all purpose flour with salt and pepper. Toss the tofu cubes with flour mixture and spray with oil.
- Pre heat the air fryer at 390 degree F.
- Transfer the tofu to air fryer basket. Air fry for about 10 to 12 minutes or until golden brown.
- Meanwhile prepare dipping sauce by mixing all the dipping sauce ingredients and refrigerate.
- Serve tofu with peanut dipping sauce. Relish.

195.Air Fried Cream Cheese Mini Multi Sweet Peppers

Serving: 4 to 6 Prep time: 7 minutes Total time: 15 minutes
Nutritional Value: Energy: 100 calories Carbs: 2.5 g Proteins: 3.6 g Fats: 8.6 g Sodium: 160 mg

Ingredients
- Bulk Italian sausage: 8 ounces
- Petite Multi colored sweet pepper: 1 package
- Softened cream cheese: 1 package
- Divided olive oil: 2 tbsp.
- Shredded Cheddar cheese: ½ cup
- Crumbled blue cheese: 1 tbsp.
- Finely chopped fresh chives: 1 tbsp.
- Minced garlic cloves: 1 clove
- Powdered black pepper: ¼ tsp.
- Panko bread crumbs: 2 tbsp.

Directions
- Bring to simmer the sausage in a skillet until crumbled.
- Pre heat the air fryer to 350 degree F.
- Split the multi colored sweet pepper lengthwise into 2 halves. Paint with olive oil slightly and air fry for 3 to 5 minutes.
- Meanwhile whisk together sausage, cream cheese, cheddar cheese, blue cheese, chives, garlic and black pepper. In another bowl, mic panko bread crumbs with olive oil.
- Scoop in the cheese mixture into the splited sweet peppers and dredge with panko bread crumbs.
- Air fry for 5 minutes again, shake and again fry for 3 minutes. Serve with favorite dipping. Relish.

196.Air fried corn on the cob

Serving: 2 Prep time: 4 minutes Total time: 15 minutes.
Nutritional Value: Energy: 145 calories Carbs: 9.4 g Proteins: 2 g Fats: 12 g Sodium: 103 mg

Ingredients
- Sliced Corn ears: 2
- Mayonnaise: ¼ cup
- Crumbled cojita cheese: 2 tsp.
- Lemon juice: 1 tsp.
- Chili powder: ¼ tsp.
- Fresh Cilantro: 4 sprigs

Directions
- Pre heat the air fryer to 400 degree F for 3 mins.
- Whisk together mayonnaise, lime juice, chili powder and cojita cheese. Dip each corn in the mixture.
- Air fry in the pre heated air fryer for 8 minutes. Flip the sides and again fry for 5 minutes.

197.Air fried Corn Nuts

Serving: Prep time: 3 minutes Total time: 20 minutes.
Nutritional Value: Energy: 225 calories, Carbs: 35.9 g, Proteins: 6 g, Fats: 7.5 g Sodium: 438 mg

Ingredients
- Goya giant white corn: 14 ounce
- Vegetable oil: 3 tbsp.
- Kosher salt: 1 ½ tsp.

Directions
- Dwell the corn in water for overnight.
- Drain and pat dry with paper towel.
- Pre heat the air fryer to 400 F.
- Coat the corn with oil and salt, transfer to air fryer basket and air fry for 10 minutes. Jerk the basket and fry for 7 minutes more. Relish

198.Air fried toasted broccoli and cauliflower

Serving: 6 Prep time: 4 minutes Total time: 22 minutes.
Nutritional Value: Energy: 69 calories, Carbs: 5.8 g Proteins: 2.4 g Fats: 4.7 g Sodium: 104 mg

Ingredients
- Sliced Cauliflower: 3 cups
- Diced Broccoli: 3 cups
- Garlic powder: ½ tsp.
- Sea salt: ¼ tsp.
- Paprika: ¼ tsp.
- Ground black pepper: 1/8 tsp.
- Olive oil: 2 tbsp.

Directions
- Pre heat the air fryer at 400 degree F.
- Combine broccoli, cauliflower, olive oil, paprika, sea salt, black pepper and garlic powder.
- Pour the mixture in the pre heated air fryer basket and air fry for 12 minutes. Jerk and again fry for 6 minutes.

199.Air fried roasted Okra

Serving: Prep time: 3 minutes Total time: 6 minutes.
Nutritional Value: Energy: 112 calories, Carbs: 16 g, Proteins: 4.7 g, Fats: 5 g, Sodium 600 mg

Ingredients
- Sliced okra: ½ pound
- Olive oil: 1 tsp.
- Salt and black pepper: to taste

Directions
- Pre heat the air fryer at 350 degree F for 5 min.
- Season okra with olive oil, pepper, and salt.
- Air fry for mins, toss and again air fry for 3 mins. Relish.

200.Air fried Vegetable pakoras

Serving: 8 Prep time: 15 minutes Total time: minutes 30.
Nutritional Value: Energy: 80 calories, Carbs: 14.4 g, Proteins: 4.3 g Fats: 1.1 g Sodium: 890 mg

Ingredients
- Diced cauliflower: 2 cups
- Minced yellow potatoes: 1 cup
- Chickpea flour: 1 ¼ cups
- Chopped red onion: ½
- Minced garlic clove: 1
- Curry powder: 1 tsp.
- Coriander: 1 tsp.
- Cumin: ½ tsp.
- Powdered cayenne pepper: ½ tsp.
- Water: ¾ cup

Directions
- Combine cauliflower, red onion, potatoes, garlic, chickpea flour, salt, coriander, cayenne, cumin and water in a container and let it rest for 10 to 12 mins.
- Pre heat the air fryer to 350 degree F for 3 mins.
- Spray the air fryer basket with cooking spray. Place cauliflower mixture into basket via a scoop.
- Air fry for 8 mins, turn the sides and again cook for 5 mins. Serve with sauce. Relish.

201.Air Fried Jack Cheese Egg Rolls

Serving: 16 Prep time: 10 minutes Total time: 20 to 25 minutes.
Nutritional Value: Energy: 215 calories, Carbs: 26 g, Proteins: 10.5 g, Fats: 7.6 g, Sodium: 627 mg

Ingredients

- Thawed frozen corns: 2 cups
- Drained spinach: 1 can
- Shredded jalapeno jack cheese: 1 ½ cups
- Rinsed and drained Clack beans: 1 can
- Shredded cheddar cheese: 1 cup
- Drained and diced green chiles: 1 can
- Sliced and chopped green onions: 4
- Kosher salt: 1 tsp.
- Ground cumin: 1 tsp.
- Chili powder: 1 tsp.
- Egg roll wrappers: 1 packet

Directions

- Combine beans, spinach, corns, jack cheese, cheddar cheese, green chiles, green onions, salt, cumin, and chili powder in a basin for filling.
- Pre heat the air fryer at 390 degree F.
- Take an egg roll wrapper, brush all the sides with beaten egg. Fill the mixture in the center of wrapper. Turn 1 edge over mixture and tuck in the sides to give the shape of roll. Repeat with remaining.
- Place rolls in air fryer basket and air fry for 6 to 7 minutes. Turn over the sides and again air fry until golden brown for 4 minutes.

202.Air Fried Bloated Mushroom With Tangy Cream

Serving: 24 Prep time: 10 minutes Total time: 20 minutes.
Nutritional Value: Energy: 43 calories, Carbs: 1.6 g, Proteins: 2.5 g, Fats: 3 g, Sodium: 55 mg

Ingredients

- De-cap and de-stem mushrooms: 24
- Diced orange or red bell pepper: ½
- Diced onion: ½
- Peeled and chopped carrot: 1
- Sliced and diced bacons: 2 slices
- Shredded cheddar cheese: 1 cup
- Sour cream: ½ cup
- Shredded cheddar cheese: 1 ½ tbsp.

Directions

- Pre heat the air fryer at 350 degree F.

- Combine mushroom stem. Bell pepper, onion, carrot, and bacon in a skillet over medium to low heat. Cook for 4 minutes and add up cheddar cheese and sour cream and cook until creamy consistent mixture.
- Fill the mixture in mushroom caps and top with more cheddar cheese. Place in the air fryer and fry for 8 minutes. Relish.

203.Air fried Buffalo wing Chickpeas

Serving: 4 Prep time: 5 minutes Total time: 65 minutes.
Nutritional Value: Energy: 176 calories, Carbs: 33.5 g, Proteins: 7 g, Fats: 1.5 g, Sodium: 1034 mg

Ingredients

- Drained and rinsed canned chickpeas: 1 can
- Buffalo wing sauce: 2 tbsp.
- Dry ranch dressing: 1 tbsp.

Directions

- Pre heat the air fryer at 350 degrees F.

- Pat dry the chickpeas with a paper towel. Season the chickpeas with buffalo wing sauce and ranch dressing powder.
- Transfer the chickpeas to the pre heated air fryer and air fry for about 8 minutes. Jerk the air fryer basket and again air fry for about 5 minutes. Dish out and Relish

204.Air fried Cauliflower tots

Serving: 4 Prep time: 6 minutes Total time: 6 minutes.
Nutritional Value: Energy: 148 calories, Carbs: 20 g Proteins: 2.8 g, fats: 6 g, Sodium: 495 mg

Ingredients

- Frozen cauliflower tots: 1 packet
- Cooking spray

Directions

- Pre heat your air fryer to 400 F. Spray the air fryer basket with cooking spray.

- Place cauliflower tots in the basket such that no piece touch the other.
- Air fry for 6 minutes. Toss over and again fry for 3 minutes. Relish

205.Air fried Korean styled Chicken wings

Serving: 4 Prep time: 10 minutes Total time: 50 minutes.
Nutritional Value: Energy: 345 calories, Carbs: 44.7 g, Proteins: 16 g Fats: 11.4 g Sodium: 1245 mg

Ingredients

- For wings:
- Chicken wings: 2 pounds
- Kosher salt: 1 tsp.
- Garlic powder: 1 tsp.
- Black pepper: ½ tsp.
- Onion powder: 1 tsp.
- Cornstarch: ½ cup
- For Sauce:
- Gochujang Korean hot pepper sauce: 3 tbsp.
- Mike's hot honey: ¼ cup
- Brown sugar: 1 tbsp.
- Soy sauce: 1 tbsp.
- Minced garlic: 2 tsp.
- Lemon juice: 1 tsp.
- Minced fresh ginger root: 1 tsp.
- Chopped green onions: ¼ cup
- Kosher Salt: ½ tsp.

- Black pepper: ¼ tsp.

Directions

- Preheat the air fryer to 400 degree F.
- Marinate the chicken wings with salt, black pepper, garlic powder and onion powder. Then coat with cornstarch.
- Air fry in the pre heated air fryer for 10 minutes, jerk the wings and the again fry for 8 minutes.
- Meanwhile prepare the sauce by combining gochujang, brown sugar, hot honey, soy sauce, lemon juice, garlic and ginger, salt and black paper in a skillet and simmer over medium heat. Then add green onion and stir.
- Pour the sauce over the wings. Garnish with toasted sesame seeds and green onion. Rel

206. Keto prime rib

Serves: 3 — Preparation time: 40 minutes — Meal Type: Main course/Lunch.
NUTRITIONAL VALUE PER SERVING: Calories: 421 kcal— Total Fat: 42g — Total Carbs: 9g— Protein: 20g

Ingredients:
- 2 pounds of standing ribs
- 4 tablespoons of kosher salt
- A teaspoon of olive oil
- 1 ½ teaspoon of black pepper
- 3 bunches of fresh rosemary

Directions
- Preheat oven to 450˚F.
- Mix salt, pepper, and a teaspoon of the oil in a small bowl.
- Rub the salt and pepper mixture on the rib very well.
- Place rosemary in the bottom of the roast pan, then place rib in the roast pan.
- Roast at 450˚ for 30 minutes.
- Reduce heat to 350˚F and simmer for 2 hours.
- Take out from oven and cover in foil for 25 minutes.
- Serve hot.

207. Keto crispy Chicken Thighs

Serves: 4 — Preparation time: 30 minutes — Meal Type: Main course/Lunch
NUTRITIONAL VALUE PER SERVING: Calories: 473 kcal— Total Fat: 42g — Total Carbs: 3.1g— Protein: 19g

Ingredients:
- 8 pieces of deboned chicken thighs deboned. You can cut into two pieces each
- 6 teaspoons KFC seasoning to taste
- 4 eggs
- 2 1/2 cups of almond flour
- 3 cups of olive oil

Directions
- Pour the olive oil into the deep fryer or a deep pot, and heat it on a medium flame.
- In a separate bowl, mix in 1 cup of the almond flour with 1 tablespoon KFC seasoning.
- Whisk the eggs in another bowl.
- Place your chicken in the almond flour and seasoning, completely coating it.
- Dip the chicken in the eggs, and set it aside.
- Deep fry the chicken until golden brown.
- Serve hot.

208. Low Carb Beef Stew

Serves: 4 — Preparation time: 2 hours   Meal Type: Main Course/Lunch/Soup.
NUTRITIONAL VALUE PER SERVING: Calories: 332 kcal— Total Fat: 32.3g — Total Carbs: 4.6g— Protein: 21g

Ingredients:
- 1 ½ pound of trimmed beef chuck roast
- 7 ounces whole mushrooms, quartered
- 6 ounces celery root, peeled and cubed into 3/4-inch pieces (or sub turnips or radishes)
- 3 large onions
- 3 sliced rib celery
- 3 ounces of carrot [sliced]
- 2 sliced cloves of garlic
- 3 tablespoons of tomato paste
- 4 tablespoons of olive oil or bacon grease
- 6 cups beef broth
- 2 bay leaves
- 1 teaspoon of dried thyme
- Salt and pepper to taste

Directions
- Mix in 1 tablespoon of oil into the beef, and mix well.
- Heat oil in a pan, and sauté mushrooms until tender.
- Leave them in the oil for two minutes, then stir for another two minutes.
- Take the mushrooms out, and put them in a bowl.
- In the same bowl, add in the celery root, onions, rib celery, carrot, and garlic, mix well.
- Heat oil in a pot.
- Add your beef inside in small batches. If you need more oil, add. The aim is to fry the beef until brown.
- When it is all browned, mix in thyme, bay leaves, tomato paste, and salt and pepper to taste. Stir for 20 minutes.
- You should have bits stuck to the bottom of the pot. Pour in a little broth and use it to scrape the bits stuck to the bottom.
- Pour in the rest of the broth and simmer for 1 hour to 1 ½ hour.
- Serve hot.

209. Chicken peanut apple sauce

NUTRITIONAL VALUE PER SERVING: Calories: 50 kal; Fat: 2 grams; Cholesterol: 0.060 grams; Sodium: 0.203 grams; Carbohydrates: 13 grams; Dietary Fiber: 2 grams; Sugar: 10 grams; Protein: 3 grams.Preparation time: 1 ½ hours

Ingredients:
- 3 pounds of chicken pieces
- ¼ cups of mustard
- ⅛ cups of brown sugar
- ¼ cups of brown sugar
- ½ cups of peanuts (powdered)
- Salt (To taste)
- Pepper (as desired)
- 1 jar of unsweetened applesauce
- Water

Directions
- Defreeze your chicken ahead if needed
- Wash the chicken thoroughly
- Place chicken in a sauté pan with water and cook on medium heat.
- When it is almost completely cooked, add apple sauce, mustard, brown sugar and the powdered peanuts.
- Stir well to achieve uniformity.
- Continue to cook over medium heat until it is 75ºc hot
- Let it down after 5 minutes
- Serve warm

210. Spinach Salmon Nugget

Serves: 8 — Preparation time: 40 minutes — Meal Type: Main course/Lunch.
NUTRITIONAL VALUE PER SERVING: Calories: 446 kcal— Total Fat: 42.8g — Total Carbs: 2.7g— Protein: 25.2g

Ingredients:
- 2 eggs
- 2 cups of chopped spinach
- 1 pound of salmon fillet
- 1 tablespoon of pepper
- 1 tablespoon minced garlic
- 1 cup of extra virgin olive oil

Directions
- Cut the salmon fillet into pieces, or in cubes.
- Place the salmon in a food processor, and add pepper and garlic, then blend until smooth.
- Preheat a steamer.
- In a separate bowl, whisk two eggs lightly.
- Add the eggs to the salmon and pepper mixture.
- Add in chopped spinach, and stir until fully mixed.
- Place the salmon and egg mixture into a steamer, and steam on low heat for ten minutes.
- Take off and let it cool. Make nuggets out of this mixture of medium size.
- Preheat a frying pan, heat extra virgin olive oil. Then, fry the nuggets until crisp and brown.
- Take out the salmon on a paper towel, or use a strainer to drain the surplus oil away.
- Serve warm and enjoy.

211. Cheesy- turkey breast

Serves: 6 — Preparation time: 20 minutes — Meal Type: Main course/Lunch.
NUTRITIONAL VALUE PER SERVING: Calories: 667 kcal — Total Fat: 41.5g — Total Carbs: 6.4g— Protein: 49.9g

Ingredients:
- 3 cups of chopped roasted turkey breast
- 3 cups of shredded cheddar cheese
- 3 cups white of shredded cheddar cheese
- 2 cups of shredded parmesan cheese

Directions
- Prepare a baking sheet by rubbing butter or spraying with non-stick cooking spray.
- Preheat oven to 350°F.
- Mix cheddar cheese, white cheddar cheese, and parmesan cheese together.
- Place 1 tablespoon of the cheese combo in a pile on a baking sheet. Be sure to leave space between cheese piles.
- Bake for 6-10 minutes, until the moment they turn golden brown from the edges, then take them off.
- You can use the turkey as topping for nacho.

212. Low-carb shrimp pad Thai with shirataki noodles

Serves: 1-2 — Preparation time: 30 minutes — Meal Type: Main course/Lunch.
NUTRITIONAL VALUE PER SERVING: Calories: 392 kcal— Total Fat: 35.5g — Total Carbs: 7.4g— Protein: 16.6g

Ingredients:
- 7 ounces of Shirataki fettuccini noodles
- 9 shrimps of medium size
- 2 chopped green onions
- 2 tablespoons of coconut aminos
- 1 minced clove of garlic
- 1 ½ tablespoon of Brain Octane Oil
- 1 egg
- 1 small juiced lime
- ½ teaspoon cashew butter
- ¼ teaspoon crushed red pepper
- ¼ cup cilantro

Directions
- Cook the noodles as the package instructs, and set aside.
- In a bowl, mix ¾ of the brain octane oil with half of the lime juice. Pour in the coconut aminos followed by garlic and pepper. Then, add butter and mix well.
- Heat a skillet and add the rest of the brain oil. Put in the shrimps and a pinch of salt to taste, and cook for 1 ½ - 2 minutes from each side.
- Take out the shrimps and place in a bowl without taking the skillet off.
- Whisk eggs, and pour in the same skillet. Softly scramble the eggs and put the shrimps back in it followed by the cooked noodles.
- Add the onions and cilantro, stir well, and drizzle lime juice over the skillet.
- Add salt and pepper to taste, and serve hot.

213. Crispy almond chicken with tomato onion sauce

Serves: 3 — Preparation time: 40 minutes — Meal Type: Main course/Lunch.
NUTRITIONAL VALUE PER SERVING: Calories: 444 kcal— Total Fat: 52g — Total Carbs: 8.2g— Protein: 14.5g

Ingredients:
- 1 pound of boneless chicken thighs
- ¾ cup extra virgin olive oil, to fry
- ½ cup of tomato puree
- ¼ teaspoon pepper
- ¼ cup almond flour [keep some extra at hand]
- 1 large egg
- 1 large diced onion
- Salt

Directions
- Cut the chicken into strips.
- Crack and beat the egg.
- Place the strips one after the other in the egg, and then roll in the almond flour.
- Preheat a skillet and heat the oil in it.
- Fry the chicken, until golden brown. Place in a strainer or on a paper towel.
- In another pan, heat oil.
- Sauté onions, until lightly brown.
- Add tomato puree, let it simmer on low flame for few minutes, then add pepper.
- After a while, take off and drizzle on the chicken.

214. Fish balls with chives and lemon garlic creamy sauce

Serves: 3 — Preparation time: 35 minutes — Meal Type: Main course/Lunch.
NUTRITIONAL VALUE PER SERVING: Calories: 322 kcal— Total Fat: 29.9g — Total Carbs: 3.2g— Protein: 27.2g

Ingredients:
- ½ pound fish fillet
- 5 tablespoons extra virgin olive oil
- 1 medium-sized diced onion
- 1 ½ tablespoon of minced garlic
- ½ cup of chives
- 1 large egg
- 3-tablespoons of coconut flour
- 2 tablespoons lemon juice
- 1 ¾ cups of coconut milk

Directions
- Preheat a skillet, then pour in 3 tablespoons of extra virgin olive oil and heat it.
- Add in the chopped onions and sauté until tender. Set aside.
- Preheat the oven to 350°F. Prepare a baking tray and line it with an aluminium foil. Be sure to spray with cooking spray or rub lightly with butter or oil.

- Cut the fish fillet into small pieces, blend it in a food processor until smooth.
- Add in onions, egg, half chives and 1 ½ tablespoon of coconut flour in a food processor, pulse once more, until well blended and smooth.
- Roll into balls and place on the baking tray, and bake for 20 -25 minutes.
- Add the remaining coconut milk into the coconut flour and mix well.
- Preheat a pan with remaining extra virgin olive oil.
- Add garlic stirring lightly, then add the coconut milk and flour mixture, let it boil.
- Reduce the heat to the smallest flame, and drizzle lemon juice on top.
- Stir well, and take it off the flame.
- Place fish balls on a plate, then pour the sauce over them as you desire.
- Serve warm.

215. Keto Bread Grass-Fed Collagen Bread

Serves: 2-4 — Preparation time: 2 hours — Meal Type: Main course/Lunch.
NUTRITIONAL VALUE PER SERVING: Calories: 223 kcal— Total Fat: 20g — Total Carbs: 10.2g— Protein: 15.5g

Ingredients:
- 7 tablespoons of almond flour
- 5 eggs
- 1 tablespoon of coconut oil
- 1 teaspoon of baking powder
- 1 teaspoon xanthan gum
- Pinch Himalayan pink salt
- Pinch of stevia
- ½ cup of unflavored grass-fed collagen protein

Directions
- Preheat the oven to 325°F.
- Grease a glass or ceramic loaf dish with cooking spray or coconut oil or butter or ghee.
- In a bowl, crack eggs and separate egg whites.
- Beat the egg whites completely.

- In another bowl, pour in the dry ingredients together and mix well.
- Take another bowl, and mix wet ingredients such as the egg yolks and the liquid coconut oil.
- Pour in the dry batch and wet batch into the egg whites' mixture.
- You may add a pinch of stevia. Stevia will reduce the flavour of the eggs. It is optional, though. Mix until batter forms.
- Pour the batter into the oiled or lined dish and place in the oven, and bake for 40 minutes.
- Since we didn't oil the sides to let it rise well, the bread may stick, and you would need a knife to do get it out well

216. Keto whey bread

Serves: 6 — Preparation time: 2 ½ hours — Meal Type: Main course/Lunch.
NUTRITIONAL VALUE PER SERVING: Calories: 244 kcal— Total Fat: 19g — Total Carbs: 4.2g— Protein: 5.5g

Ingredients
- 12 grams of a cup of unflavored whey protein powder
- 11 egg whites
- 5 tablespoons of melted butter
- 2 teaspoons of baking powder
- 1¼ cups of almond flour
- 2 egg yolks
- 1 teaspoon of vanilla flavour
- 1 tablespoon of confectioners erythritol
- ¼ teaspoon of cream of tartar
- Pinch salt

Directions
- Preheat the oven to 325°F, and grease a baking pan with baking spray or rub butter on it.

- Beat 12 eggs yolks with the cream of tartar well. Set aside.
- Put in all the dry ingredients in a bowl and stir until mixed.
- Mix in the egg yolks into the dry ingredients.
- Add in the melted butter and blend until the ingredients are thoroughly mixed.
- Pour in the whisked eggs whites and mix well
- Pour the batter into the baking pan, and bake it for 1 hour and 30 minutes.
- Take out and let it cool on a cake rack.
- Eat as you desire.

217. Almond Keto Bread

Serves: 6 — Preparation time: 1 hour — Meal Type: Main course/Lunch.
NUTRITIONAL VALUE PER SERVING: Calories: 294 kcal— Total Fat: 25g — Total Carbs: 12g— Protein: 7.2g

Ingredients:
- 8 eggs
- ½ cup of almond milk
- 1 teaspoon of salt
- 2 cups of almond flour
- 1 tablespoon Vanilla powder extract
- ½ cup of melted butter
- 1 ¼ tablespoon of baking powder

Directions
- Preheat the oven to 325°F, and grease a baking pan with baking spray or rub butter on it.
- Put the eggs in a bowl, mix well.

- In another bowl, mix the almond flour, salt, and vanilla extract together.
- Then, mix the butter in a separate bowl, and pour the eggs mixture in it whisking thoroughly.
- Pour the dry ingredients in the eggs and butter and mix well.
- Then, add the almond milk and baking powder, mix well.
- Pour the mixture in the pan and bake for 30 minutes.
- Take out and let it cool on the cake rack before slicing.

218. Cauliflower rice

Serves: 2 — Preparation time: 20 minutes — Meal Type: Main course/Lunch.
NUTRITIONAL VALUE PER SERVING: Calories: 204 kcal— Total Fat: 11g — Total Carbs: 4.2g— Protein: 1.5g

Ingredients:
- 1 head of cauliflower
- 1 tablespoon of olive oil or grass-fed butter
- Salt to taste

Directions
- Slice the cauliflower into small pieces with a sharp knife, add in a food processor and process it until fully broken.
- If any pieces left unprocessed, put them back in and process again.
- Preheat a large pan, and heat olive oil in it.
- Add in your processed cauliflower with a pinch of salt.
- Cover and cook for 4-8 minutes.
- Then, serve warm.

219. Olive-Flavoured Pork Broth

Serves: 5 — Preparation time: 1 hour — Meal Type: Main course/Lunch.
NUTRITIONAL VALUE PER SERVING: Calories: 274 kcal— Total Fat: 19g — Total Carbs: 3.2g— Protein: 19.5g

Ingredients:
- 8 boneless pork chops
- 8 ounces of ragu
- 3 chopped garlic cloves
- 2 sliced onions
- 1/8 cup of olive oil
- ¾ cup of sliced olives
- ½ cup of beef broth
- ¼ teaspoon of cinnamon

Directions
- Cut the pork into big pieces, but suitable for eating.
- Preheat the skillet and heat oil in it.
- Place in the pork and fry both sides until brown. Set aside.
- Take out the extra oil from the skillet, until two spoonful remains.
- Put in the onions and garlic and sauté until onions become tender.
- Add in the broth, meat, ragu, cinnamon, and olives, and stir.
- Cover and simmer for 20 minutes.
- Serve hot.

220. Grilled beef roast

Serves: 4 — Preparation time: 1 ½ hour — Meal Type: Main course/Lunch.
NUTRITIONAL VALUE PER SERVING: Calories: 592 kcal— Total Fat: 53.9g — Total Carbs: 1.3g— Protein: 26.4g

Ingredients:
- 2 pounds of boneless beef roast
- 1/8 cup of fresh sage leaves
- ¼ cup of rosemary leaves
- 3 peeled garlic cloves, peeled
- 1 lemon
- 1 tablespoon of salt

Directions
- Juice the lemon. Set aside.
- Put in rosemary, sage, and garlic into the blender and blend till smooth.
- Put in salt and the lemon juice into the blender, and fully blend again.
- Coat the beef with the mixture well.
- Place the meat on the grill and cover for an hour, or until cooked well.
- Serve hot.

221. Keto chicken breasts

Serves: 4 — Preparation time: 1 ½ hour — Meal Type: Main course/Lunch.
NUTRITIONAL VALUE PER SERVING: Calories: 592 kcal — Total Fat: 29g — Total Carbs: 53g — Protein: 2.5g

Ingredients:
- 2 pounds of chicken breasts
- 2 minced garlic cloves
- 2 ¼ tablespoons of dried oregano
- 2 ¼ tablespoons of keto mustard
- 1 ¼ cups olive oil
- Salt to taste
- 1 cup lemon of juice

Directions
- Mix in the mustard, oregano, and garlic in a mixing bowl well.
- When fully mixed, drop in your oil, lemon juice, salt to taste, mix well.
- Put the meat in a zip lock bag, then pour in the mixture. Coat well.
- Seal and marinate for at least eight hours.
- Preheat the oven to 350 F, and bake for sixty minutes.

222. Keto Mushroom Soup

Serves: 4 — Preparation time: 1 ½ hour — Meal Type: Main course/Lunch.
NUTRITIONAL VALUE PER SERVING: Calories: 464 kcal — Total Fat: 65.5g — Total Carbs: 1.5g— Protein: 13.5g

Ingredients:
- 31 ounces of chicken broth
- 11 mushrooms
- 2 crushed garlic cloves
- 2 cups of heavy whipping cream
- 1 tablespoon of sherry
- 1 diced onion
- 1 teaspoon of salt
- 1 teaspoon of black pepper
- ½ cup of butter
- ½ teaspoon of thyme
- ¼ cup of vegetable stock

Direction
- Slice 9 mushrooms, and slice 2 separately.
- In a heated pan, add in the butter, then onions, garlic, and the sliced mushrooms. Sauté for 3-5 minutes.
- Pour in chicken broth and vegetable stock and stir on high flame. Then, add in sherry, thyme, salt and pepper.
- Reduce your heat to a low level, and simmer for 5 more minutes.
- Pour in the cream gently, and stir to thicken.
- Throw in your 2 sliced mushrooms and steam for a minute or two.
- You can serve this soup with Keto bread.

223. Cheesy bacon ranch chicken

Serves: 3 — Preparation time: 1 hour — Meal Type: Main course/Lunch.
NUTRITIONAL VALUE PER SERVING: Calories: 592 kcal— Total Fat: 53g — Total Carbs: 29g— Protein: 25g

Ingredients:
- 8 boneless and skinned chicken breasts
- 1 cup of olive oil
- 8 thick slices bacon
- 3 cups of shredded mozzarella
- 1 ¼ tablespoon of ranch seasoning
- 1 small chopped onion
- Chopped chives
- Kosher salt or pink salt
- Black pepper

Directions
- Preheat skillet and heat little oil, and cook bacon evenly on both sides.
- Save 4 tablespoons of drippings and put the others away.
- Add in salt and pepper in a bowl and rub it over chicken to season.
- Put ½ oil on the flame to cook the chicken from each side, for 5 to 7 minutes.
- When ready, reduce the heat and put in the ranch seasoning, then add mozzarella.
- Cover and cook on a low flame for 3-5 minutes.
- Put in bacon fat and chopped chives, then bacon and cover it.
- Take off and serve warm.

224. Keto pork chops

Serves: 3 — Preparation time: 1 hour — Meal Type: Main course/Lunch.
NUTRITIONAL VALUE PER SERVING: Calories: 594 kcal— Total Fat: 53g — Total Carbs: 28g— Protein: 27g

Ingredients:
- 8 boneless pork loin chops
- 3 minced cloves of garlic
- 1/8 a cup of extra-virgin olive oil
- 2 tablespoons of rosemary
- Kosher salt
- Black pepper
- 1 cup of butter

Directions
- Preheat oven to 375°.
- Coat pork with salt and pepper generously in a bowl.
- Microwave butter in for 10-20 seconds to melt. Add in rosemary and garlic, mix and set aside.
- In a skillet, pour in olive oil and put the seasoned pork inside, and fry till golden on each side
- Preheat oven to 145°
- Take out fried pork and coat generously with butter and garlic.
- Place in a pan, bake for 10-12 minutes.
- Serve with more garlic butter.

225. Broiled Salmon

Serves: 4 — Preparation time: 1 ½ hour — Meal Type: Main course/Lunch.
NUTRITIONAL VALUE PER SERVING: Calories: 492 kcal— Total Fat: 50g — Total Carbs: 39g— Protein: 22g

Ingredients:
- 4 ounces of salmon fillets
- 1 tablespoon of grainy mustard
- 1 tablespoon of minced shallots
- 2 teaspoons of chopped thyme leaves
- 2 minced cloves of garlic
- 2 teaspoons of chopped rosemary
- Juice of ½ a lemon
- Kosher salt
- Black pepper
- Lemon slices

Direction
- Preheat your broiler.
- Take a bowl, mix in mustard, shallot, garlic, rosemary, and thyme together. Then, add lemon juice, salt and pepper, and mix well.
- Lay your fillets and spread the marinade all over.
- Broil for 7 to 8 minutes.

226. Keto taco casserole

Serves: 4 — Preparation time: 1 ½ hour — Meal Type: Main course/Lunch.
NUTRITIONAL VALUE PER SERVING: Calories: 298 kcal— Total Fat: 18.7g — Total Carbs: 10.8g— Protein: 22.6g

Ingredients:
- 6 eggs
- 2 cups of shredded Mexican cheese
- 2 tablespoons of chopped parsley leaves
- 2 pounds of ground beef
- 2 tablespoons of kosher salt
- 2 tablespoons of extra-virgin olive oil
- 2 tablespoons of taco seasoning mix
- 1 seeded and minced jalapeño
- 1 sliced jalapeño
- 1 cup of sour cream
- Small diced yellow onion
- Black pepper

Direction
- Crack and beat six eggs lightly.
- Preheat an oven to 350°.
- Meanwhile, place a skillet on medium heat, heat oil, and add onions. Fry until tender.
- Then add in the ground beef, sauté for few seconds until the color change, then add salt and pepper to taste.
- Sprinkle in taco seasoning and jalapeño and stir well.
- Add eggs in the meat, and mix well.
- Put the mixture in a baking dish, sprinkle some cheese on the tip, then bake until set, or for 25 minutes.

227. Garlicky Lemon Mahi-Mahi

Serves: 3 — Preparation time: 1 ½ hour — Meal Type: Main course/Lunch.
NUTRITIONAL VALUE PER SERVING: Calories: 592 kcal— Total Fat: 53g — Total Carbs: 19g— Protein: 33g

Ingredients:
- 6 tablespoons of butter
- 5 tablespoons of extra-virgin olive oil
- 4 ounces of mahi-mahi fillets
- 3 minced cloves of garlic
- Kosher salt
- Black pepper
- 2 pounds of asparagus
- 2 sliced lemons
- Zest and juice of 2 lemons
- 1 teaspoon of crushed red pepper flakes 1 tablespoon of chopped parsley

Directions
- Melt 3 tablespoons of butter and olive oil in a microwave.
- Heat a skillet and put in mahi-mahi, then sprinkle black pepper.
- Cook for 4 to 5 minutes on each side. When done, move to a plate.
- In another skillet, add remaining oil and add in the asparagus, stir fry for 2-3 minutes. Take out in a plate.
- In the same skillet, pour in the remaining butter, and add garlic, red pepper, lemon, zest, juice, and parsley.
- Add in the mahi-mahi and asparagus and stir together. Serve hot.

228. Keto Shrimp Alfredo

Serves: 3 — Preparation time: 25 minutes — Meal Type: Main course/Lunch.
NUTRITIONAL VALUE PER SERVING: Calories: 442 kcal— Total Fat: 53g — Total Carbs: 3g— Protein: 26g

Ingredients:
- 1 pound of wild shrimp
- 3 tablespoons of organic grass-fed whey
- 1 ½ cups of frozen asparagus
- 1 cup of heavy cream
- ½ cup of parmesan cheese
- Sea salt
- Black pepper
- 2 ground garlic cloves
- 1 small diced onion

Directions
- Peel and devein the shrimps, coat them well with salt and pepper. Let it cover in a bowl for 20 minutes.
- Preheat a skillet. Put in butter, garlic, and onions.
- When butter is melted, put in shrimp and stir fry till for 3 minutes.
- Pour in heavy cream and stir well. Then, add ion cheese and stir till cheese melts.
- Serve hot.

229. Broccoli Salmon

Serves: 3 — Preparation time: 30 minutes — Meal Type: Main course/Lunch.
NUTRITIONAL VALUE PER SERVING: Calories: 374 kcal— Total Fat: 20.5g — Total Carbs: 14g— Protein: 26.6g

Ingredients:
- 8 ounces of cooked salmon
- 2 celery stalks
- 1 tablespoon of olive oil
- 1 head of medium-sized broccoli
- 1 tablespoon of Brain octane
- ½ teaspoon of thyme
- ¼ teaspoon of curry powder
- ½ teaspoon of black pepper
- ½ teaspoon of salt
- ½ trimmed leak
- ¼ of an avocado
- ½ of an onion sliced

Directions
- Mix curry, thyme, pepper, salt, and set aside.
- Slice avocado into small pieces.
- Add in leek, broccoli and celery in a saucepan and boil it until soft.
- Drain excess water, leaving only about 1 cup of liquid.
- Using some saved water, blend the veggies in a blender halfway between smooth. Do not use up all the water. Then, put in the blended spices, and mix well.
- In a saucepan, pour oil, and sauté onion until soft, then add blended veggies. Then, add sliced avocado and let it steam.
- Add in salmon, steam for 1 minute, then serve hot with rice or alone.

230. Beef -stuffed onions

Serves: 5 — Preparation time: 30 minutes — Meal Type: Main course/Lunch.
NUTRITIONAL VALUE PER SERVING: Calories: 281 kcal— Total Fat: 26g — Total Carbs: 10g— Protein: 17g

Ingredients:
- 5 onions (medium-sized)
- ¾ pound of ground beef
- 2 medium eggs
- Italian seasoning to taste
- 2 spoons of olive oil
- Salt
- Black pepper
- ¼ cup of ground pork
- 4 tablespoons parmesan cheese
- Worcestershire sauce to taste
- 2 ounces of quartered cheddar cheese

Directions
- Preheat oven to 350°F.
- Slice off the ends of each onion, peel, and remove layers. Take out the inner layers, so the onion is hollow and bottomless. Place it in a casserole dish.
- In another bowl, whisk eggs lightly.
- In another bowl, mix the two kinds of cheese.
- In another bowl, put in the ground beef, eggs mixture, olive oil, ground pork, and Worcestershire sauce, ¼ teaspoon of salt and other seasonings to taste, and mix well.
- Fully stuff each onion with the mix of beef and egg.
- Make a space in the stuffing for cheese balls and put inside.
- Cover the onion with another meat layer, and bake for 30-45 minutes.

231. Bacon-Parmesan Spaghetti Squash

Serves: 4 — Preparation time: 2 hours — Meal Type: Main course/Lunch.
NUTRITIONAL VALUE PER SERVING: Calories: 288 kcal— Total Fat: 18.5g — Total Carbs: 3.5g— Protein: 22g

Ingredients:
- 2 pounds spaghetti squash
- 2 pounds bacon
- ½ cup of butter
- 2 cups of shredded parmesan cheese
- Salt
- Black pepper

Directions
- Preheat oven to 375°F, and line a baking sheet with parchment paper or foil and spray with baking spray.
- Cut off the stem end of the spaghetti squash, slice into rings no more than an inch wide, and take out the seeds.
- Lay the sliced rings down on the baking sheet, bake for 40-45 minutes. It is ready when the strands separate easily when a fork is used to scrape it. Let it cool.
- Cut up the bacon into pieces, and cook them pan until crispy. Take out and let it cool.
- Take off the shell on each ring, and separate each strand with a fork and put them in a bowl.
- Heat the strands in a microwave to get them warm, then put in butter and stir around till the butter melts.
- Pour in parmesan cheese and bacon crumbles, and add salt and pepper to your taste.
- Enjoy.

232. Cheese-mushroom pork chops

Serves: 4 — Preparation time: 2 hours — Meal Type: Main course/Lunch.
NUTRITIONAL VALUE PER SERVING: Calories: 495 kcal— Total Fat: 35g — Total Carbs: 6g— Protein: 38g

Ingredients:
- 10 ounces of white mushrooms
- 6 tablespoons of butter
- 4 boneless pork chops
- 2 tablespoons of sour cream
- ¾ cup of shredded mozzarella cheese
- ½ teaspoon of ground ginger
- 1 teaspoon of brain octane oil
- 1 small chopped
- 1 clove garlic minced
- Salt to taste
- Black pepper to taste

Directions
- Slice the mushrooms and set aside.
- Put in dry seasonings in a bowl and mix well.
- Season the pork chops with the above seasoning mix.
- In a skillet, melt four tablespoons of butter, then add in brain octane oil.
- Add in chops and cook until brown. Take out and set aside.
- Preheat oven to 350°F.
- Add butter in the same skillet, and add garlic, onions and mushrooms, sauté until onions are soft and water evaporates from mushrooms. Then, add seasonings to taste.
- Remove from heat, and add in the sour cream, stir well.
- Coat the pork generously with mushroom mixture, place it on a baking sheet.
- Then, sprinkle cheese on top, and bake for 10 -15 minutes in a preheated oven at 350°F.

233. Keto turkey meatballs

Serves: 2 — Preparation time: 30 minutes — Meal Type: Main course/Lunch.
NUTRITIONAL VALUE PER SERVING: Calories: 135 kcal— Total Fat: 57g — Total Carbs: 6g— Protein: 75g

Ingredients:
- 1 pound of ground turkey
- 1 tablespoon of fish sauce
- 1 diced onion
- 2 tablespoons of soy sauce
- ½ almond flour
- 1/8 cup of ground beef
- ½ teaspoon of garlic powder
- ½ teaspoon of salt
- ½ teaspoon of ground ginger
- ½ teaspoon of thyme
- ½ teaspoon of curry
- 5 tablespoons of olive oil

Directions
- Combine ground turkey, fish sauce, 1 diced onion, soy sauce, ground beef, seasonings, oil, and flour in a large mixing bowl. Mix it thoroughly.
- Form meatballs depending on preferred size.
- Heat skillet and pour in 3 tablespoons of oil [you may need more depending on the size of meat balls].
- Cook meatballs until evenly browned on each side. Serve hot.

234. Turkey Breasts with Salsa

Serves: 4 — Preparation time: 40 minutes — Meal Type: Main course/Lunch.
NUTRITIONAL VALUE PER SERVING: Calories: 189 kcal— Total Fat: 18.6g — Total Carbs: 7.5g— Protein: 19.4g

Ingredients:
- 4 boneless turkey. Skinned.
- 3 tablespoons olive oil
- Salt
- Pepper
- For salsa:
- 6 chopped tomatoes
- ½ diced onions
- 5 ounces of pitted and chopped olives
- 2 crushed garlic cloves
- 2 tablespoons of chopped basil
- 1 large diced
- Pepper
- Salt

Directions
- In a bowl, put salt, pepper and 3 spoons of oil, mix together and coat the turkey with this mixture.
- Place it on a preheated grill, and grill for ten minutes.
- In another bowl, mix garlic, olives, tomatoes, pepper, and drop the rest of the oil. Sprinkle salt and toss. Serve this salsa with turkey is warm.

235. Cauliflower chicken broth

Serves: 2 — Preparation time: 30 minutes — Meal Type: Main course/Lunch.
NUTRITIONAL VALUE PER SERVING: Calories: 73 kcal— Total Fat: 11g — Total Carbs: 4g— Protein: 3g

Ingredients:
- 7 cups romaine lettuce chopped
- 4 tablespoons of ghee
- 4 cups chicken broth
- 2 minced garlic cloves
- 2 cups of chopped cauliflower
- ½ of an onion
- 1½ tablespoon of chopped basil
- 1 tablespoon of chopped parsley
- 1 teaspoon salt
- 1/8 teaspoon of black pepper
- 1 tablespoon of olive oil

Directions
- In a skillet, heat ghee, then add 1 tablespoon of olive oil.
- Stir fry the onion and garlic until the onion is soft.
- Put in basil and parsley, salt and pepper to taste, and stir for a minute.
- Pour in lettuce and cauliflower stirring continuously.
- Then add in the broth, and cover and cook on a low flame for some minutes.
- Serve hot.

236. Coconut Crab Cakes

Serves: 4 — Preparation time: 1 hour — Meal Type: Main course/Lunch.
NUTRITIONAL VALUE PER SERVING: Calories: 311 kcal— Total Fat: 39g — Total Carbs: 2g— Protein: 6.9g

Ingredients:
- 1 tablespoon of minced garlic
- 2 pasteurized eggs
- 2 teaspoons of brain octane oil
- ¾ cup of coconut flakes
- ¾ cup chopped of spinach
- ¼ pound crabmeat
- ¼ cup of chopped leek
- ½ cup extra virgin olive oil
- ½ teaspoon of pepper
- ¼ onion diced
- Salt

Directions
- Pour the crabmeat in a bowl, then add in the coconut flakes and mix well.
- Whisk eggs in a bowl, then mix in leek and spinach.
- Season the egg mixture with pepper, 2 pinches of salt, and garlic.
- Then, pour the eggs into the crab and stir well.
- Preheat a pan, heat extra virgin olive, and fry the crab evenly from each side until golden brown. Remove from pan and serve hot.

237. Grilled lamb

Serves: 2 — Preparation time: 30 minutes — Meal Type: Main course/Lunch.
NUTRITIONAL VALUE PER SERVING: Calories: 299 kcal— Total Fat: 17.6g — Total Carbs: 0.5g— Protein: 33.5g

Ingredients:
- 2 pounds of lamb
- 5 spoons of ghee butter
- 3 tablespoons of Keto mustard
- 2 minced garlic cloves
- 1 ½ tablespoon of chopped basil
- ½ tablespoon of pepper
- 3 tablespoons of olive oil
- ½ teaspoon of salt

Directions
- Mix butter, mustard, and basil with a pinch of salt to taste. Then, set aside.
- Mix garlic, salt, and pepper together. Then, add a teaspoon of oil.
- Season the lamb generously with this mix.
- Grill the lamb on medium heat for five minutes, until fully cooked.
- Take butter mix and spread generously on chops and serve hot.

238. Chicken breasts with salsa

Serves: 4 — Preparation time: 45 minutes — Meal Type: Main course/Lunch.
NUTRITIONAL VALUE PER SERVING: Calories: 159 kcal— Total Fat: 17.6g — Total Carbs: 8.5g— Protein: 18.5g

Ingredients:
- 4 boneless chickens. Skinned.
- 4 tablespoons olive oil
- ½ tablespoon of ghee
- Salt
- Pepper
- For salsa:
- 2 crushed garlic cloves
- 2 tablespoons of chopped basil
- 5 ounces of olives
- 1 large diced
- 6 tomatoes
- Pepper
- Salt

Directions
- Pit and chop your olives, then chop tomatoes in a plate.
- In a bowl, put salt, pepper and 3 spoons of oil, and mix well. Then coat chicken with this mix.
- Place on a preheated grill for 5 minutes. Take chicken out and coat with ghee. Use a brush and put back it.
- Grill for another 6-8 minutes.
- In another bowl, mix garlic, olives, tomatoes, pepper, and drop the rest of the oil. Sprinkle salt and toss.
- Serve hot.

239. Chicken Spinach salad

Serves: 3 — Preparation time: 15 minutes — Meal Type: Main course/Lunch.
NUTRITIONAL VALUE PER SERVING. Calories: 303 kcal— Total Fat: 28.9g — Total Carbs: 4.6g— Protein: 43.3g

Ingredients:
- 2 ½ cups of spinach
- 4 ½ ounces of boiled chicken
- 2 boiled eggs
- ½ cup of chopped cucumber
- 3 slices of bacon
- 1 small avocado
- 1 tablespoon olive oil
- ½ teaspoon of Brain Octane oil
- Pinch of Salt
- Pepper

Direction
- Dice the boiled eggs.
- Slice boiled chicken, bacon, avocado, spinach, and cucumber, and combine them in a bowl. Then add diced boiled eggs.
- Drizzle with some oil. Mix well.
- Add salt and pepper to taste.
- Enjoy.

240. Keto Fish Cake

Serves: 4 — Preparation time: 30 minutes — Meal Type: Main course/Lunch.
NUTRITIONAL VALUE PER SERVING. Calories: 303 kcal— Total Fat: 28.9g — Total Carbs: 6g— Protein: 33.3g

Ingredients:
- 3 tablespoons of grated parmesan cheese
- 3 tablespoons of Keto mayonnaise
- 3 tablespoons olive oil of
- 2 tablespoons almond flour
- 1 stock cube
- 1 pound of firm tilapia
- 1 egg
- 1 teaspoon Keto mustard
- ½ teaspoon of Worcestershire sauce
- 1½ tablespoons fresh chopped parsley
- Salt pepper

Directions
- Chop the fish into bit size.
- In a bowl, put the fish, cheese, mayonnaise, egg and blend. Then, add the almond flour and mustard, mix well.
- Add in the parsley, Worcestershire sauce, sprinkle stock cube and a pinch of salt. Mould the mixture together into small disks.
- Heat oil in a pan lightly, then fry each side of disk evenly.
- Serve warm with sauce or salsa.

241. Keto mushroom chicken soup

Serves: 4 — Preparation time: 1 hour — Meal Type: Main course/Lunch
NUTRITIONAL VALUE PER SERVING. Calories: 136 kcal— Total Fat: 7g — Total Carbs: 4g— Protein: 19.9g

Ingredients:
- 6 cups of chicken stock
- 5 slices of chopped bacon
- 4 cups cooked chicken breast, chopped
- 3 cups of fat water
- 2 cups of chopped celery root
- 2 cups of sliced yellow squash
- 2 tablespoons of olive oil
- ½ teaspoon of brain octane oil
- ¼ cup of chopped basil
- ¼ cup of chopped onion
- ¼ cup of chopped tomatoes
- 1 tablespoon of ground garlic
- 1 cup of sliced white mushrooms
- 1 cup green beans, cut into 1-inch pieces
- Salt
- Black pepper

Directions
- Heat oil in a skillet, add in half of the onions, sauté until soft.
- Put in bacon and fry for a minute and a half.
- Then, add in onions, garlic, tomatoes, and mushrooms, stir fry for three minutes.
- Put in stock and fat water with rest of the ingredients, let it simmer for 10-15 minutes. Serve hot.

242. Lamb breasts with salsa

Serves: 4 — Preparation time: 50 minutes — Meal Type: Main course/Lunch.
NUTRITIONAL VALUE PER SERVING. Calories: 189 kcal— Total Fat: 20.6g — Total Carbs: 4.5g— Protein: 19.4g

Ingredients:
- For lamb:
- 4 boneless lamb. Skinned.
- 3 tablespoons olive oil
- Salt
- Pepper
- For salsa:
- 6 chopped tomatoes
- ½ diced onions
- 5 ounces of pitted and chopped olives
- 2 crushed garlic cloves
- 2 tablespoons of chopped basil
- 1 large diced
- Pepper
- Salt

Directions
- Preheat oven to 300°C.
- In a bowl, put salt, pepper and 3 spoons of oil, mix and coat the lamb.
- Place in grill, and grill for 45 minutes to an hour.
- In another bowl, mix garlic, olives, tomatoes, pepper, and drop the rest of the oil. Sprinkle salt and toss.
- Mix the veggies with the grilled lamb, and serve warm.

243. Cheesy- chicken roast

Serves: 4 — Preparation time: 30 minutes — Meal Type: Main course/Lunch.
NUTRITIONAL VALUE PER SERVING. Calories: 667 kcal— Total Fat: 49.9g — Total Carbs: 6.4g— Protein: 41.5g

Ingredients:
- 3 cups of chopped roasted chicken
- 2 cups of shredded cheddar cheese
- 2 cups white of shredded cheddar cheese
- 3 cups of shredded parmesan cheese

Directions
- Preheat oven to 350°F, and prepare a baking sheet. Be sure to rub butter or to spray with non-stick cooking spray.
- In a bowl, put in all the cheese and mix well.
- Microwave the cheese till it melts
- Put in the chicken and toss thoroughly.
- Put 2 tablespoons of the cheese chicken combo in a pile on the baking sheet. Be sure to leave space between piles.
- Bake for 4-6 minutes. The moment they turn golden brown at the edges, take them off.
- Serve hot.

244. Keto catfish soup

Serves: 2 — Preparation time: 30 minutes — Meal Type: Main course/Lunch.
NUTRITIONAL VALUE PER SERVING. Calories: 175 kcal— Total Fat: 57g — Total Carbs: 4g— Protein: 14.5g

Ingredients:
- 1 medium catfish
- 5 tablespoons of olive oil
- 1 lime
- 3 cups of water
- 1 habanero pepper
- 1 small onion
- Keto stock cubes
- 1 basil leaf salt
- Ground ginger
- 1 clove of grains of Selim
- 1 rough-skinned plum
- 1 calabash nutmeg
- 1 grain of paradise
- Black pepper

Directions

- Put together the grains of Selim, rough-skinned plum, calabash nutmeg, the grain of paradise and black pepper. Grind in a food grinder without water until powdered.
- Chop the onion and pepper, then cut the lime in two pieces, wash the catfish with half lemon juice and rinse with water.
- In a pot, put in the catfish, powdered seasonings, olive oil, cups of water, chopped onion, ginger, basil leaf, and chopped pepper. Then, put in salt and stock cubes to taste.
- Boil for 30-40 minutes, then serve hot.

245: Chicken salad

Yields: 6 servings Prep time: 10 minutes Cook time: 20 minutes.
Nutrition value per serving. Net: Calories: 279 net Net Fats: 19 g Net carbs: 10 g Net Proteins: 25 g

Ingredients
- 2 lbs. chicken breast
- 3 celery stalks, diced
- ½ cup Mayonnaise
- 2 teaspoon brown mustard
- ½ teaspoon salt
- 2 tablespoon Dill, fresh and chopped
- ¼ Cup Pecans, chopped

Directions
- Preheat oven to 450 degrees °F, and prepare a baking tray by lining it with parchment paper.

- Bake the chicken for 15 minutes, or until it is well cooked.
- Combine the celery, mayonnaise, mustard, and salt in a mixing bowl. Let it sit in the refrigerator to cool.
- Take out the chicken from the oven when done, and slice into bite-sized chunks. Let it cool, then mix in with mayonnaise mixture.
- Let it cool overnight in the fridge for best results; however, it can be eaten straight away.

246: Slow Cooker Lemon Thyme Chicken

Yields: 4 servings Prepare time: 10 minutes Cook time: 4 hours.

Nutrition Value per serving Calories: 120 net Fat: 8 g net. Protein: 12 g net Carbs: 1 g net

Ingredients
- 10-15 cloves of garlic
- 2 sliced lemons
- ½ teaspoon of ground pepper
- 1 teaspoon of thyme
- 3 ½ -pound whole chicken

Directions
- Put lemon and garlic at the base of the slow cooker.
- Mix all the spices, and marinate the chicken with this rub.
- Put the chicken in the slow cooker, cover it, and cook for 4 hours on a low flame.
- Take out the chicken and serve hot.

247: Slow Cooker Balsamic Oregano Chicken

Yields: 4 servings Prep time: 10 minutes Cook time: 4 hours 15 minutes.
Nutrition Value per serving. Calories: 190 net Fat: 6 g net Protein: 26 g net Carbohydrates: 6 g net

Ingredients
- 6 pieces of boneless, skinless chicken
- 2 cans of diced tomatoes
- 1 large onion, thinly sliced
- 4 cloves of garlic
- ½ cup of balsamic vinegar
- 1 tablespoon of olive oil
- 1 tablespoon of dried rosemary
- 1 teaspoon of dried basil
- ½ teaspoon of thyme

- Salt and pepper

Directions
- Mix all of the ingredients except chicken.
- Put chicken at the base of the slow cooker.
- Pour the prepared mixture on the top of the chicken, and cook for 4 hours.
- When cooked, let it rest for 15 minutes, then serve.

248. Sous Vide Chicken Avocado And Lettuce

Servings: 4. Serve with cilantro, avocado and cucumber.
Nutritional Values: calories 217kcal, fats 13g, carbs 11g, protein 14g. Preparation time: 8 minutes Cooking time: 12 minutes

Ingredients:
- 3 tablespoons coconut cream
- 2 teaspoons fish sauce
- 1/2 teaspoon turmeric powder
- 1 teaspoon grated ginger
- Cucumber slices
- Cilantro for serving
- 1 pound boneless chicken
- 2 garlic cloves
- 1 sliced avocado
- Lettuce leaves
- 1/2 cup spinach

Directions:
- Bring the chicken, fish sauce, turmeric, garlic, coconut cream, ginger and spinach in a food processor and pulse.

- In a canning glass, grease with coconut oil and add 1tbsp of the chopped mixture into the jars.
- Fill water in the sous vide container and set the temperature to 196F.
- Properly close the glass jars to make air impermeable.
- Submerge the jars into the water bath and cook for 13 minutes.
- Remove the jars and keep to cool.
- Open the jars and remove the muffins.
- Add the lettuce leaves and drizzle with lime juice.

249. Sous Vide Chicken and Lemon soup

Nutritional Values: calories 366kcal, fats 3g, carbs 10g, protein 5g.
Preparation time: 20 minutes Cooking time: 50 minutes Servings: 8

Ingredients:
- 3 celery stalks
- 1/2 onion
- 3 boneless chicken breasts
- 1 tablespoon lemon zest
- 2 tablespoon lemon juice
- 3 carrots
- 3 garlic cloves cup chicken broth
- 3 thyme sprigs
- 2 tablespoon olive oil
- Salt
- Pepper
- 4 cup spinach
- 3 tablespoon dill

Directions:
- In a Dutch oven, pour the oil and add garlic, onion, carrots, and celery and cook for 7 minutes.
- Add the thyme and broth and simmer for 31 minutes.
- Fill water in the sous vide container and set the temperature to 196F.
- Gently put the chicken, salt and pepper to the sous vide bath and cook for 21 minutes.
- Remove the chicken from the bag and cut it into small sizes.
- Add the cut chicken pieces to the soup and cook for 11 minutes.
- Add the juice, dill, lemon zest, lemon juice, salt and pepper.
- Transfer to a serving plate and serve with garlic toast.

250. Sous Vide Lime-Honey Chicken Wings

Servings: 4. Preparation time: 20 minutes Cooking time: 45 minutes
Nutritional Values: calories 210kcal, fats 7g, carbs 7g, protein 19g

Ingredients:
- 1 tablespoon lime zest
- 3 tablespoon sesame oil
- 16 chicken wings
- Salt
- Pepper
- 1/2 cup honey
- 1/4 cup lime juice
- 1/4 cup soy sauce
- 2 tablespoon grated ginger
- 3 minced garlic cloves
- 2 sliced scallions

Directions:
- Get a small bowl and mix all the ingredients except the chicken wings.
- Pour the mixed ingredients into the zip lock bag and allow it to marinate in the refrigerator for 6 hours.
- After 6 hours, remove it from the refrigerator and keep it aside.
- Fill water in the sous vide container and set to 196F
- Immerse the bag in the water bath and cook for 41 minutes.
- Preheat the oven to 398F.
- Carefully pour the remaining marinade.
- Cook for 4 minutes.
- Serve immediately while still warm.

251. Sous Vide Chicken Tamari

Servings4: Preparation time: 30 minutes Cooking time: 15 minutes
Nutritional Values: calories 200kcal, fats 10g, protein 25g.

Ingredients:
- 2 tablespoon grated ginger
- 1 tablespoon sesame oil
- For Sauce: 3/4 cup cashews
- 1/2 cup almond butter
- 1 tablespoon maple syrup
- 2 tablespoons tamari
- 1 1/2 tablespoon fish sauce
- 3 crushed garlic cloves
- 1 1/2 tablespoon grated ginger
- 1 3/4 pound diced boneless chicken
- 1 1/2 teaspoon lime zest
- 1 1/2 tablespoon lime juice
- 1 tablespoon coconut oil
- 1 1/2 tablespoon turmeric powder
- 2 tablespoon tamari
- 2 chopped red chili
- 1 1/2 tablespoon coriander powder
- 1 teaspoon cumin powder
- Salt
- Pepper
- Coriander leaves

Directions:
- In a deep bowl, add and mix all the dry ingredients for the chicken.
- Add oil into the bowl and toss the diced boneless chicken in it and keep to marinate for 1 hour 55 minutes.
- Fill the sous vide container with water and set to 196F.
- Gently place the chicken in the zip lock bag and seal it by removing excess air.
- Immerse it in the water bath and cook for 11 minutes.
- In a bowl, add and mix the ingredients needed for the sauce and beat until a smooth blend forms.
- Preheat the grill and thread the chicken pieces in a skewer.
- Grill for 6 minutes and it turns brown.
- Transfer the chicken to a platter and serve with cashew sauce.

252. Sous Vide Goose Breast And Bacon

Servings: 5Preparation time: 10 minutes Cooking time: 10 minutes
Nutritional Values: calories 202kcal, fats 10g, proteins 25g.

Ingredients:
- 1 pound goose breast
- 1 cup bacon strips
- 1/4 cup olive oil Toothpicks
- Salt and pepper

Directions:
- Carefully chop the goose breast into small bite-sized chunks.
- Fold the goose in the bacon and secure with toothpick.
- Lightly rub the olive oil on the bacon and place it in a zip lock bag.
- Fill water in the sous vide container set to 196F.
- Submerge the bag and cook 11 minutes.
- Serve while it is still hot.

253. Sous Vide Orange Sauce And Duck

Servings: 4 Preparation time: 10 minutes Cooking time: 30 minutes

Nutritional Values: calories 600kcal, fats 42g, protein 29g.

Ingredients:
- Salt and pepper as per taste
- 3/4 cup orange juice
- 1 cup orange marmalade
- 1 tablespoon cornstarch
- 1 tablespoon paprika
- 4 duck breasts
- 3/4 cup chicken broth

Directions:
- In a saucepan, pour the orange juice, the orange marmalade and the chicken broth and mix thoroughly.
- Cook for 16 minutes over high heat.
- Add the cornstarch, stir and cook until it begins to thicken.
- Then, add the duck breast, the paprika, salt and pepper and put it in the zip lock bag by removing all air.
- Fill the sous vide container with water and set to 196F.
- Immerse the bag in the bath water and cook for 30 minutes.
- Remove the duck breast and transfer it to a platter.
- Pour the orange mixture over the duck breast.
- Serve and enjoy!

254. Sous Vide Turkey Mushroom Burgers

Servings: 4 Preparation time: 35 minutes Cooking time: 15 minutes

Nutritional Values: calories 500kcal, fats 26g, carbs 28g, protein 40g.

Ingredients:
- 4 English muffins
- Salt, pepper, mayonnaise and mustard as per taste
- 3 tablespoon parsley
- 1 1/4 pound ground turkey 2 tablespoon olive oil
- 1 mushroom cap
- Sliced avocado for serving
- 1 tablespoon shallot
- 1 teaspoon Worcestershire sauce slices cheddar cheese

Directions:
- Pulse the parsley, the shallot and mushroom together.
- Pour the olive oil, turkey, Worcestershire sauce, pepper and salt.
- Fill the sous vide container with water and set to 196F.
- Gently put the mixture into the zip lock bag. Remove excess air and seal.
- Submerge the bags into the water vide bath and cook for 29 minutes.
- Then grill the patties for 6 minutes on both sides. Put the slices carefully on the patty and cook for 3 minutes.
- Divide the muffin into half and spread with mustard and mayonnaise.
- Use the avocado as topping.
- Serve and enjoy.

255. Sous Vide Duck Garlic Cacciatore

Servings: 4 Preparation time: 50 minutes Cooking time: 90 minutes

Nutritional Values: calories 450kcal, fats 25g, carbs 13g, protein 42g.

Ingredients:
- 4 smashed garlic cloves
- 2 chopped celery
- 1 duck cut into
- 2 chopped carrots
- flour,
- 8 pieces
- 3 cups crushed tomatoes
- pepper
- 4 tablespoons butter
- 1 chopped yellow onion
- 1 cup dry red wine
- olive oil
- 3/4 pounds mushrooms
- 2 sprigs parsley
- Salt

Directions:
- Serve immediately and enjoy!
- In a large bowl, put the chopped ducks and sprinkle with salt and pepper.
- Fill water in the sous vide container and set to 196
- Put the chopped duck a large zip lock bag and seal by removing excess air.
- Immerse the bag in the sous vide bath and cook for 29 minutes.
- In a saucepan pan, add and stir the onion, celery, carrots, red wine and garlic and cook or 6 minutes.
- Add the mushrooms and the crushed tomatoes into the pan and stir.
- Add the duck, the parsley and the butter and cook for 58 minutes.
- Remove and place on a serving plate.

256. Sous Vide Ginger Chicken And Spinach

Servings: 4. Preparation time: 10 minutes Cooking time: 20 minutes

Nutritional Values: calories 430kcal, protein 34g, carbs 39g, fats 15g.

Ingredients:
- 2 tablespoons of canola oil
- 1 1/4 pound chopped boneless chicken
- pepper
- 1 1/4 cup baby spinach
- 1 tablespoon chopped ginger
- 2 tablespoon miso
- Salt
- 3 cup cooked brown rice
- 1 chopped garlic cloves

Directions:
- Pour the canola oil in a pan and heat. Add the garlic and ginger to the pan and cook for 4 minutes over medium heat.
- Fill water in the sous vide container and set to 196F.
- Put the chicken in the zip lock bag and seal by removing excess air.
- Place it gently in the sous vide water bath and cook for 11 minutes.
- In a deep bowl, add and mix the miso with 2 tbsp o water and beat until smooth paste is formed.
- In a saucepan, add spinach and the chicken and cook for 4 minutes, string frequently to avoid burning.
- Remove and transfer to a serving platter.
- Serve immediately and enjoy!

257. Sous Vide Rosemary Flavored Turkey

Servings: 8. Preparation time: 20 minutes Cooking time: 45 hours

Ingredients:
- 3 garlic heads
- 2 tablespoon olive oil
- 2 carrots
- 6 sprig sage
- 3/4 cup chicken broth
- Salt and pepper as per taste
- 1 turkey
- 3 onions
- 6 sprigs rosemary
- 2 stalks celery

Directions:
- In the cavity of the turkey, put the onion, garlic and herbs.
- In a bowl, pour the olive oil and toss the piece of turkey in it.
- Sprinkle the turkey with salt.

258.Roasted Butternut Squash Hummus

Servings: 1. Preparation Time: 10 minutes Cook time: 25 minutes

Ingredients
- Butternut squash: 275 gm (peeled and cut in 2cm dice)
- Chickpeas: 400 gm can
- Mild curry powder: ½ tsp
- Ground coriander: ½ tsp
- Ground cumin: 1 tsp
- Smoked paprika: ¼ tsp
- Tahini: 1 tbsp
- Garlic cloves: 2
- Lemon juice: 2 tbsp
- Olive oil
- Salt: as per your taste
- Fresh coriander: for serving
- Smoked paprika: for serving

Directions
- Preheat the oven to 200C
- Put the diced butternut squash on a baking dish and bake for 20-25 minutes
- Drain chickpeas and collect the chickpea juice and set aside
- Take a blending bowl and add ground coriander, drained chickpeas, curry powder, cumin, tahini, paprika, and garlic cloves
- Now add the butternut squash (roasted) leaving about a handful behind for serving
- Add approximately 3 tbsp of chickpea juice into the blending bowl
- Blend them all together to give the smooth consistency
- Transfer to serving bowl and top with salt and lemon juice
- Serve with the chickpeas and roasted butternut squash, smoked paprika, olive oil, and chopped coriander

259.Jackfruit Burger

Preparation Time: 10 minutes Cook time: 35 minutes Servings: 4Ingredients Burger buns: 4 Tinned jackfruit: 400 gm

Ingredients
- Brown onion: 1
- Ground cumin: 1 tsp
- Chinese five-spice: 1 tsp
- Smoked paprika: 2 tsp
- Cloves garlic: 2
- Vegetable oil: 2 tbsp
- Cayenne pepper: 1 tsp
- Tomato ketchup: 400 gm
- Soy sauce: 10 gm
- White wine vinegar: 20 gm
- Marmite: 5 gm
- Red onion sliced into rounds: 1
- Water: 20 gm
- White wine vinegar: 50 gm
- Salt: 1 tsp
- Sugar: 1 tsp
- Finely sliced red cabbage
- Cucumber rounds
- Vegan mayonnaise

Directions
- For the pickled onions, add all the ingredients in the saucepan and bring to boil – remove from the heat and let it sit quietly to cool
- Add vegetable oil in a separate pan and include garlic and onion till they soften
- Add the ketchup, vinegar, and spices to them
- Drain the tinned jackfruit liquid and add to the pan and simmer for twenty minutes
- Pull the jackfruit apart using tongs and add soy sauce and marmite at the top and leave it aside
- Cut the burger buns from between and char them on a grill
- Add pickled onions, jackfruits, and other garnishing items and enjoy

260. Sous Vide Spicy Adobo Chicken

Servings: 2 Preparation time: 5 minutes Cooking Time: 120 minutes.

Nutrition Values: Calories: 320 Carbohydrate: 33g Protein: 16g Fat: 14g Sugar: 3g Sodium: 255mg

Ingredients
- ½ tablespoon molasses
- 2 garlic cloves, crushed
- ¼ teaspoon whole black peppercorns
- 2 chicken leg quarters
- ¼ cup dark soy sauce Salt as needed
- ½ Worcestershire sauce 1 bay leaf
- ¼ cup white vinegar
- 1 tablespoon canola oil

Directions:
- In a bowl, add and mix the garlic, bay leaf, soy sauce, peppercorns, Worcestershire, molasses, bay leaf and salt.
- In a large zip lock bag, add the chicken legs with the marinade and refrigerate for 11 to 12 hours.
- Fill water in the sous vide container and preheat to 165F.
- Immerse the zip lock sealed chicken into the preheated water bath and heat for 120 minutes.
- Once done, remove the bag from the water bath and air dry the chicken for 12 to 16 minutes.
- Using a nonstick pan, sear with the canola oil over medium heat.
- Transfer the sauce from zip lock bag to the nonstick pan and cook according to desire.
- Serve in a serving bowl with the sauce and enjoy!

261. Sous Vide Greek Meatballs

Servings: 4 Preparation time: 20 minutes Cooking Time: 120 minutes\

Nutrition Values: Calories: 238 Carbohydrate: 3g Protein: 8g Fat: 21g Sugar: 2g Sodium: 332mg

Ingredients
- 2 garlic cloves, minced
- 1 teaspoon fresh oregano, minced
- 1 tablespoon extra-virgin olive oil
- 1 lb. ground chicken
- ¼ cup panko bread crumbs Lemon wedges for serving
- ½ teaspoon freshly ground black pepper
- 1 teaspoon kosher salt
- ½ teaspoon grated lemon zest

Directions:
- Fill the sous vide container with water and preheat the water to the temperature not 147F.
- Put the olive oil, chicken , garlic, lemon zest, pepper, salt and Oregon into a bowl and mix thoroughly.
- Add and combine with the panko breadcrumbs.
- Using your hands, form the mixture into 14 balls.
- Put the balls gently into a zip lock bag and seal after squeezing out the excess air.
- Immerse the bag into the water bath and cook underwater water for 120 seconds.
- Once cooked, remove the bag from the water bath and remove the balls from the bag.
- Line foil on the bottom of a baking sheet and transfer the balls to the sheet.
- Set the broiler temperature to high heat and broil for 6 or 7 minutes nor until balls turn brown.
- Transfer nto a platter and serve with lemon wedges.

262.Smoked Tofu and Warm Lentil Salad

Preparation Time: 15 minutes. Cook time: 35 minutes Servings: 4

Ingredients
- Smoked tofu: 200 gm
- Puy lentils: 350 gm
- Medium leek: 1
- Medium carrots: 3
- Onion: 1
- Garlic cloves: 3
- Wholegrain mustard: 3 tsp
- Bay leaves: 2
- Dried thyme: 2 tsp
- Balsamic vinegar: 2 tbsp
- Olive oil: 5 tbsp
- Vegetable broth: 750 ml
- Capers: 2-3 tbsp
- Fresh parsley leaves
- Salt & pepper: as per your taste

Directions
- Take a large pot and add vegetable broth and lentils
- Let the lentils cook on medium heat for 15 minutes or more till they are cooked completely
- When the lentils are done, remove the excess liquid and keep them aside but covered
- In a dish, heat some olive oil and fry garlic cloves and onion till they become soft
- Finely chop the leek, and peel carrots and turn them into small pieces
- In the garlic and onion, add the vegetable along with thyme and bay leaves and cook on medium heat till vegetables become soft
- Now add lentils and smoked tofu
- Combine them all well
- Take a separate bowl and add olive oil, mustard, garlic clove crushed, and balsamic vinegar
- Pour this dressing to the lentil salad with the parsley leaves and capers
- Add salt and pepper and serve hot

263.Mexican Tofu Scramble

Preparation Time: 5 minutes Cook time: 15 minutes Servings: 6

Ingredients
- Plain tofu: 400 gm
- Kidney beans: 400 gm can
- Garlic cloves: 2
- Turmeric: ½ tsp
- Nutritional yeast: 2 tbsp
- Corn: 170 gm can
- Red onion: 1
- Chipotle pepper: 1
- Red pepper: 1
- Flour tortillas
- Salt & pepper: as per your taste
- Bunch of fresh coriander
- Olive oil

Directions
- Take a large frying pan and add chopped onion, garlic, and chipotle till they turn golden brown
- Cut the red pepper in half cm pieces and add to onions and cook for 5 minutes
- Take another bowl and add drained tofu to it
- Scramble tofu using a fork and add nutritional yeast and turmeric
- Drain the kidney beans and rinse them along with corn and add them to the frying pan followed by tofu
- Mix them all well and cook on the low heat just to make them warm
- Add salt and pepper to taste
- Place on warm tortillas and put coriander leaves on top when serving

264.Goat Cheese Figs Pizza

Preparation Time: 20 minutes. Cook time: 80 minutes Servings: 1

Ingredients
- Fresh figs: 200 gm
- Fresh rosemary: 1 tbsp (finely chopped)
- Red onion: 1
- Hard goat cheese: 80 gm
- Rocket: 1 small bag
- Pine nuts: 2 tbsp
- Maple syrup: 1 tbsp
- Olive oil: 2 tbsp
- Balsamic vinegar: 1 tbsp
- Bread flour: 2 ½ cup
- Active dry yeast: 2 tbsp
- Warm water: 1 cup
- Olive oil: 2 tbsp
- Salt: 1 tbsp
- Sugar: 1 tsp

Directions
- Prepare the pizza crust by adding all the pizza crust ingredient in a bowl and knead with warm water
- Place it in the airtight container and leave for an hour or two
- At 220C, preheat the oven
- Take a saucepan and heat olive oil in it and fry the red onion
- Add balsamic vinegar and maple syrup till it becomes caramelized
- When the onions are cooked, put them in a bowl and add chopped rosemary
- Spread the pizza dough on the pizza pan
- Spread the onions on the pizza dough with the figs and goat cheese on top along with pine nuts
- Bake for 15 minutes
- Add rocket on top just before serving the pizza

265.Roasted Eggplant and Tomatoes

Preparation Time: 10 minutes Cook time: 45 minutes Servings: 6

Ingredients
- Eggplant: 1 medium – cut into medium pieces
- Tomatoes: 4 medium – cut into 6 pieces each
- Yellow onion: 1 medium – cut into ¼ inch pieces
- Unpasteurized sweet white miso: 2 tbsp
- Honey: 1 tsp
- Olive oil: 3 tbsp
- Freshly squeezed lemon juice: 1 tbsp
- Garlic clove, grated or pressed: 1 large
- Round coriander: 1 tsp
- Red chili pepper flakes: 1 tsp
- Ground turmeric: ½ tsp
- Fine sea salt: ½ tsp
- Cooked chickpeas: ¾ US cup
- Chopped fresh flat-leaf parsley
- Whole-milk yogurt for serving

Directions
- Preheat the oven to 200C
- Take a large baking sheet and line it with parchment paper
- Add tomatoes, eggplant, and onion on it
- Take a small bowl and add oil, lemon juice, mirin, miso, red chili pepper flakes, coriander, salt, and turmeric and stir and sprinkle on the vegetables to coat them evenly
- Roast the vegetables for 20 minutes till they turn brown
- Remove from the oven and toss them and again roast for 15 minutes
- Sprinkle chickpeas on top with a bit of salt and roast again for 5 minutes only
- Serve them with herbs on top and yogurt on the side
- Save the leftover in the airtight jar in the fridge

266 Sous Vide Ginger Duck Breast

Servings: 2 Preparation time: 20 minutes Cooking Time: 120 minutes.

Nutrition Values: Calories: 365 Carbohydrate: 19g Protein: 18g Fat: 25g Sugar: 13g Sodium: 63mg

Ingredients
- 1½ teaspoons sesame oil
- 1-inch fresh ginger, peeled and sliced thinly
- Kosher salt and pepper as needed
- 2 garlic cloves, thinly sliced
- 2 boneless duck breasts

Directions:
- Fill water in the sous vide container and preheat to 135F.
- In a bowl, add and sprinkle the duck breast with pepper and salt.

- Transfer the duck breast into a cooking pouch and add the sesame oil, garlic and ginger.
- Seal the bag using a vacuum sealer.
- Immerse the bag into the water bath and cook underwater for 120 minutes.
- Once cooked, remove the duck breast and do away with the ginger and garlic.
- Place a nonstick frying pan over high heat and place the duck breast into the pan.
- Cook and flip each side for 30 seconds.
- Keep the duck breast on a cutting board for 5 minutes.
- Cut and serve with any dish of choice.

267.Roasted Tofu and Cauliflower with Gribiche Sauce

Preparation Time: 10 minutes. Cook time: 35 minutes Servings: 4

Ingredients
- Medium cauliflower: 1
- Garlic cloves crushed: 2
- Plain tofu: 400 gm
- Nutritional yeast: 2 tbsp
- Garlic cloves crushed: 2
- Extra olive oil
- Turmeric: ½ tsp
- Dijon mustard: 2 tsp
- Extra virgin olive oil: 6 tbsp
- Cider vinegar: 2 tsp
- Finely chopped parsley: 5 tbsp
- Finely chopped gherkins in vinegar: 4 tbsp
- Finely chopped capers: 2 tbsp

Directions
- Preheat the oven to 200C
- Drain tofu and press to release as much liquid as you can

- Divide the cauliflower to its small florets
- Line the baking tray with the cauliflower florets and also include crushed garlic
- Brush with olive oil and roast for 30 minutes and turn after 15 minutes
- In the meantime, prepare the sauce by adding all the gribiche sauce ingredients and mix well and put aside
- Make tofu scramble just before after 20 minutes of placing cauliflower in the oven
- Take a bowl and mash tofu using a fork
- In a frying pan, add a bit of olive oil and add the mashed tofu
- Add crushed garlic, turmeric, and yeast and stir well
- Cook on medium heat for a while
- Serve immediately when the cauliflowers are done and place the sauce on the side

268. Low Carb Garlic Chicken

Servings: 2. Preparation Time: 15 minutes Cook Time: 40 minutes

Ingredients
- Chicken drumsticks: 1 lb
- Olive oil: 1 tbsp
- Salt: ¼ tbsp or as per your taste
- Pepper: ¼ tbsp or as per your taste
- Lemon juice: ½ tbsp
- Garlic: 3 cloves
- Fresh parsley: ¼ cup chopped finely

Directions
- Preheat the oven at 225C
- Grease the baking pan
- Add the chicken drumsticks into the pan and add salt and pepper as per your taste
- Further, add olive oil and lemon juice over the chicken drumsticks
- In the end, sprinkle parsley and garlic
- Bake the drumsticks until they turn golden
- Baking time depends on your baking temperature – usually, 30-40 minutes would be enough
- Serve with salad or a delicious cauliflower mash

269. Paprika Chicken with Garlic Mayo

Preparation Time: 15 minutes Cook Time: 40 minutes Servings: 2

Ingredients
- Chicken drumsticks: 1 lb
- Peeled Rutabaga: 2-3 inch cut
- Salt: ¼ tbsp or as per your taste
- Pepper: ¼ tbsp or as per your taste
- Olive oil: 2 tbsp
- Paprika powder: ½ tbsp
- Vegan Mayonnaise: 1 cup
- Garlic powder: 1 tsp
- Paprika powder: 1 tsp
- Salt: ¼ tbsp or as per your taste
- Pepper: ¼ tbsp or as per your taste

Directions
- Preheat the oven at 200C
- In a baking dish, add the drumsticks and the rutabaga
- Now mix salt, paprika powder, pepper, and olive oil
- Bake your preparations for over 40 minutes
- For paprika and garlic mayo, mix all the ingredients in vegan mayonnaise and serve with the roasted chicken drumsticks and rutabaga

270. Buffalo Chicken

Preparation Time: 10 minutes. Cook Time: 30 minutes Servings: 2

Ingredients
- Chicken wings or drumsticks: 1 lb
- Peeled Rutabaga: 2-3 inch cut
- Salt: ¼ tbsp or as per your taste
- Coconut oil or olive oil: 1 tbsp
- Paprika powder: ½ tbsp
- Tomato paste: ½ tbsp
- White vinegar: 1 tbsp
- Oil to grease the dish: 2 tbsp

Directions
- Preheat the oven at 225C
- Take a big bowl and add all the ingredients in it with the chicken
- Grease the baking pan
- Place the coated chicken in the baking pan and bake till golden brown for around 30 minutes or more

271. Sous Vide Jamaican Jerk Chicken

Servings: 3 Preparation time: 5 minutes Cooking Time: 190 minutes

Nutrition Values: Calories: 330 Carbohydrate: 4g Protein: 24g Fat: 23g Sugar: 1g Sodium: 311mg

Ingredients
- 2 lbs. chicken wings
- ¼ cup fresh cilantro for garnishing, chopped
- 2 tablespoons jerk seasoning

Directions:
- Fill your sous vide container with water and preheat to 146F.
- Gently add the chicken and jerk seasoning into a cooking pouch and seal using a vacuum sealer.
- Submerge the cooking bag into the preheated water bath and cook for 3 hours.
- Remove the bag from the bath when cooking time elapses and remove the chicken wings from the bag.
- Pat dry the wings and using a towel.
- Heat grill to high heat and place the wings in it.
- Reduce the grill heat to medium and cook the wings until crispy or light brown.
- Transfer the grill to a platter and add some jerk paste.
- Embellish with sliced cilantro and serve.

272. Sous Vide Chicken Caprese

Servings: 2 Preparation time: 5 minutes Cooking Time: 45 minutes

Nutrition Values: Calories: 440 Carbohydrate: 5g Protein: 30g Fat: 33g Sugar: 3g Sodium: 524mg

Ingredients
- 2 chicken breasts, boneless, skinless Salt and pepper as needed
- 2 teaspoons unsalted butter 4 cups lettuce
- large tomato, sliced
- oz fresh mozzarella, sliced
- tablespoons red onion, diced Fresh basil leaves
- 1 tablespoon extra-virgin olive oil 2 lemon wedges for serving

Directions:
- Fill the sous vide container with water and set the temperature to 146F.
- Sprinkle the chicken with pepper and salt in a bowl and transfer the chicken to a zip lock bag.
- Seal the bag using a vacuum sealer and immerse the bag into the preheated water bath.
- Cook for 46 minutes.
- Remove the bag from the water bath and drain the cooking liquid.
- Get a frying pan placed over medium to high heat.
- Put the butter into the pan and melt.
- Transfer the chicken breast to the melted butter and sear until golden brown.
- Transfer into a serving platter.
- Divide and distribute the lettuce onto the breast. Top with red onion, basil, mozzarella and tomato.
- Serve and enjoy with lemon wedges.

273: Easy Buffalo Wings

Servings2 Prep time: 1 hour. Cook time: 20 minutes.
Nutritional value per serving Calories: 620 net Protein: 48 g net Fat: 46 g net Carbs: 1 g net

Ingredients
- 6 Chicken Wings, 6 Drumettes, and 6 Wingettes
- 2 tablespoons of Butter
- 1/2 cup of Hot Sauce
- Paprika
- Garlic Powder
- Pepper and Salt to taste
- Cayenne (optional)

Directions
- Slice each chicken into wings and drums and remove the tips.
- Marinate the chicken with hot sauce and all spices. Keep it in the refrigerator for 1 hour for margination.
- Set broiler on high and put oven rack 6 inches below from the broiler.
- Line the baking tray with aluminum paper. Place wings on it, ensuring enough space in between them, so that heat can reach each chicken piece evenly from all sides.
- Then, cook for 8 minutes under the broiler until the wings turn golden brown.
- Melt butter in the microwave and pour half of it on the chicken. Add rest to the hot sauce. Add cayenne, if you like spicy.
- Turn the chicken and broil from the other side for 8 minutes more.
- When chicken turned brown from all sides, take it off the heat.
- Pour the rest of the butter and hot sauce mixture on it and coat evenly. Serve hot.

274: Stuffed Chicken Breast and smoked ham

Yields: 4 servings Prep time: 10 minutes Cook time: 30 minutes.
Nutrition Value per serving Calories: 427.5 net Fat: 13.6 g net Protein: 36.0 g net Carbohydrates: 3.5 g net

Ingredients
- 1 lb. chicken breasts
- 1 teaspoon salt
- 1 teaspoon black pepper
- 1 cup cream cheese
- 1 tablespoon fresh thyme
- ¼ cup fresh basil
- 2 cloves garlic, crushed and minced
- 1 cup smoked ham, diced
- 1 tablespoon olive oil

Directions
- Line the baking pan with aluminium foil, and preheat the oven to 350 degrees °F.
- Take each chicken breast and slice along one side, about two-thirds of the way in to create a space to stuff the chicken.
- Sprinkle salt and pepper on the chicken to season it.
- Combine cream cheese, thyme, basil, garlic and ham in a medium bowl, mix well.
- Fill each chicken with stuffing in equal amounts and tie all around with the cooking twine.
- Heat olive oil in a pan over medium heat, add chicken and cook for 2 to 3 minutes from each side, or until the chicken is lightly browned.
- Take out the chicken on the prepared baking dish and place in the oven.
- Bake for almost 20 minutes, or until the chicken is thoroughly cooked.

275: Slow Cooker Butter Chicken

Yields: 6 servings Prep time: 10 minutes Cook time: 5 hours.
Nutrition Value per serving: Net Carbs: 5.5 g net Fat: 19.4 g net Protein: 37 g net Carbohydrates: 20.6 g net

Ingredients
- 4 tablespoons unsalted butter
- 2 onions, diced
- 2 pounds boneless, skinless chicken breasts
- A 2-inch piece of ginger, cut into 1/2-inch pieces
- 4 garlic cloves
- ½ cup sliced almonds
- 1 cup plain yoghurt
- 2 teaspoons graham spice
- 1 teaspoon salt
- 1 can diced tomatoes, drained
- ¼ cup heavy cream

Directions
- Cut the chicken breasts into small pieces.
- Melt butter in a pan, add onions and sauté until brown.
- Add ginger, garlic, yoghurt, almonds, graham spices and salt in the food processor, blend until smooth. Then, add tomatoes and mix again.
- Gently put the chicken on the bottom of the slow cooker. Pour the blended mixture on top of the chicken, and cook for 4 to 5 hours on low flame.
- When done, serve it with cooked rice.

276: Slow Cooker Chicken Hearts

Yields: 3 servings Prep time: 5 minutes Cook time: 6 hours.
Nutrition Value per serving: Calories: 249.9 net Fat: 3 g net Protein: 38.7 g net Net carbs: 9.7 g net

Ingredients
- 7 tablespoons full-fat Greek yoghurt
- 2 tablespoons heavy cream or coconut milk
- ½ cup chicken stock
- ¼ tablespoon cayenne pepper
- ¼ tablespoon paprika
- ½ teaspoon salt
- ½ tablespoon Dijon mustard
- 2 cloves garlic, minced
- 1 lb. chicken hearts, cut into thirds
- ½ lb. whole mushrooms, sliced
- ½ onion, thinly sliced

Directions
- Put onions and mushrooms on the bottom of the slow cooker, then put the chicken on it.
- Then, add spices, garlic and mustard in it along with the chicken broth.
- Cover the pot and let it cook for 6 hours.
- Remove from the heat and let it rest for 4 to 5 minutes, then pour yoghurt and cream. Serve.

277: Chicken Crust Pizza with Bacon

Yields 4 servings Prep time: 5 minutes Cook time: 30 minutes.
Nutrition Value per serving: Calories: 360 net Fat: 5.9 g net Protein: 2.7 g net Net carbs: 0.7 g net

Ingredients
- 1/2-pound chicken mince
- 1/2 cup Parmesan cheese, freshly grated
- 1/2 cup Mozzarella cheese, grated
- Salt and ground black pepper, to taste
- 1 bell pepper, sliced
- 2 slices Canadian bacon, chopped
- 1 tomato, chopped
- 1 teaspoon oregano
- 1/2 teaspoon basil

Directions
- Mix the chicken mince, cheese, salt, and black pepper together in a mixing bowl.
- Spread the cheese-chicken mixture on a lined baking pan and press it evenly.
- Bake it in a preheated oven, at 390 degrees °F for 20 minutes.
- Then top it with bell pepper, bacon, tomato, oregano, and basil.
- Bake it for 10 minutes more and serve hot.

278: Tangy Classic Chicken Drumettes

Yields 4 servings Prep time: 5 minutes Cook time: 35 minutes.
Nutrition Value per serving Calories: 209 net Fat: 12.2 g net Protein: 0.1 g net Carbs: 0.4 g net

Ingredients
- 1-pound chicken drumettes
- 1 tablespoon olive oil
- 2 tablespoons butter, melted
- 1 garlic cloves, sliced
- Fresh juice of 1/2 lemon
- 2 tablespoons white wine
- Salt and ground black pepper, to taste
- 1 tablespoon fresh scallions, chopped

Directions
- Preheat the oven to 440 degrees °F.

- Place the chicken in the pre-lined baking pan. Then, sprinkle olive oil and melted butter.
- Then, add garlic, lemon, wine, salt, and black pepper.
- Bake for about 35 minutes.
- Take out and garnish with fresh scallions. Serve hot.

279. Crispy Chicken Fillets in Tomato Sauce

Yields 3 servings Prep time: 5 minutes Cook time: 10 minutes.
Nutrition Value per serving: Calories: 359 net Fat: 23.6 g net Carbs: 1.2 g net Protein: 30.4 g net

Ingredients
- 2 tablespoons double cream
- 1 egg
- 2-ounces pork rinds, crushed
- 2 ounces Romano cheese, grated
- Sea salt and ground black pepper, to taste
- 1 teaspoon cayenne pepper
- 1 teaspoon dried parsley
- 1 garlic clove, halved
- 1/2-pound chicken fillets
- 2 tablespoons olive oil
- 1 large-sized Roma tomato, pureed
- Bread crumbs

Directions
- Whisk together cream and egg in a small bowl.
- Mix the crushed pork rinds, Romano cheese, black pepper, salt, cayenne

pepper, and dried parsley in another bowl.
- Rub the garlic cloves on the chicken from all over. Then, dip the chicken fillets in the egg mixture, then, coat the chicken with bread crumbs from all sides.
- Warm the olive oil along with ghee in a pan over normal heat.
- When thoroughly hot, cook chicken fillets for 2 to 4 minutes from each side.
- Take out the cooked chicken fillets on a pre-greased baking pan. Top with the pureed tomato, and bake for about 2 to 3 minutes until thoroughly warmed.
- Serve hot.

280: Slow Cooker Lemon Garlic Chicken

Yields: 2 servings Prep time: 10 minutes Cook time: 6 to 7 hours in low flame or 3 to 4 hours on high flame.
Nutrition Value per serving Calories: 274 net Fat: 16.7 g net Protein: 26.9 g net Carbs: 3.4 g net

Ingredients
- 1 pound of chicken breast
- 3/8 cup chicken broth
- 1-1/2 tablespoons lemon juice
- 1/ 2 lemon, sliced
- 1 tablespoon garlic, minced
- 1/2 teaspoon basil
- 1/4 teaspoon salt
- 1/8 teaspoon pepper
- 1/4 teaspoon garlic powder
- 1/4 teaspoon oregano
- 4 tablespoon melted butter

Directions
- Mix all spices and melted butter in a bowl, and thoroughly coat the chicken breast with it.
- Heat butter in a pan and cook coated chicken breast for about 7 to 10 minutes from each side.
- Now put the chicken breast in a slow cooker, and place lemon slices on top of it. Then, add the chicken broth in the slow cooker, and let it cook for 6 to 7 hours on low flame.

281: Chicken and Waffles with Hollandaise

Yields: 4 servings Prep time: 15 minutes Cook time: 45 minutes.
Nutrition Value per serving: Calories: 639 g net Fats: 48 g net Carbs: 2 g net Proteins: 60 g net

Ingredients
- 1 cup coconut oil or bacon fat, for frying
- 2 large eggs
- 1½ cups grated Parmesan cheese (or pork dust if dairy-free)
- ¼ teaspoon ground black pepper
- 1 pound boneless, skinless chicken thighs
- 3 cups shredded zucchini
- Fine sea salt
- 1 cup powdered Parmesan cheese (or pork dust if dairy-free)
- 2 tablespoons unsalted butter (or coconut oil if dairy-free), softened
- 2 large eggs, beaten
- ½ cup Hollandaise, for serving
- 1 cup bacon fat, beef tallow, duck fat, or lard (or unsalted butter or ghee if not dairy-sensitive)
- 4 large egg yolks
- ½ cup lemon juice
- ½ teaspoon fine sea salt
- ¼ teaspoon ground black pepper

Directions
- Slice the chicken thighs into small pieces.
- Beat an egg in a bowl, set aside.
- In another bowl, mix an egg with grated parmesan and pepper.
- Evenly coat each chicken pieces first in egg then in egg and cheese mixture.
- Heat one cup of coconut oil in a skillet, and fry the chicken pieces until it turns golden from all sides. Take out in a plate and set aside.
- Put shredded zucchini in a sieve and dash with salt. Let it sit for 4 minutes until the moisture dries out
- Heat the waffle iron, and put 3 to 4 spoons of zucchini in the centre of the waffle iron. Close the lid until it turns brown and take a waffle shape.
- Put the chicken on top of each waffle, once they are ready. Set aside
- Now to make hollandaise, heat fat in a pan over high heat.
- Blend egg yolks and lemon juice in a food processor or blender, until it turned into a smooth paste. Pour the fat slowly while pulsating the blender on low speed. Then, add salt and pepper. Pulse again to mix thoroughly.
- Pour hollandaise on the waffles and serve.

282: Cordon Bleu Lasagna

Yields: 10 servings Prep time: 12 minutes Cook time: 1 hour 40 minutes.
Nutrition Value per serving Calories: 314 net Fats: 26 g net Carbs: 3 g net Protein: 16 g net

Ingredients
- To make chicken
- 3 tablespoons bacon fat, lard, or ghee
- 4 chicken leg quarters (about 3 pounds)
- 1½ teaspoons salt
- ½ teaspoon ground black pepper
- ¼ cup diced onions
- 1 teaspoon minced garlic
- 1 cup of chicken bone broth.
- To make the sauce
- ¼ cup (½ stick) unsalted butter
- 1½ ounces cream cheese (3 tablespoons)
- ¼ cup beef or chicken bone broth
- 1 cup shredded Swiss cheese
- Salt to taste
- ground black pepper
- To make lasagna
- 1 large zucchini (about 10 inches long), trimmed and sliced lengthwise into ¼-inch planks
- 1 (4-ounce) package sliced Swiss cheese
- 1 (4-ounce) package thin-sliced ham

Directions
- Thoroughly season chicken legs with salt and pepper.
- Heat the bacon fat in a deep pan, and fry chicken legs for 7 to 8 minutes, or until it turned golden brown.
- Put onions and garlic in the same pan with chicken legs, and sauté until it turns light golden. Keep stirring continuously.
- Now, add the broth and cover. Let it simmer for an hour or so, or until the chicken meat falls off the bones.
- Shred the chicken to pieces, and set aside.
- To make the sauce, combine cream cheese, butter and bone broth in another pan and cook while stirring continuously until it thickens. Add Swiss cheese and stir again to allow the cheese to melt completely. Then, add salt and pepper to taste in the sauce. Set aside.
- Preheat the oven to 350 degrees °F.
- To make lasagna, put the zucchini layers in casserole dishes, and pour half of the sauce over the zucchini.
- Then, top it with Swiss cheese slices; then with ham; then put a layer of shredded chicken; and finally, pour the remaining sauce over it.
- Bake the lasagna for 20 minutes and serve hot.

283: Poulet Grand-Mère

Yields: 4 servings Prep time: 15 minutes Cook time: 30 minutes.
Nutrition Value per serving: Calories: 489 net Fats: 42 g net Carbs: 3 g net Proteins: 23 g net

Ingredients
- 4 bone-in, skin-on chicken thighs
- 1 teaspoon salt
- ¼ cup ghee (or coconut oil if dairy-free)
- 4 sprigs of fresh thyme, plus extra for garnish
- 4 strips thick-cut bacon, diced
- ¼ cup sliced onions
- 1 cup sliced mushrooms
- Ground black pepper
- 2 cups of chicken bone broth
- 2 tablespoons melted ghee or unsalted butter

Directions
- Preheat the oven to 350 degrees °F.
- Dash the chicken thighs with salt.
- Melt ghee in a skillet and add thyme and chicken in it. Let it cook 2 minutes from each side until it turns golden in colour. While cooking, try to retain the moisture of the chicken by occasionally pouring the ghee over the chicken with the help of a spoon.
- Take the chicken off the skillet, and place it on a baking tray to bake the chicken for 7 to 8 minutes.
- Meanwhile, sauté the diced bacon in the leftover ghee in the skillet for about 4 minutes. Add in the onions and sauté until soft. Then, mix in the mushrooms and cook for another 3 minutes and season it with salt and pepper.
- Finally, add the broth to the skillet. Let it simmer and thicken before serving with the chicken.

284.Electric Smoked Pig Shots

Ingredients
- Thickly cut bacon, sliced in half
- Sausage links; thoroughly smoked and cut into a thick round measuring ½ inches
- Barbecue sauce
- ½ cup of grated cheese
- 8 ounces of cream cheese
- 2 tbsp of Jeff's original rub
- 2 tbsp of chopped jalapenos

Directions
- Take a mixing bowl and add both the types of cheese along with the original rub and chopped jalapenos. Mix everything well
- Now take the bacon and wrap half-pieces around the slices of sausage
- Secure this wrapping with a toothpick
- In these cups, add in the cream cheese but make sure not to fill it to the brim or else it may overflow while smoking
- Set the smoker for indirect cooking by keeping the temperature in the range of 250 to 275 F
- Keep these pig shots on the smoker grate and cook for almost 90 minutes. Check if the bacon has cooked thoroughly
- Glaze it with barbecue sauce and let it cook for another 10 minutes to allow the sauce to seep in
- Serve

285.Electric Smoked Eggs

Ingredients
- 12 eggs

Directions
- Preheat your smoker by pushing the temperature to 325 degrees F
- Now place the egg directly on the grates of the grill and cook for half an hour
- Remove the cooked eggs and place them directly into an ice bath. Let them chill completely
- Now reduce the temperature of your smoker to 175 degrees
- Peel the eggs and then once again put them back to the grill
- Smoke them for further half an hour
- Serve and enjoy

286.Vegan Cheddar Garlic Wings

Servings: 2 Preparation Time: 15 minutes Cook Time: 30 minutes

Ingredients
- Chicken wings: 1 lb
- Vegan cheddar cheese: 1/6 cup freshly grated
- Olive oil: 1 tbsp
- Garlic: ½ clove minced
- Garlic powder: 1/8 tsp
- Salt: ½ tsp

Directions
- Preheat the oven at 225C
- Add olive oil and spices to the chicken in a big bowl
- Put the marinated chicken in the refrigerator for 30 minutes at least
- In a preheated oven, bake the chicken for 25 minutes till it turns golden brown
- You can also grill the chicken wings
- Place the cooked wings in a bowl and add cheddar cheese on top
- Serve hot

287.Pan Fry Chicken and Cabbage Cucumber Plate

Servings: 2 Preparation Time: 15 minutes Cook Time: 20 minutes

Ingredients
- Chicken pieces: 1 lb
- Green cabbage: 7 oz. fresh
- Red onion: 1
- Cucumber: 1
- Olive oil: 1 tbsp
- Vegan Mayonnaise: ½ cup
- Salt: As per your taste
- Pepper: As per your taste

Directions
- Finely chop the cabbage and cucumber and place on a plate
- Thinly slice a red onion and add it to the cabbage
- Pan-fry the chicken pieces over low heat for 15 minutes with salt and pepper and turn after regular intervals of 3-4 minutes
- Add the chicken and mayonnaise to the vegetables and add salt and pepper
- In the end, pour olive oil over this yummy dish

288.Crispy Chicken Leg with Broccoli and Cherry Tomatoes

Servings: 2. Preparation Time: 15 minutes Cook Time: 50 minutes

Ingredients
- Chicken legs: 4 (each piece at least 4-6 oz)
- Italian seasoning: 3 tbsp
- Broccoli: 500 gm
- Cherry tomatoes: 250 gm
- Olive oil: 1 tbsp
- Salt: as per your taste
- Pepper: as per your taste

Directions
- Preheat the oven to 200C
- Add olive oil and spices to the chicken legs
- Place tomatoes cut in four pieces and chicken legs in a greased baking dish
- Bake for 40-45 minutes till the chicken is done
- In the meanwhile, cut the broccoli with its stem, add some salt in water and boil the broccoli for 5 minutes and strain and set aside
- Serve the done chicken legs with broccoli

289.Beef Cabbage Casserole

Servings: 2 Preparation Time: 10 minutes Cook Time: 40 minutes

Ingredients
- Ground Beef: 250 gm
- Green Cabbage: 500 gm
- Cooking oil: 4 tbsp
- Onion powder: ½ tsp
- Paprika: 1 tsp
- White wine vinegar: ½ tbsp
- Ground black pepper: as per your taste
- Salt: as per your taste
- Leafy greens: as your recipe demands
- Cheddar cheese: half cup

Directions
- Preheat the oven to 225C
- Chop the cabbage finely
- In a large wok, fry the cabbage in the 2 tbsp cooking oil over a medium heat
- Fry till soft but not till it turns brown – approximately it will take 8-10 minutes
- Add all the seasoning to the cabbage and fry for a minute and set aside
- Use the rest of the oil to sauté the ground beef and fry on medium-low heat till done
- Now add cabbage to the meat and mix well
- Remove the pan from the stove and add salt and pepper as per your flavor
- Add the cheese on the preparation and bake for 20 minutes
- Serve the dish with leafy greens

290.Lemongrass Chicken Rice

Serving: 2 Preparation Time: 30 minutes Cook Time: 10 minutes

Ingredients
- Chicken breasts: 2
- Lemongrass: 2 stalks chopped
- Soy sauce: 2 tbsp
- Garlic: 1 clove chopped
- Sesame oil: 1 tbsp
- Carrots: 1 cup julienned
- Daikon: 1 cup julienned
- Sugar: ¼ cup
- Salt: a pinch
- Water: 1 cup
- White vinegar: ½ cup
- Brown rice: 2 cup cooked
- Cucumber: 1 cup slices
- Hoisin sauce: as per your taste
- Jalapeño: 1 seeded and sliced
- Fresh cilantro: a few stems
- Sriracha mayo: ¼ cup mayo plus 1 tsp sriracha

Directions
- Take the chicken ingredients and combine them all excluding chicken
- Rub them on the chicken and place in the refrigerator for half an hour
- Make the slaw in the meanwhile by combining all the ingredients together in a bowl and put in the refrigerator as well
- Take out the chicken and make its thin slices
- Cook the chicken slices on the medium heat in a bit of olive oil
- Assemble your serving dish with the bed of rice, then place chicken, then slaw and pour all the remaining assembly ingredients on the top

291.Stir-Fry Beef Cauliflower

Servings: 3 Preparation Time: 10 minutes Cook Time: 40 minutes

Ingredients
- Cauliflower: 750 gm
- Ground beef: 500 gm
- Olive oil: 6 tbsp
- Onion powder: 1 tsp
- Garlic: 2 cloves crushed
- Crushed chili flakes: 1 tbsp
- White wine vinegar: 1 tbsp
- Ginger: 1 tbsp finely grated
- Green Onion: 3 chopped in half-inch slice
- Sesame oil: 1 tbsp
- Ground black pepper: as per your taste
- Salt: as per your taste

Directions
- Divide the cauliflower into florets and fry it in the half of the oil – it should just become brown
- Add all the seasonings to the cauliflower and continue stirring for a minute then remove it from the flame
- In a separate pan, add rest of the oil and add chili flakes, garlic, and ginger; sauté the mixture for one minute
- Now add ground meat till it turns brown on the low heat
- Add cauliflower and green onions to the meat and mix everything well
- Add salt, pepper, and sesame oil before serving

292.Beef Veggie Chili Recipe

Servings: 4. Preparation Time: 30 minutes Cook Time: 1 hour 30 minutes

Ingredients
- Red lentils: 150 gm
- Onion: 1 chopped
- Mixed beans: 400 gm can
- Lean minced beef: 250 g
- Tomatoes: 400 gm can
- Potatoes: 4 (large)
- Garlic cloves: 2 crushed
- Chipotle paste: 2 tbsp
- Olive oil: 2 tbsp
- Vegetable stock: 500 ml
- Sun-dried tomato paste: 2 tbsp
- Butternut squash: 500 gm (peeled and cubed)
- Red peppers: 2 (chopped without seed)
- Celery: 2 sticks
- Coriander leaves
- Worcestershire sauce: 2 tbsp
- Sour cream: 150 ml

Directions
- At 200 °C, heat the oven
- Put potatoes in the foil and brush with 1 tbsp oil and dust sea salt
- Wrap the potatoes and bake for 1.5 hours till they become soft
- Take a large pan and add the remaining oil
- Fry onion for a few minutes and garlic and minced beef
- Fry till the beef turn brown
- Now add tomatoes, vegetable stock, chipotle paste, lentils, Worcestershire sauce, and sun-dried tomato paste
- Stir for a minute or two and include pepper, celery, peppers, and beans and bring to boil
- Cover and place in the oven for an hour
- Cross each potato from the top and add chili, sour cream, and coriander leaves and serve with mince and veggies

293.Sausage with Broccoli and Cauliflower
Servings: 2. Preparation Time: 15 minutes. Cook Time: 25 minutes

Ingredients
- Broccoli in Florets: 200 gm
- Cauliflower in Florets: 300 gm
- Shredded cheese: half cup
- Sausages: 150 gm precooked
- Leek: Half
- Dijon mustard: 2/3 tbsp
- Yellow onion: 1
- Sour cream: 1/3 cup.
- Salt: as per your taste
- Pepper: as per your taste
- Fresh Thyme: 1 ½ tbsp
- Oil for frying: 2 tbsp

Directions
- At 200C, preheat the oven
- Chop down onion and leek
- Make 1" chunks of the cauliflower and broccoli florets
- Slice sausages into 1" pieces
- Put two pans on the heat with the cooking oil and fry vegetables in one and sausages in another
- Arrange the vegetables on a baking dish, mix the sour cream and mustard together and pour on top of vegetables
- Add cheese and sausage on top of the vegetables and sprinkle with thyme
- Bake the dish in the oven for 10 minutes

294.Electric Smoky Jalapeno Popper Mac And Cheese

Ingredients
- 1/2 pound of diced bacon
- 8 oz of elbow macaroni noodles; uncooked
- 1 thinly sliced jalapeno
- 2 jalapenos seeds; removed and finely diced
- 1 link of bratwurst; uncooked, casing removed
- 1 cup of whole milk
- 2 cups of shredded marbled cheddar
- 1 8 oz brick cream cheese
- 1/4 cup of crushed butter
- 1 cup of heavy cream
- 1 tsp of garlic powder
- 1 tsp of rub
- 1 tsp of salt
- 1/2 tsp of black pepper
- 1 cup of water

Directions
- Take the smoker and preheat it to 225 degrees
- Now take a 12-inch cast-iron skillet and put it over medium heat
- Brown both the bacon and the sausage
- Now add in the diced jalapenos and cook it for a couple of minutes until it softens
- Stir the cream cheese to the mix and do so until it has thoroughly combined
- Now, add noodles, along with milk, water, and cream
- Cook it while making sure to stir uniformly
- Now turn off the heat and add salt, garlic powder, pepper, and cheese until you find everything has melted and mixed evenly.
- Sprinkle sweet rub, thin jalapeno slices, and the buttered crackers
- Now take the Mac and cheese and place it in the smoker. Smoke for 30 minutes
- Increase the grill temperature to 400 degrees and bake for 10 minutes
- Serve

295.Electric Smoker Brisket Baked Beans

Ingredients
- 4 strips of artisanal bacon; thick-sliced, cut crosswise into 1/4-inch silvers
- 3 stemmed, seeded, and diced jalapenos
- 1 stemmed, seeded poblano Chile; cut into 1/4-inch dice
- 1 peeled large onion, cut into 1/4-inch dice
- 1 red or yellow bell pepper, stemmed, seeded, and cut into 1/4-inch dice
- ½ cup of cilantro; chopped fresh
- 2 cloves of peeled and minced garlic
- 2 cups of chopped barbecue brisket
- ½ cup of dark beer, plus extra as needed
- 15 ounces of drained navy beans
- 15 ounces of baked beans
- 15 ounces of drained red kidney beans
- 15 ounces of drained black beans
- 2/3 cup of packed brown sugar, plus extra as needed
- 1 ½ cups of sweet red barbecue sauce
- 1/3 cup of Dijon mustard

- Coarse salt (sea or kosher) and freshly ground black pepper

Direction
- Take a large Dutch oven and put it on medium to high heat.
- Add bacon to it and cook it for 3 minutes while making sure to stir occasionally
- Now add poblano, jalapenos, onion, garlic, bell pepper, and ¼ cup of chopped cilantro to it and cook for 3 to 4 minutes
- Now add the beans to the bacon mixture
- Add in the barbecue sauce along with beer, sugar, brisket, and mustard
- Now set the smoker to pre-heat and push the temperature to 275 degrees F
- Smoke the beans until they look thick, concentrated, and are richly flavored
- Now add the right seasoning along with salt, pepper, and sugar
- Sprinkle with the leftover ¼ cup of chopped cilantro
- Serve

296.Electric Smoked Pineapple Rings

Ingredients
- 1 whole pineapple
- 1 tsp of kosher salt
- 2 to 3 tbsp of maple syrup

Directions
- Take the pineapple and cut the top and bottom parts
- Now cut the pineapple in the half by slicing it right through the diameter at the center
- Get rid of the cores of each half and also discard the outer skin

- Now slice it into rounds measuring ¼ to ½ inches in thickness
- Place these pineapple rings in a fresh clean bowl and coat them with maple syrup. Season it with salt.
- Now take these rings and place them on a sheet pan and get the smoker ready
- Preheat the smoker and then let the rings smoke for 60 to 90 minutes
- Remove the plate and let it cool for 10 minutes
- Serve along with side dish like ham slices

297. Electric Smoked Pork Shoulder

Ingredients
- 4 to 5 lbs of boneless pork shoulder
- For the dry rub
- 2 tbsp of packed dark brown sugar
- ½ tbsp of granulated sugar
- ½ tbsp of celery seeds
- 1/8 cup of paprika
- 1 tbsp of cumin
- ½ tbsp of ground black pepper
- 2 tbsp of kosher salt
- ½ tbsp of dried oregano
- 1 tbsp of dark chili powder

Directions
- Take a shaker and mix all the ingredients of the dry rub in it
- Now take the pork shoulder and get rid of the excess fat with the help of a sharp knife
- Now slather the rub generously over the pork. Make sure to save some of the extra dry rub to be used later
- Cover the pork and refrigerate it for nearly 12 hours
- Now remove the pork from the fridge a minimum of 1 hour before cooking
- Follow the instructions of your smoker and preheat it by pushing the temperature to 250 degrees F
- Now keep the pork shoulder on the grate and keep the temperature at 250 degrees
- Smoke it for almost 60 to 90 minutes per pound
- Remove the pork from the smoker and wrap it in a butcher paper and place it in a cooler for an hour
- Shred-it well while making sure to pull it across the strands
- Serve

298. Applewood Electric Smoked Pork

Ingredients
- 4 to 6 pounds of pork loin; whole boneless
- Unsweetened apple juice
- 2 tbsp of safflower oil
- 1 tbsp of Chinese five-spice powder
- ¼ tsp of nutmeg
- 2 tsp of sea salt
- ½ tsp of garlic powder
- 1 tsp of black pepper; cracked
- Water

Directions
- Take the pork loin and rinse it thoroughly in cold water and then pat it dry to get rid of all moisture
- Now trim any silver skin and get rid of the excess fat. Make sure to leave ¼" of fat for preserving the flavor
- Take a sheet pan and place the loin on it
- Now take a small bowl and mix the spices and herbs in it
- Rub this mixture all over the loin and let it rest for an hour at the room temperature
- Now preheat the smoker by keeping the temperature to 225 degrees F
- Take a bowl at the very base of the smoker and add 50% apple juice and 50% wart. Also, add wood chips to the side of the tray in the electric smoker
- New place the pork loin on the middle rack and make sure that the fat side is up. Insert the probe thermometer to it
- Let it cook for 3 hours. You should let the internal temperature reach 155 degrees F
- When smoked well, move it to a cutting board and use aluminum foil to tent it
- Let the meat rest for 20 minutes and then slice
- Serve

299. Pulled Pork On An Electric Smoker

Ingredients
- 8-pound pork shoulder roast
- 1 quart of apple cider
- For the BBQ rub
- 1 chopped onion
- 5 tbsp of white sugar
- 1 tbsp of onion powder
- 1 tbsp of garlic powder
- 5 tbsp of light brown sugar
- 2 tbsp of paprika
- 2 tbsp of kosher salt
- 1 tbsp of black pepper; freshly ground
- 3 cups hickory chips, well soaked in water

Directions
- Take a large pot and add apple cider in ample amount to cover the pork shoulder completely in it
- Now take a bowl and add white and brown sugar along with onion powder, paprika, garlic powder, salt, and black pepper and mix thoroughly.
- Mix nearly ¼ cup of this sugar rub into the cider and keep the remaining rub aside
- Cover the pot and refrigerate it for 12 hours
- Now put the smoker on preheat with the temperature pushed to 210 degrees F
- Now add the right quantity of wood chips to the smoker
- Take the water pan inside the smoker and add cider brine to it along with onion and ¼ cup of the sugar rub
- Spread the leftover rub on the pork shoulder
- Place the pork shoulder right at the center of the smoker
- Smoke it for approx 8 hours
- Add more hickory chips and liquid if needed
- Transfer the pork to a large platter and let it cool for half an hour
- Slice and serve

300. Dry Rubbed And Electric Smoked Pork Chops

Ingredients

- 4 pork chops measuring 1 – ½" thick
- 1 tbsp of onion powder
- 2 tbsp of mustard
- 1 tbsp of brown sugar
- 2 tsp of garlic powder
- 2 tbsp of extra virgin olive oil
- 1 tbsp of smoked paprika
- 1 ½ tbsp of sea salt
- 2 tsp of freshly ground pepper
- Water
- Hickory chips

Directions

- Take a large bowl and add salt, along with onion powder, sugar, garlic powder, paprika, and pepper. Mix it well to combine thoroughly.
- Now take another small bowl and add mustard along with extra virgin olive oil
- Take the pork chops and rinse them thoroughly in cold water
- Pat it dry by using clean paper towels
- Now coat each of the chops with the mixture of oil and mustard.
- Now take the dry rub and cover the chops with the dry rub and make sure that it sticks well to the mustard and oil.
- Place this well-seasoned pork on the rack and set it at room temperature.
- Now prepare the smoker by filling it with hickory chips. The water bowl should be filled halfway along
- Preheat the smoker by raising the temperature to 250 degrees F
- Now keep the rack in the smoker and let it smoke for 90 minutes. The internal temperature should reach 145 degrees F.
- Smoke it for 30 minutes longer if you feel that the temperature hasn't reached the desired level
- Replenish chips and water if needed
- Take the pork chops and put them on a cutting board.
- Tent them with foil and let it rest for 10 minutes
- Serve

301. Grilled Lemon Pepper Pork Tenderloin(Electric Smoker)

Ingredients

- 2 lbs of pork tenderloin
- 2 tbsp of olive oil
- 2 lemon zest
- 1 clove of minced garlic
- 1 tsp of lemon juice
- 1 tsp of minced fresh parsley
- ½ tsp of kosher salt
- 1 tsp of black pepper

Directions

- Take a small-sized bowl and add all ingredients in it except pork tenderloin. Whisk it well
- Take the tenderloin now and trim the silver skin to get rid of all kind of excess fat present in it
- Now place this in a zip lock bag of appropriate size
- The prepared marinade should now be poured over the tenderloin and once again zip the bag
- Keep it in the fridge and let it marinate for a couple of hours
- Now put the smoker to preheat and push the temperature to 375 degrees F
- Take off the tenderloin from the bag and discard the marinade
- Put the tenderloin on the grate of the grill and smoke it for 20 minutes
- Make sure to flip it after 10 minutes to ensure even cooking on both sides
- The internal temperature should reach 145 degrees F before you move it out of the smoker
- Add the sauce and let it rest for 10 minutes
- Serve

302. Electric Smoked Ham With Maple And Mustard Glaze

Ingredients

- 10 to 16 pounds baked ham; bone-in
- 2 tbsp of brown mustard; spicy
- ½ cup of cane sugar; raw turbinado
- ½ cup of pure maple syrup
- ¼ cup of pineapple juice

Directions

- Take the ham off the packaging and rinse it under cold water to get rid of any kind of extra seasoning and preservative.
- Pat it dry with clean paper towels
- Place the ham on the lined sheet pan making sure to keep the flat side down
- Let it come to room temperature for half an hour
- Place the water in a pan at the bottom part of the smoker and make sure to load the trays with wooden chips
- Preheat the smoker by pushing the temperature to 250 degrees F
- Now keep the ham in the lower end of the smoker and also add a digital
- thermometer in the thick part of the ham.
- Smoke the ham until the internal temperature reaches 130 degrees F. It is likely to take an hour and a half.
- Now take a saucepan and add all other ingredients except for ham and glaze them by whisking it well and simmering them
- Let it thicken so that it looks like runny syrup
- Now remove the ham from the smoker when the temperature has reached 130 degrees F
- Coat it with glaze appropriately
- Once again return the ham to the smoker till the internal temperature reaches 140 degrees F
- Now take the ham to the cutting board and then tent it with foil for 10 minutes
- Slice and serve

303.Chicken Cauliflower Alfredo

Servings: 4. Preparation Time: 10 minutes. Cook Time: 30 minutes

Ingredients
- Chicken breasts: 1 ½ lb
- Cauliflower: 1 ½ lb
- Baby spinach: 1 cup
- Cooking oil: 4 tbsp
- Garlic: 4 cloves
- Heavy whipping cream: 1 ½ cup
- Cheese: ½ cup
- Salt: as per your taste
- Pepper: as per your taste

Directions
- Cut chicken breast into strips
- Add cooking oil to the frying pan and cook garlic and chicken
- Let the chicken rest in a plate once cooked
- Cook baby spinach to the point where it shrinks and let it rest
- Add cream to the frying pan and boil it for a couple of minutes
- Now put the chicken, spinach, and cheeses in the pan and add pepper and salt as per your need
- On low heat parboil the cauliflower and divide it into small florets as big as a walnut
- Add the sauce and the chicken mix well and serve

304.Healthy Spinach Curry

Servings: 2. Preparation Time: 10 minutes Cook Time: 15 minutes

Ingredients
- Fresh spinach: 500 gm
- Green curry paste: 3 tbsp
- Olive oil: 2 tbsp
- Cheese: ½ cup.
- Cumin seeds: 1 tbsp
- Salt: as per your taste
- Pepper: as per your taste

Directions
- Mix the olive oil and curry paste in a medium-sized bowl
- Cut cubes of cheese and put them in the paste mixture
- Cook the pasta mixture in a skillet for 5 to 7 minutes on medium heat until the cubes start melting
- In a dry skillet, put cumin seeds on toast as until smoke rises from them, and they start releasing the aroma
- Add spinach and olive oil with the seeds
- Stir till the spinach is completely cooked
- Put in little salt and pepper
- Sprinkle the spinach on plates over the curried cheese

305 Creamed spinach

Servings: 3Preparation Time: 5 minutes. Cook Time: 10 minutes

Ingredients
- Olive oil: 4 tbsp
- Yellow onion: 1 minced
- Fresh spinach: 500 gm (rinsed, dried and trimmed)
- Heavy whipping cream: ¼ cup
- Vegetable broth: ¼ cup
- Garlic powder: ¼ tbsp
- Cheese: 1 tbsp

Directions
- Heat olive oil in a large skillet over medium heat
- Put in the minced onion and cook for nearly 3 minutes until it's soft
- Now put in the spinach as it is cooking add cream cheese and heavy cream to the spinach and stir till both are melted
- Add broth and garlic powder and cook until everything is creamy and smooth
- Set the pan aside and garnish with freshly grated cheese
- Serve with tortillas

306.Electric Smoked Chicken Breasts

Ingredients
- 4 pounds on chicken breasts; bone-in and skin on
- 2 tbsp of brown sugar
- ¼ cup of kosher salt
- 1 tbsp of cider vinegar
- For the dry rub
- ½ tsp of onion powder
- 1 tsp of paprika
- ½ tsp of garlic powder
- 1 tsp of black pepper
- 1 tbsp of brown sugar

Directions
- Take a large bowl and add brown sugar along with apple cider vinegar, kosher salt, and water. Mix well until both salt and sugar dissolve thoroughly.
- Take the chicken breasts and place them in brine. Make sure to cover it thoroughly and refrigerate it for 4 hours.
- Pre-heat your electric smoker and let the temperature reach 225 degrees F
- Now take the chicken breasts and remove them from brine and rinse them thoroughly with cold water
- Pay it dry with clean paper towels
- Take a bowl and mix black pepper, salt, brown sugar, onion powder, paprika, and garlic powder.
- Now sprinkle this dry rub all over the chicken breast
- Place it on the grill rack making sure that the skin side faces up on the grill
- Smoke these breasts until the juices run clear and the internal temperature reaches 165 degrees. This should take approx 4 hours
- Serve

307.Applewood Electric Smoked Chicken

Ingredients
- 4 to 5 pounds whole chicken
- ¼ cup of packed dark brown sugar
- 1 tbsp of garlic powder
- 2 tbsp of chili powder
- 1 tbsp of oregano
- 1 tbsp of paprika; smoked
- 1 tsp of salt
- 1 tbsp of onion powder

Directions
- Remove the insides of the chicken and then run cold water over it and rinse it thoroughly
- Pat it dry with the help of clean paper towels
- Now take the whole chicken and place it on the cutting board. Cut it right down the middle of the breast and then place it in a glass dish measuring 9x13
- Now take a small bowl and add all the dry ingredients and mix it well
- Sprinkle this rub all over the chicken while still in the glass dish
- Place a plastic wrap over the dish and refrigerate it overnight. Ideally, marinate it for nearly 12 hours
- Once it has marinated, put the smoker on preheat and let the temperature reach 225 degrees
- Place the chicken on the rack making sure that the breast side is up
- Smoke it for about 4 to 5 hours and the temperature should reach 225 degrees
- Smoke it till the internal temperature reaches 165 degrees
- Let it sit for 10 minutes
- Slice and serve

308.BBQ Chicken Breasts(Smoker)

Ingredients
- 4 chicken breasts; boneless, skinless
- ½ cup of BBQ sauce
- Extra virgin olive oil
- Kosher salt
- Freshly ground black pepper

Directions
- Preheat the smoker and push the temperature to 450 degrees F
- Now take the chicken breasts and drizzle them with extra virgin olive oil
- Make sure to rub it thoroughly and also season it with salt and pepper appropriately
- Now take these chicken breasts and place them on the grill
- Cover and cook it for 5 to 6 minutes until they easily let go of the grates
- Now flip it and cook for further 5 minutes
- Baste it with bbq sauce, flip it and cook it for 2 minutes each side
- Repeat on the other side
- Smoke it till the internal temperature rises to 165 degrees F
- Transfer to a fresh plate and cover it with foil and let it rest for some time
- Serve with more BBQ sauce

309.Sweet Chili Lime Grilled Chicken (Smoker)

Ingredients
- 4 chicken breasts; skinless and boneless
- Green onions; thinly sliced
- 2 lime juice
- Lime wedges
- ¾ cup of sweet chili sauce
- 1/3 cup of soy sauce; low sodium,
- Vegetable oil

Directions
- Take a large bowl and mix soy sauce, chili juice, and lime juice in it. Set ¼ cup of the marinade aside to be used later
- Now take a resealable plastic bag and add chicken to it. Add marinade to it and let it marinate in the fridge overnight
- Now put the smoker on preheat and make sure to oil the grates
- Grill the chicken by basting it with marinade.
- Grill for 8 minutes per side
- Baste with the leftover marinade and garnish it with green onions
- Serve with lime wedges

310.Electric Smoked Flank Steak With Mushrooms

Ingredients
- 1 cup of freshly sliced mushrooms
- 1 cup of green beans
- 2 mid-sized tomatoes
- ¼ cup of olive oil
- Salt
- Pepper

Directions
- Set the smoker to preheat and push the temperature to 350 degrees F
- Take the meat and tenderize it on both the sides with the help of a mallet
- Season it with salt and pepper
- Grill it for 15 minutes per side
- Now add sliced mushrooms, green beans, and tomatoes to it and brush it with olive oil
- Add more salt if needed
- Place it on the frogmat and allow it to cook for the next 15 minutes
- Serve

311.Butter chicken Indian style

Servings: 2. Preparation Time: 10 minutes Cook Time: 20 minutes

Ingredients
- Boneless chicken thighs: 500 grams cut in cubes
- Tomato: ½ chopped
- Yellow onion: ½ chopped
- Fresh ginger: ½ tbsp chopped
- Garlic clove: tbsp chopped
- Tomato paste: 1/3 tbsp
- Garam masala seasoning: 1/3 tbsp
- Chili powder: ¼ tbsp
- Cooking oil: 2 tbsp
- Butter: 2 tbsp
- Fresh cilantro: ¼ cup (optional)
- Cream: ½ cup
- Salt: as per your taste

Directions
- Add onion, ginger, tomato paste, garlic and tomato with spices in a food processor
- Blend till the mixture is smooth
- Pour in the cream and run the processor for a few seconds
- Put the chicken for marinating with the mixture you just made for a minimum of 20 minutes, the more the better
- Heat oil on medium heat in a frying pan
- Take out the chicken from marinade (leaving the gravy), and put in a frying pan
- Simmer the chicken for 15 minutes on medium heat until it gets fully cooked
- Add salt as per your needs
- For garnishing, add cream, melted butter, and cilantro from the top

312.Cauliflower and Mushroom Risotto

Servings: 4. Preparation Time: 15 minutes Cook Time: 30 minutes

Ingredients
- Large Cauliflower: 1
- Vegetable stock: 1 cup
- Mushrooms: 1 cup
- Garlic: 2 cloves
- Shallot: 1
- Heavy whipping cream: 1 cup
- White Wine: ¾ cup
- Cheese: 2 ½ oz grated
- Salt: as per your taste
- Pepper: as per your taste
- Fresh Thyme: as per your taste
- Cooking oil: as per you need

Directions
- Boil the vegetable stock and let it rest
- Chop down the mushrooms and fry them in little oil until they turn golden
- Chop down garlic and shallot and add them to fried mushrooms
- Now pour in the grated cauliflower to the mixture
- Add half of the white wine and the boiled stock
- Let simmer uncovered till the liquid comes to boil
- Put in the rest of white wine.
- Add cream from the top and simmer until the cauliflower gets tender and the liquid becomes dry
- Take it out from the heat and put in the cheese and sprinkle with fresh thyme

313.Barbecued Whole Chicken (Smoker)

Ingredients
- 2 boiler chickens weighing 3 to 4 pounds each
- Salt
- Pepper
- For the BBQ sauce
- 2 finely chopped small-sized onions
- 2 cups of ketchup
- ¼ tsp of garlic powder
- 2 tbsp of canola oil
- 1 tsp of ground mustard
- 2 tbsp of brown sugar
- 1/8 tsp of hot pepper sauce
- ¼ cup of lemon juice
- 2 tbsp of water
- 1/8 tsp of salt
- ¼ tsp of pepper

Directions
- Take the chicken pieces and season it with salt and pepper
- Put the smoker on preheat and then grill the chicken piece for 20 minutes making sure to keep the skin side down and leaving it uncovered
- Take a small-sized saucepan and heat oil in it over medium flame
- Now add onions to it and sauté it till it turns tender
- Mix the remaining ingredients to the sauce and bring it to boil for 10 minutes
- Now turn the chicken and brush it with BBQ sauce
- Grill for 20 more minutes and brush it with sauce. Make sure the internal temperature reaches 165 degrees F
- Serve

314.Hellfire Chicken Wings(Smoker)

Ingredients
- For hellfire chicken wings
- 3 lbs of chicken wings
- 2 tbsp of vegetable oil
- For the rub
- 1 tbsp of paprika
- 1 tsp of garlic; granulated
- 1 tsp of celery seed
- 1 tsp of onion powder
- 2 tsp of brown sugar
- 1 tsp of cayenne pepper
- 1 tsp of salt
- 1 tsp of ground black pepper
- For the sauce
- ½ cup of cilantro leaves
- 2-4 jalapeno poppers; sliced in a crosswise manner
- ½ cup of hot sauce
- 2 tbsp of unsalted butter

Directions
- Cut the tips off the chicken wings and discard them
- Cut through the joint cut each of the wings into two different pieces
- Keep this in a clean mixing bowl and pour oil over it
- Now take a small-sized bowl and add onion powder along with celery seed, cayenne, sugar, paprika, granulated garlic, salt, and pepper to it
- Take this dry rub mixture and sprinkle it all over the chicken.
- Toss it gently and coat the wings
- Now put the smoker on ore heat and make sure the temperature reaches 350 degrees F
- Now grill the wings for 45 minutes till you find that the skin has turned golden brown and it has cooked well
- Make it a point to turn it midway
- Now take a small saucepan and then melt the butter. Make sure to keep the flame on medium-low
- Add jalapenos and cook for 3 minutes
- Stir in cilantro
- Pour this sauce all over the wings and toss it to coat well
- Serve

315.Sweet And Sour Chicken Drumstick

Ingredients
- 8 pieces of chicken drumstick
- Minced garlic
- Minced ginger
- 2 tbsp of rice wine vinegar
- Juice of ½ lemons
- ½ juiced lime
- 3 tbsp of brown sugar
- ¼ cup of soy sauce
- 2 tbsp of honey
- 1 cup of ketchup
- 1 tbsp of sweet heat rub

Directions
- Take a fresh mixing bowl and add ketchup, soy sauce, rice wine vinegar, honey, brown sugar, lemon, garlic, ginger, and sweet heat rub and mix well
- Keep one half of this mixture aside to be used as a dipping sauce later
- Take the remaining half and keep it a plastic bag which can be re-sealed
- Now add drumsticks to this bag and seal it again
- Refrigerate it overnight
- Now take the chicken from this bag and discard the marinade
- Preheat the grill and set the temperature to 225 degrees F
- Put the chicken on the grate and smoke it for 2 to 3 hours. Make sure to turn it in between
- Remove from the grill and let it sit for 10 minutes
- Add more sauce
- Serve

316.Electric Smoked Turkey Recipe

Ingredients
- 12 lb of whole turkey with neck and giblets removed
- 1 quartered; lemon
- 3 cups of chicken broth
- 1 quartered domino
- 4 springs of fresh herb
- ½ cup of BBQ rub
- Fresh herbs for garnishing purpose
- Cooking spray

Directions
- Preheat your smoker by pushing the temperature to 250 degrees F. Ideally, use applewood chips
- Now take a disposable aluminum pan and coat it thoroughly with cooking spray.
- Take the turkey and place it on the pan. Make sure to properly tuck the wings inside the body
- Now stuff the cavity present inside the turkey with lemon, herbs, and onions and then tie the legs together with the help of twine
- Take the BBQ rub and sprinkle it all over turkey's surface
- Place this turkey in the smoker and let it cook for 6 to 7 hours
- You can blast it with chicken broth every 45 minutes or so
- Keep a thermometer in the thickest part of the thigh of the turkey and keep smoking it till the temperature reads 165 degrees F
- If the turkey gets too dark, cover it with the help of foil
- Now take the turkey out of the smoker and let it rest for 10 minutes
- Garnish with herbs and serve

317.Authentic Electric Smoked Turkey

Ingredients
- 12-16 lbs of frozen turkey with giblets removed completely
- ½ cup of Worcester sauce
- 1 cup of rub
- 1 ½ tbsp of minced garlic
- 1 cup of sugar
- 3 gal of water
- 2 tbsp of canola oil

Directions
- Check if the turkey is fully thawed and the giblets have all been removed if not do so
- Now take a non-metallic bucket of 5-gallon capacity and pour 3 gallons of water in it
- Now add the rub and mix it till the rub has been dissolved thoroughly
- Now add sugar, garlic, and the Worcestershire sauce to it
- Take the turkey and place it in the bucket containing the brine. Make sure to push the breast side down
- When the turkey has been completely submerged, you need to cover it and then refrigerate it overnight
- Take out the turkey and remove the brine. Pat it dry with clean paper towels
- Rub canola oil all over the turkey and then place it in a disposable roasting pan while the breast side should face upwards
- Put the smoker to preheat and raise the temperature to 225 degrees F
- Now keep the turkey in the grill and smoke it for 2 to 3 hours
- Increase the temperature to 350 degrees F and cook it for a further 4 hours
- Insert a thermometer in the thickest part of the breast and check when the internal temperature reaches 165 degrees F
- Now remove it from the grill and let it rest for 15 minutes
- Serve

318.Turkey In An Electric Smoker

Ingredients
- 10 pound of whole turkey with neck and giblets removed
- 1 quartered apple
- 4 cloves of crushed garlic
- 1 quartered onion
- 2 cans of cola-flavored carbonated beverage measuring 12 fluid ounces each
- ½ cup of butter
- 1 tbsp of garlic powder
- 1 tbsp of salt
- 2 tbsp of seasoned salt
- 1 tbsp of ground black pepper

Directions
- Put the smoker to pre-heat and raise the temperature to 225 to 250 degrees F
- Take the turkey and thoroughly rinse it under cold water
- Make sure to rub the crushed garlic all over the outside of the bird
- Now sprinkle it with seasoned salt
- Take a roasting pan and fill the cavity of the turkey with apple, onion, butter, cola, garlic powder, salt, and black pepper. Cover it with a foil; make sure not to do it too tight
- Now smoke the turkey at 250 degrees for 10 hours
- Insert a thermometer in the thickest area of the thigh and keep smoking it until you find the internal temperature reaches 180 degrees F
- Make sure to baste it every 1 to 2 hours with juices present in the roasting pan
- Remove from smoker and let it rest for some time
- Serve

319.Juicy Thanksgiving Turkey

Ingredients
- 15 pound of whole turkey with necks and giblet thoroughly removed
- 1 chopped onion
- 2 stalk of chopped celery
- 1 chopped carrot
- 1 orange, cut into wedges
- 14.5 ounce can of chicken broth
- 2 tbsp of dried parsley
- 1 tbsp of lemon pepper
- 2 tbsp of dried sage; rubbed
- 2 tbsp of dried rosemary
- 2 tbsp of thyme leaves; dried
- 1 tsp of salt
- 750 ml champagne bottle

Directions
- Put the smoker on preheat and let the temperature reach 350 degrees F
- Take the turkey and line it with aluminum foil in a way that it is completely wrapped
- Now take a small bowl and add parsley, thyme, rosemary, lemon pepper, sage, and salt in it. Mix well
- Take the herb mixture and rub it inside the turkey's cavity
- Now stuff it with celery, carrot, orange, and onion
- Take the chicken broth along with champagne and pour it over the turkey all the while making sure that some of it seep in the cavity
- Seal it again with the foil
- Now smoke it in the grill for 3 hours or so until you feel that the juices now run clear
- Take off the foil and then let it smoke again for 30 minutes or so
- Insert a thermometer in the thickest area of the thigh and smoke it till the temperature reads 180 degrees F
- Now take off the turkey from the smoker and cover it with a double sheet of foil
- Let it rest for 15 minutes
- Slice and serve

320.Easy Electric Smoked Fish

Ingredients
- 4-5 pounds of mackerel skin-on fillets
- ½ cup of salt
- 1 quart of water
- ½ cup of white granulated sugar
- Paprika

Directions
- Take the brine and mix it well over low flame making sure that both sugar and salt has dissolved thoroughly
- Now let it cool for some time
- Take the fish and submerge it in the brine that has cooled
- Let it fridge overnight
- Now take off the fish and remove the fillets and rinse it lightly
- Pat it dry and then sprinkle paprika over it
- Preheat the smoker and get it ready by adding wooden chips
- Now smoke the fish for nearly 3 hours until the internal temperature reads 160 degrees F
- Take the fish out of the grill
- Serve

321.Electric Smoked Seafood Ceviche

Ingredients
- 1 lb of sea scallops
- 1 juiced orange
- 1 lb of peeled and deveined shrimp
- 1 juiced lemon
- 1 diced avocado
- ½ minced red onion
- 1 juiced and zester lime
- 1 tbsp of chopped cilantro
- 1 tsp of onion powder
- 1 tsp of garlic powder
- 1 tbsp of canola oil
- 2 tsp of salt
- ½ tsp of black pepper
- 1 pinch of crushed red pepper

Directions
- Take a bowl and mix scallops, canola oil, and shrimp to it
- Now put the smoker on preheat and keep the temperature to 180 degrees Celsius
- Now put both the shrimp and scallop on the grill and smoke it for 4-5 minutes
- Take a large mixing bowl and add all other ingredients and mix well
- Now turn the grill to 325 degrees and let it smoke for an additional 5 minutes
- Now allow both the shrimp and scallop to cool and cut it in half slicing along with width and them mix it with the ingredients present in the bowl
- Refrigerate the ceviche for a couple of hours to allow the flavors to infuse properly
- Serve

322.Electric Smoked Eel

Ingredients
- 2 lb of eel; completely gutted and skin scarped toughly
- 1 gallon of water
- Salt

Directions
- Take the eel fish and make sure that the skin has been scraped thoroughly to remove all possible traces of slime. It should be thoroughly rinsed with water and check if it is well gutted.
- Now take 1 gallon of water and 2.2 lbs of salt to it, this makes 80 degrees brine
- The cleaned eels need to be brined for 2 hours
- Rinse them again and then the fish should be impaled on a stick, starting from the stomach to up the head
- Let the fish dry for 1 to 2 hours
- Now preheat the smoker and get it ready
- Smoke the eel for 3 hours at 140 degrees F
- The temperature should be kept high at the start and then once the fish has hardened, the temperature needs to be lowered
- Remove from the grill and let it sit for 5 minutes
- Serve

323.Electric Smoked Catfish Recipe

Ingredients

- 4 large fillets of catfish
- 1 quart of buttermilk
- 1 tsp of lemon peels; dehydrated
- 2 tbsp of hot sauce
- Olive oil
- 2 tsp of dried oregano
- 1 tsp of kosher salt
- ½ tsp of ground black pepper
- Orange dill sauce to serve

Directions

- Take a casserole dish and add hot sauce to buttermilk and mix well
- Now add catfish fillets and then cover it with plastic wrap and fridge it for an hour
- Now remove the catfish and pat it dry with clean paper towels
- Set the smoker to preheat and keep the flame to medium-low
- Take a small bowl and add lemon peel along with oregano, salt, and pepper
- Coat the fish with olive oil and then sprinkle the seasoning evenly over it
- Now preheat the smoker and make it ready
- Pour the catfish in the grill and let it smoke well for 45 minutes
- Remove the fish from the grill and put it on the serving platter
- Serve with dill sauce

324.Smoked Catfish With Herb Marinade

Ingredients

- 4 fillets of catfish
- 1 clove of minced garlic
- 1 tsp of cayenne pepper
- 1 cup of oil
- 1 tbsp of thyme
- ½ cup of red wine vinegar
- 1 tbsp of basil
- 1 juiced lemon
- 3 tbsp of sugar
- 2 tbsp of oregano
- 1 tbsp of salt
- 1 tsp of black pepper

Directions

- Take all the ingredients for the marinade and mix them well
- Now take the catfish and place it in a bowl
- Pour marinade over the fish and turn it to ensure that the catfish is evenly coated
- Cover the fish with plastic wrap and then fridge it for an hour
- Put the smoker on preheat and set the temperature to 225 degrees F
- Now put the catfish on the racks and let it smoke for 2 and a half hour
- Set aside and serve

325.Cajun Electric Smoked Catfish

Ingredients

- 4-8 fillets of catfish
- 1 cup of hot sauce
- Cajun seasoning
- 1 cup of salt
- Water
- Salt and black pepper

Directions

- Take a couple of casserole dishes and fill half of it with water on room temperature
- Put ½ a cup of salt in each of the dishes and then put the catfish fillets inside the saltwater mix
- Set the dish in the fridge for 4 hours to brine them well. The brine is important as it prevents the fish from drying out
  completely and thereby enhances the flavor
- Take the catfish out of the fridge and get rid of the brine mixture. Pat it dry
- Sprinkle Cajun seasoning and then season it with salt and pepper on the top of fillets and then drizzle it with hot sauce
- Now set the smoke to preheat and put the catfish on the grill. Lower the temperature a little as this will enable slow cooking. Smoke it for 2 to 2.5 hours
- When the fish has turned flaky white, take it off the smoker and let it sit for 15 minutes
- Serve

326.Grilled Lobster Tail

Ingredients

- 10 ounces of lobster tail
- ¼ tsp of old bay seasoning
- 1 tsp of freshly chopped parsley
- 2 tbsp of melted butter
- ¼ tsp of sea salt

Directions

- Preheat the smoker and make sure that the temperature stays close to 450 degrees
- Now take the lobster and slice it from the middle
- Season it with the right amount of salt and old bay
- Keep the tail on the grate of the grill. You should make sure that it is the meat side which faces downwards and should touch the grill
- Grill it for around 15 minutes until you feel that the internal temperature has reached close to 140 degrees
- Now take off the lobster from the grill and drizzle with the right amount of melted butter
- Sprinkle chopped parsley on top of it
- Serve

327.Smoked Rainbow Trout With A Wet Brine

Ingredients

- 2 boned rainbow trout fillet
- 4 cloves of minced garlic
- 8 cups of water
- 1 tbsp of sriracha sauce
- ½ cup of white sugar
- 1 tsp of thyme
- 2 tbsp of soy sauce
- 1 tbsp of paprika
- 1/3 cup of kosher salt
- 1 tbsp of black pepper

Directions

- Take a bowl and mix sugar, salt, and spices to water and mix it well
- Now take a dish and place the fish facing skin side down and then add in the brine
- Flip the fish a few times and then cover it with a plastic wrap
- Place the whole thing in the fridge and let it marinate overnight
- Rinse this fish thoroughly and then place it in a cool dry place for an hour
- Set the smoker to preheat and now put it on the grill of the smoker
- Smoke it for 3 to 4 hours till the internal temperature reaches 145 degrees
- Serve

328. Dry cherry and almond scones supreme

Meal type: Snack Preparation time: 20 mins.
NUTRITIONAL VALUE. Serving size: 12 scones; Calories: 133kal; protein 33.48g; Carbohydrate: 11.1g; Fat 5g.

Ingredients:
- 1 egg
- 1 egg white
- 1 scoop of unjury protein powder
- 1 cup of chopped and very dried cherries
- ¼ cup canola oil
- ½ cup granular stevia
- ½ cup low fat butter milk
- ½ teaspoon almond extract
- ½ cup non fat instant powdered milk
- ½ tea spoon baking soda
- 2 cups of wheat flour

Directions
- Preheat your oven to approximately 350 degrees celcius. Try not to exceed this figure
- Apply a non-stick cooking spray on your cookie sheet
- Whisk your eggs and egg white together in a mixing bowl
- Put in butter milk, canola oil, and stevia into separate bowl
- Mix with hand mixer or wooden spoon till well combined
- Pour in eggs and mix again
- Pour in protein powder, powdered milk, and mix well
- Put in wheat flour and mix lightly
- Put in almond extract and mix lightly
- Put in baking soda and mix
- From this, mold out 12 scones
- Lace on lined and sprayed baking sheet and bake for 20-25 minute

329. Gingered ham

Meal type: Lunch. Preparation time: 3 hours
NUTRITIONAL VALUE. Serving size: 8 servings; Calories: 470 kal; protein 63 g; Carbohydrate: 2g; Fat 23.4g.

Ingredients:
- 6 pounds of boneless gammon joint
- 7 black peppercorns
- 5 cloves
- 3 teaspoons of grated root ginger
- 2 cups of ginger beer; sugar free
- 1 medium onion, diced
- Small root ginger; peeled

Directions
- Slice ginger
- Preheat the oven to 160C or 325F
- Get out roasting pan and spray with low fat baking spray
- Pour in half1 ½ of ginger beer
- Place onions, sliced ginger, cloves, and peppercorns
- Cover with two layers of foil
- Bake for 2 ½ hours be sure to baste once
- Remove and discard all juices
- Set aside
- Increase oven to 200C/400F
- Pour remaining root beer, jam, grated ginger in skillet and let boil
- When it boils reduce heat to low and let the glaze simmer for 6 minutes
- Take off skin from ham. Do not touch the fat layer
- Rub half the glaze on it and bake for another ten minutes without cover
- Take out and rub the rest of the glaze and bake for another ten minutes serve warm

330. Lamb potato hotpot

Meal type: Lunch Preparation time: 20 mins.
NUTRITIONAL VALUE. Serving size: 6 servings; Calories: 133kal; protein 32.1g; Carbohydrate: 29g; Fat 6.2g.

Ingredients:
- 3 bay leaves
- 3 tablespoons oil canola
- 2 onions, thinly sliced
- 2 carrots
- 2 ½ cups of meat stock
- 1 ½ pounds of potatoes
- ½ tablespoon thyme
- 1 ½ pounds of lamb
- 1 tablespoon protein powder
- 1 tablespoon Worcestershire sauce
- Salt and pepper to taste

Directions
- Thinly slice onions and set aside
- Dice lamb and set aside
- Chop carrots and set aside
- Pour in canola oil into oven-safe skillet
- Put in onions, carrot and lam
- Add salt and pepper to taste
- Fry for 5-8 minutes
- Put in protein powder
- Preheat the oven to 200 C/400 F
- Stir fry for 1 minute
- Pour in stock and the Worcestershire sauce
- Cover and let simmer for 15-20 mins
- Slice potatoes into very thin slices
- Place potatoes in stacks in the pots decoratively
- Put in pinch of salt and pepper
- Cover and take off heat
- Place in oven and bake for 1.5 hours
- Take out and place on low heat for thirty minutes

331. Baked chicken and bacon

Meal type: Snack Preparation time: 1 hour.
NUTRITIONAL VALUE. Serving size: 1 serving; Calories: 252 kal; protein 39.7g; Carbohydrate: 4.1g; Fat 8.8g.

Ingredients:
- 4 ounces of chicken; skinless and boneless
- 2 slices of bacon
- ½ teaspoon grated ginger
- ½ teaspoon grated garlic
- 2 teaspoons salsa
- 1 slice tomato
- 1 heaped tbsp grated reduced-fat hard cheese or shredded low-fat mozzarella cheese
- 1 small tomato, sliced
- 2 tablespoons mozzarella cheese
- Salt and pepper to taste

Directions
- Dice bacon
- Preheat the oven to 190 C/375 F
- Spread out foil and spray low-fat cooking spray
- Put in chicken
- Place bacon all over the chicken at both sides and all over
- Rub garlic and ginger
- Sprinkle salt and pepper
- Wrap tightly
- Leave for 15 minutes
- Unwrap and place in non-stick baking sheet
- Pour pesto sauce over it
- Cover with foil
- Bake for 15 minutes
- Take out and sprinkle cheese
- Place tomatoes
- Bake for 14 minutes

332. Protein yogurt cookies

Meal type: Snack. Preparation time: 1 hour

NUTRITIONAL VALUE. Serving size: 12 cookies, 3 servings; Calories: 287; Total Fat: 6g; Total Carbs:4.5g; Protein: 23.8g

Ingredients:
- ¼ cup of protein powder
- ¼ teaspoon baking powder
- 3 eggs
- 5 tablespoons of no fat yogurt

Directions:
- Crack the eggs separate egg whites from the yolk
- Beat the whites till they get bubbly
- Set aside
- In the yolks of the eggs, put in the yoghurt
- Mix well
- Combine both bowl's contents and mix well
- Put in protein powder mix lightly
- Put in baking powder and mix till dough forms
- The result should be somewhat thick
- With a spoon, line out scoops of the baking tray that has parchment
- Lightly spread out the scoops so they are like cookies. They will be very light so apply no pressure
- Bake for 25- 30 minutes
- Take out and leave to cool for an hour

333. Protein vanilla cookies

Serves 4Preparation time: 40 mins.

NUTRITIONAL VALUE.; Calories: 175; Total Fat: 9g; Total Carbs: 5.5g; Protein: 16.8g. Meal type: Snack

Ingredients:
- 8 tablespoons of low fat cocoa powder
- 1 tablespoon of wheat powder
- 6 tablespoons of canola oil
- 1 flat teaspoon of baking powder
- 2 eggs
- 1 tablespoon confectioners swerve
- 1 1/3 cups of protein powder
- Teaspoon of vanilla extract

Directions:
- Crack and mix the eggs
- Pour eggs in oil to the eggs
- Put in vanilla extract
- Mix very well
- Add cocoa powder
- Add confectioners swerve
- Add protein powder
- Mix very well
- Add baking powder
- Mix till dough forms
- Spread out and cut out your cookies
- Top with the rest of your chocolate chips
- Bake for 8 to 10 minutes
- They will come out very soft
- Set them down and let them cool so they can harden

334. Vanilla frozen yogurt

NUTRITIONAL VALUE.Serves5; Calories: 190; Protein: 60g; Carbs: 14g; Fat: 4.6g

Meal type: Desert. Preparation time: 20 mins

Ingredients:
- ¼ cup of fat-free heavy cream
- 2 tablespoons of stevia
- 1 teaspoon of vanilla extract
- ¾ cup of skimmed milk
- ¾ cup of fat free yogurt

Directions:
- Pour in the vanilla extract and stevia into the blender
- Pour in skimmed milk, fat-free yogurt, and then the heavy cream and blend for 10—20 seconds
- Get out popsicle ice tray
- Pour in liquid, put in possible sticks and freeze

335. Vegan salad dressing

Meal type: Breakfast. Preparation time: 20 mins.

NUTRITIONAL VALUE. Serving size: 4; Calories: 58 kal; protein 2 8g; Carbohydrate: 11g; Fat 0g.

Ingredients:
- 2 teaspoons Dijon mustard
- 1/2 cup rice vinegar
- 3 cloves garlic (minced)
- Salt to taste
- Pepper to taste

Directions
- Directions
- Mince garlic
- Pour in mustard, vinegar, garlic, salt, and pepper to taste

336. Shrimp Pepper Soup

NUTRITIONAL VALUE. Serving size: 2 serving; Calories: 190 kal; protein 25; Carbohydrate: 15 g;Fat 09g.

Meal type: Breakfast. Preparation time: 20 mins

Ingredients:
- 3 ounces fresh shrimp, peeled, cleaned, tails removed
- 1 tablespoon canola oil
- 2 garlic cloves; minced
- 1 clove of minced garlic
- 2 cup of vegetable broth
- 1 tablespoon soy sauce
- 1/2cup baby spinach
- 1 tablespoon lemon juice
- 1 tablespoon chopped parsley

Directions:
- Heat canola oil in skillet on medium heat
- Pour in garlic and ginger
- Stir fry till brown
- Pour in broth, and soy sauce
- Boil and add shrimp
- Let shrimps boil for 3 minutes
- Put in lemon juice and spinach
- Sprinkle parsley and serve

337. Beef Canola Burger

Meal type: Breakfast/ Lunch. Preparation time: 20 mins.

NUTRITIONAL VALUE. Fat: 19g; Carbohydrates: 9g; Calories: 687 kal; Protein: 39g

Ingredients:
- 2 pounds of lean ground beef
- 2 tablespoons canola oil
- 2 cloves of garlic, minced
- 3 tablespoons Worcestershire sauce
- 1 teaspoon of black pepper
- 1 tablespoon of salt

Directions:
- In a bowl pour in the meat, sauce, pepper, and garlic and 2 spoons of oil
- Sprinkle in salt to taste.
- Mix the ingredients very well
- Pour out the mixture on a clean board and mold into patties
- Place on a grill. Cook each side for around seven minutes
- You can eat with wheat buns

338.Smoked Tuna Steaks

Ingredients
- 6 tuna steaks each 1 inch thick
- 12 thin slices of fresh lemon
- 1 tsp of ground garlic
- ¼ cup of extra virgin olive oil
- 3 tbsp of light brown sugar
- Lemon pepper seasoning
- 2 tbsp of kosher salt
- Water

Directions
- Take the tuna steaks and coat it with sugar and salt on all the sides
- Now place this in a sealable container and refrigerate it overnight
- Preheat the smoker by pushing the temperature to 190 degrees F. Add water to the pan in the smoker

- Now take the tuna steak and put it on a clean surface.
- Wipe off the brine and then coat it with extra virgin olive oil along with garlic powder and lemon pepper seaming
- Now keep these steaks on the smoker rack and put 2 slices of lemon on top of them
- Keep the rack back in the smoker and then smoke it for an hour
- Continue to smoke till the internal temperature reaches 145 degrees F
- Remove it to a cutting board and let it rest
- Serve

339.Smoked Albacore Tuna

Ingredients
- 6 albacore tuna fillets (8 oz)
- 1 lemon zest
- 1 orange zest
- 1 cup of brown sugar
- 1 cup of kosher salt

Directions
- Take a small bowl and add salt along with sugar and citrus zest
- Now layer the brine along with the fish while making sure that ample brine gets filled between each fillet. This is done to make sure that the fillets don't touch each other
- Fridge it for nearly 6 hours

- Now put the grill on preheat and the temperature setting should be set to smoke mode
- Now take off the fillets from the fridge and rinse the excess brine
- Pat it dry with the help of a clean paper towel and then place them on a cooling rack for approx half an hour
- Now remove the fillets from the fridge and place it on the grate to be smoked for 3 hours
- The temperate should then be raised to 225 degrees F and let them cook for one more hour till the dish seems to develop slightly browning color
- Remove it from the grill and serve immediately

340.Grilled Rockfish

Ingredients
- 6 fillets of rockfish
- ½ tsp of garlic powder
- ½ tsp of onion powder
- 6 tbsp of butter
- 2 tsp of chopped fresh dill
- 1 sliced lemon
- ¾ tsp of salt

Directions
- Put the smoker on pre-heat and push the feature to 375 degrees F
- Take the fish and place it on a baking dish that is grill safe

- Season both the sides of the fish with garlic powder, onion, dill, and salt
- Now place butter buns right on the top of each fillet
- Add lemon slices to it as well
- Take the baking dish and place it on the grill smoke for 20 minutes until the fish loses its translucency
- Now remove it from the grill and allow it to rest for 5 minutes
- Serve

341.Spicy Shrimp Skewers (Electric Smoker)

Ingredients
- 2 lbs of shrimp; peeled and deveined
- 6 oz of Thai chilies
- 6 cloves of garlic
- 1 ½ tbsp of white vinegar
- 3 tbsp of olive oil
- 2 tbsp of Napa valley rub
- 1 ½ tsp of sugar

Directions
- Take all ingredients except for the shrimp and place in a blender to churn it into a smooth taste
- Now take a fresh new bowl and then add shrimp to it along with the mixture you

blended and keep the whole thing in the fridge for minutes
- Take it out from the fridge after the time has passed and thread the shrimp on the metal skewers. This is important to grill it perfectly
- Now set the grill to preheat. Push the temperature to high as it should be around degrees F
- Now take the shrimps and the place it on the grill so that you can cook it for a couple of minutes per side
- Serve

342. Grilled German Sausage

Ingredients
- 2 eggs
- 1 lb of ground beef
- 4 lbs of 80% lean, 20% fat ground pork
- 1 tbsp of ground nutmeg
- 2 tsp of ground mace
- 1 cup of cold milk
- 1 cup of non-fat dry milk powder
- 1 tsp of ground ginger
- 1 tsp of curing salt
- 2 tbsp of salt

Directions
- Take a fresh clean bowl and add both the types of salt along with nutmeg, mace and ginger

- Now to this mix, add both milk and eggs and beat it well to make a uniform paste
- Pour this whole mixture over the ground beef and once again make sure to mix well so as to coat evenly
- Now use the meat to make sausage links out of it
- Put the smoker to preheat and push the temperature to 225 degrees F
- Smoke the whole thing for a couple of hours till you feel that it has cooked properly
- Serve

343.Grilled Shrimp With Cajun Dip

Ingredients
- ½ lb of shrimp; shelled and deveined
- ½ tbsp of bacon seasoning
- ½ tbsp of Cajun styled seasoning
- 2 tbsp of olive oil
- Scallions
- Garlic toast squares
- 1 tsp of Cajun styled seasoning
- 1 clove of grated garlic
- 1 tbsp of bacon rubs
- 1 tbsp of hot sauce
- ½ cup of mayonnaise
- 1 cup of sour cream
- 1 tsp of lemon juice

Directions
- Put the smoker to preheat and push the temperature to 350 degrees F
- Now take a fresh bowl and add lemon juice, along with the hot sauce, bacon rub, sour cream, garlic, Cajun seasoning, and mayonnaise.
- Whisk it well to make sure that everything has combined well
- Now for the shrimp take another fresh bowl and add shrimps along with bacon seasoning. Also, add olive oil and Cajun seasoning to the same bowl and toss it well so as to mix thoroughly.
- Take the dip mixture, cover it with foil, and then place it in the oven
- Keep it on the grill and cook it for almost 15 minutes
- Add shrimp to it and cook for 5 more minutes till you find that the shrimps have turned opaque
- Remove the dip from the grill and top it with scallions and shrimps
- Serve along with garlic toast squares

344.Electric Smoked Meatballs

Ingredients
- 1 pound of sausage
- 2 eggs
- 1 pound of 80/20 ground beef
- ½ cup of grated parmesan cheese
- 1 tsp of granulated garlic
- 2 tsp of Italian seasoning
- 1 cup of Italian bread crumbs

Directions
- Take all ingredients in a bowl and then make meatballs out of it that is sized uniformly
- Put the smoker on preheat and push the temperature to 275 degrees
- Put the meatballs in the smoker and continue to smoke them till the internal temperature reaches 165 degrees
- Cook for almost 45 minutes
- Serve

345.Tri-Tip Roast

Ingredients
- 3 pounds of tri-tips
- ½ tsp of cayenne
- 1 tsp of onion powder
- 1 tsp of garlic powder
- 1 ½ tsp of kosher salt
- 1 tsp of black pepper
- 1tsp of paprika

Directions
- Put the smoker to preheat and push the temperature to 250 degrees
- Now cook the tri-tip in the half and half.
- Foil it and again cook for 30 more minutes on the other side
- Now increase the temperature to 350 degrees F and cook it for half an hour again
- Let it rest for some time
- Slice well
- Serve

346.Mini Greek Vegetarian Quiches

Preparation Time: 25 minutes Cook time: 40 minutes Servings: 12

Ingredients
- Cheddar cheese: 75 gm
- Double cream: 125 ml
- Spinach leaves: 250 gm finely chopped
- Garlic: 2 cloves (chopped)
- Pine nuts: 3 tbsp
- Filo pastry: 100 gm
- Onion: 1 (medium) diced
- Olive oil
- Red pepper: 1 large roasted
- Feta: 200 gm
- Eggs: 2
- Pitted Kalamata olives: 15

Directions
- Preheat the oven to 350F and grease the muffin tray
- Take a large frying pan and heat some olive oil
- Fry the onion till it tenders
- Add spinach leaves to the onions and fry till they become soft and add garlic
- Take the filo pastry and cut them into strips that are 27cm long and 6.5cm wide
- Take two strips and brush with oil
- Fold it into half in length to 13.5 cm and put in a single muffin hole in a way that one is present over other making the angle of 45 degrees – it will cover the base completely
- Do this for the rest of the muffin holes in your muffin tray
- Crumble feta using a fork and add grated cheddar, beaten eggs, olives, red pepper, pine nuts, and double cream
- Add spinach mixture in the end and put a scoop of it into each of the filo casing
- Bake in the oven till it turns golden brown for over 25 minutes
- Remove after 5 minutes from the muffin tray and serve hot with salad

347.Quinoa Cauliflower Bites

Ingredients
- Cauliflower: 150 gm
- Quinoa: 100 gm
- Eggs:3
- Spring onions: 4
- Feta: 100 gm
- Garlic powder: ½ tsp
- Pepper: as per your taste
- Baking powder: ½ tsp

Directions
- Preheat the oven to 400F
- Take a small saucepan and heat a small amount of water
- When it starts to boil, add quinoa and simmer for 15 minutes or as per packet's instruction
- Strain the water when ready
- Finely grate the cauliflower to give it rice-like texture
- Now in a large bowl, add eggs and beat well
- Then include cauliflower rice, crumbled feta, quinoa, garlic powder, pepper, chopped spring onion, and baking powder to the eggs
- Line your muffin tray with paper baking cases
- Take a spoonful of the cauliflower mixture and put into the baking cases
- Flat the surface top with the spoon
- Bake for 25 minutes in the oven
- Leave it on the muffin tray for 10 minutes after removing from the oven
- Serve warm with salad

348.Miso Ginger Avocado and Grapefruit Salad

Ingredients
- Ripe avocado: 1 peeled and diced
- Pink grapefruit: 1
- Alfafa: 1 handful
- Watercress: 2 handfuls
- Pumpkin seeds: 25 gm
- Spring onion: 1
- Pistachios. 25 gm
- Chopped coriander leaves: a handful
- Red chili: ¼
- For Dressing:
- Soy sauce: 2 tsp
- Miso paste: 2 tsp
- Sesame oil: 2 tsp
- Freshly grated ginger: 1 tsp
- Lime juice: 3 tsp
- Olive oil: 2 tsp
- Mirin: 1 tsp
- Maple syrup: 2 tsp
- Garlic: 1 small

Directions
- Mix all the dressing ingredients together and set aside
- Peel grapefruit and remove white skin from the whole fruit and separate its segments
- Take a pan and roast pumpkin seeds and pistachios and set aside
- In a large bowl, place avocado, grapefruit segments, and watercress
- Sprinkle rest of the ingredients on top including roasted pumpkin seeds and pistachios
- Serve with the dressing

349.Creamy Cabbage

Ingredients
- Green cabbage: 500 gm
- Cooking oil: 2 tbsp
- Heavy whipping cream: 1 cup
- Fresh parsley: ½ cup chopped
- Lemon zest: 1 tbsp
- Salt: as per your taste
- Pepper: as per your taste

Directions
- Chop the cabbage
- In a frying pan, add the cooking oil and cabbage and sauté on medium heat till cabbage softens
- Now add heavy whipping cream to cabbage and heat
- When the cream is reduced add salt and pepper
- Remove from heat and sprinkle lemon zest and parsley before serving

350.Cucumber Salad

Ingredients
- Cucumbers: 2 medium-sized
- Half fat crème fraiche:3 tbsp
- Lemon juice: of 2 lemons
- Chives: as per recipe demands (finely chopped)
- Salt: as per your taste
- Pepper: as per your taste
- Garlic: 1 clove (crushed)

Directions
- Peel the cucumbers and divide them into two pieces by cutting vertically
- Remove the seeds from the center
- Make the long strips of the peeled cucumber by using a vegetable peeler
- Cut the thin slices
- Put the cucumber slices in the colander and sprinkle salt from the top
- Place some weight over them like a pan to increase the water draining
- Leave the cucumbers for over 120 minutes
- Rinse the cucumber using cold water to remove the excess salt
- Squeeze or press with your hands or with the spoon or towel to remove the extra water as much as possible
- Take a salad bowl and add lemon juice, cream, chives, and garlic
- Combine them all well
- Add cucumbers to them and mix till they combine well
- Sprinkle pepper on top
- Put it in the fridge if like it cooled

351.Perfect Electric Mix Brisket

Ingredients

- Beef broth
- Perfectly mixed pellets
- Untrimmed Brisket
- Salt and pepper

Directions

- Pour in the mixed pellets and put the smoker to preheat. Make sure to have the temperature in the range of 225 degrees
- Now take the untrimmed brisket and then trim it to ¼ inch of the whole fat which was present. Make sure that you get rid of the hard fat completely.
- Now rub this trimmed basket with salt and pepper and thereby season it well
- Place the brisket at the very center of the smoker

- Keep smoking until you can spot the presence of good bark. Ideally, the internal temperature would reach 185 degrees.
- Make a foil tent and add in any of your favorite liquid to it. Analyze the size of the brisket and then add the right amount of cooking liquid
- Now seal the brisket with the cooking liquid in the foil tent and then insert a thermometer in the brisket so that you can note the internal temperature
- Smoke it on the grill till the internal temperature reaches 200 degrees F
- Now remove it from the grill and let the brisket to rest
- Slice it across the grain when cooled
- Serve

352.Smoked 321 Ribs

Ingredients

- 3 racks of baby back ribs
- 1 ½ tbsp of maple syrup
- ½ cup of apple juice
- 1 ½ tbsp of mustard
- BBQ rub
- Coarse salt
- For the homemade glaze
- 1 cup of ketchup
- ½ cup of mustard
- ½ cup of maple syrup
- 3 tbsp of vinegar
- 1 tsp of pepper

Directions

- Take the baby back ribs and later pat them dry
- Now score the membrane that is present on the concave side of the ribs and then make it a point to peel it off
- Season the ribs with the right amount of salt and let it dry in the brine for one hour

- Now mix maple syrup, apple juice, and mustard in a spray bottle
- Take another bowl and add all ingredients for glaze inside it and keep it aside
- Put the smoker on preheat and push the temperature to 250 degrees F
- Now check the ribs and when they have brined well; splash it using the spray bottle mix
- Cover the ribs with the help of the rub and then keep them on the grates of the smoker for almost 3 hours
- Now take them out and spread glaze all over it and then cover it with foil and let it smoke for a couple of hours again
- Take off the foil and cook it for an additional hour
- Next, spread a little more glaze at the top
- Serve

353. Smoked Flank Steak With Mushrooms

Ingredients

- 1 cup of freshly sliced mushrooms
- 1 cup of green beans
- 2 tomatoes
- ¼ cup of olive oil
- Salt and pepper

Directions

- Set the smoker to preheat and push the temperature to 350 degrees
- Now take the meat and tenderize it by using a mallet. Do this on both the sides

- Season it with the right amount of salt and pepper
- Now put it on the grates of the grill and smoke it for 15 minutes each side
- Slice mushroom along with green beans and tomatoes over the meat and then lightly brush it with olive oil
- Season it with salt again
- Place it on the frog mat and then let it cook for further 15 minutes
- Serve

354: Chicken and Gravy Cobbler

Yields: 8 servings— Prep time: 20 minutes — Cook time: 25 minutes.
Nutrition value per serving: Calories: 438 net Fats: 33 g net Proteins: 28 g net Carbs: 6 g net

Ingredients

- 2 tablespoons ghee or unsalted butter (or coconut oil)
- 1½ cups sliced mushrooms
- ¼ cup diced onions
- 2 stalks celery, finely chopped
- 1 cup chopped asparagus
- 1½ pounds boneless, skinless chicken thighs, cut into ¼-inch pieces
- 1 teaspoon fine sea salt
- ½ teaspoon ground black pepper
- 4-ounces cream cheese
- ¾ cup of chicken bone broth
- 4 large egg whites
- 1 cup blanched almond flour
- 1 teaspoon baking powder
- ¼ teaspoon fine sea salt
- 3 tablespoons very cold butter (or lard if dairy-free), cut into pieces

Directions

- Preheat the oven to 400 degrees °F.
- Melt the ghee in a skillet, then add onions and mushroom in it. Sauté for 3 to 4 minutes.

- Then, add celery and asparagus while stirring continuously. Sauté for another 3 to 4 minutes.
- Season the chicken with sea salt and black pepper. Then, add into the skillet and cook until it sears well from all sides. Remove from the heat.
- Add bone broth in the skillet. Then, add in the cream cheese slowly while stirring continuously ensuring no lumps are left. You can use a whisk for this purpose. Set aside.
- To make biscuits, beat the egg whites in a bowl using an electric beater until it is fluffy and firm.
- In another bowl, mix the baking powder, almond flour and salt. Then, gently mix in the cold butter.
- Fold the flour mixture into the egg whites gently. Use an ice cream scooper or a large spoon to scoop out and shape the dough into a 2-inch round or oval-shaped biscuits.
- Set the biscuits over the chicken mixture in the skillet, and bake for 12 to 16 minutes, or until the cookies turn golden brown. Serve hot.

355: Creamy Chicken Soup

Yields: 8 servings — Prep time: 5 minutes — Cook time: 15 minutes.
Nutrition value per serving: Calories: 245 net Fats: 30 g net Protein: 36 g net Carb: 6 g net

Ingredients
- 4 tablespoons butter
- 8-ounces cream cheese, cubed
- 4 cup of chicken bone broth
- Salt to taste
- Pepper to taste
- 4 cups cooked, shredded chicken breast
- ½ cup heavy cream

Directions
- Take a deep pan and put it over medium heat. Melt butter in it, then add shredded chicken and sauté for 1 to 2 minutes, or until the chicken is well coated with the butter.
- Add cream cheese and mix well.
- When cream cheese melts, add in the bone broth and cream while stirring continuously. You can use a whisk for this purpose.
- Then, add salt and pepper and mix well.
- Serve hot into soup bowls and enjoy!

356: Saucy & crispy chicken

Yields: 4 servings— Prep time: 7 minutes plus 1 hour for marinating— Cook time: 12 minutes.
Nutrition value per serving: Calories: 544 net Fats: 42 g net— Proteins: 40 g net— Carbs: 0.2 g net

Ingredients
- ½ cup avocado oil
- ½ cup ranch dressing
- 3 tablespoons coconut aminos
- 1 tablespoon minced garlic
- 1 teaspoon coconut vinegar
- 1 teaspoon lemon juice
- 1 teaspoon ground black pepper
- 4 boneless, skinless chicken thighs, pounded to a ¾-inch thickness
- Fine sea salt
- Ground black pepper
- 2 teaspoons coconut oil or avocado oil, for frying
- ½ cup ranch dressing
- ¼ cup grated Parmesan cheese
- ½ cup pork dust
- ⅓ cup grated Parmesan cheese
- 2 tablespoons unsalted butter, melted
- 1 teaspoon garlic salt
- 1 cup shredded provolone cheese

Directions
- Mix together all the marinade ingredients except the chicken.
- Coat the chicken thoroughly with this rub, then put it in the refrigerator for 1 hour to incorporate the flavours well.
- Preheat the broiler. Take the chicken out from the refrigerator and remove the excess marinade.
- Heat coconut oil in a cast-iron skillet, add chicken and cook for 3 to 5 minutes from each side. Remove from the heat.
- For making Parmesan sauce, mix together ½ cup of ranch dressing and ¼ cup of Parmesan cheese in a bowl. Set aside.
- To make Parmesan topping, combine ⅓ cup of Parmesan cheese, garlic salt, and unsalted melted butter in another mixing bowl.
- Pour the prepared Parmesan sauce, shredded provolone cheese, and Parmesan topping on to the sautéed chicken in the skillet.
- Place the skillet in the oven and let it broil for 4 to 5 minutes. Serve when the cheese has melted.

357. Fried Chicken with Cheesy Grits

Yields: 4 servings— Prep time: 8 minutes — Cook time: 13 minutes.
Nutrition value per serving: Calories: 592 net — Fats: 46 g net— Proteins: 45 g net— Carbs: 1 g net

Ingredients
- 2 cups coconut oil or rendered keto fat, such as lard, for frying
- 1 large egg
- ½ cup powdered Parmesan cheese or pork dust
- ¼ teaspoon ground black pepper
- 4 chicken legs
- Double batch Keto Grits
- Chopped fresh herbs of choice, for garnish

Directions
- Beat an egg in a bowl. Set aside.
- Take another bowl and mix in the Parmesan cheese and pepper. Set aside.
- Heat oil in a deep frying pan (almost 4-inch deep).
- Dip the chicken legs into the egg, then into the Parmesan mixture. Ensure even coating by firmly pressing each chicken leg into the cheese mixture. Coat well from all sides.
- Fry the chicken legs in the preheated oil until the chicken is thoroughly cooked, or for 10 minutes.
- For serving, place grit on a plate and top with the chicken legs. Garnish with chopped herbs and serve.

358: Chicken Divan

Yields: 4 servings— Prep time: 5 minutes — Cook time: 30 minutes.
Nutrition value per serving: Calories: 691 net— Fats: 63 g net— Proteins: 29 g net— Carbs: 4 g net

Ingredients
- 1 cup mayonnaise
- 1 cup of chicken bone broth
- 1 cup shredded cheddar cheese
- 1 teaspoon chopped fresh chives
- 1 teaspoon fine sea salt, divided
- 1 (12-ounce) package broccoli florets
- 1 tablespoon ghee or coconut oil
- 4 (4-ounce) boneless, skinless chicken thighs, cut into 1-inch strips

Directions
- Preheat the oven to 350 degrees °F and grease a square casserole baking dish.
- Mix together the mayo, broth, cheese, chives, and ½ teaspoon of the salt in a bowl, stir well.
- Fill a pot with 1 inch of water and bring it to boil. Then, add broccoli and cover it.
- Let the broccoli become soft in the steam for 5 minutes. Drain the water, then mix the broccoli with the mayo mixture.
- Rub salt on the chicken strips.
- Heat ghee in a pan and fry each side of chicken strips for at least 3 to 4 minutes.
- Once the chicken is cooked thoroughly, add the strips to the mayo mixture and mix well.
- Place the chicken mixture in the casserole dish and bake for 20 minutes. Serve hot.

359: Smothered Fried Cabin Chicken

Yields: 4 servings— Prep time: 10 minutes — Cook time: 10 minutes
Nutrition value per serving: Calories: 517 net— Fats: 36 g net— Proteins: 45 g net— Carbs: 4 g net

Ingredients

- 4 boneless, skinless chicken thighs
- fine sea salt
- ground black pepper
- 2 large eggs
- ½ cup pork dust or powdered pork rinds
- ½ cup powdered Parmesan cheese
- 2 strips bacon, diced
- 1 cup shredded sharp cheddar cheese (dairy-free)
- ¼ cup diced tomatoes
- 2 cups leafy salad greens mix
- 1 lemon
- quartered ¼ cup ranch dressing
- Sliced green onions, for garnish
- 2 teaspoons olive oil

Directions

- Preheat the oven to 400 degrees °F.
- Gently pound the chicken to ½ inch thickness, and season each side with salt and pepper to taste.
- Beat an egg in a bowl and add salt and pepper, mix well.
- In another bowl, mix pork dust and parmesan cheese. Set aside.
- For coating, dip each chicken piece first in the egg wash, then press into the pork dust and parmesan mixture to coat thoroughly.
- Cook the diced bacon in a skillet for about 4 minutes until it becomes golden and crisp. Take out on a plate.
- In the same skillet (add more oil if required), fry each side of the coated chicken for 2 minutes, or until golden brown in colour.
- Once cooked, remove from the heat. Top the fried chicken with the fried bacon, shredded cheese, and diced tomatoes.
- Bake it in the oven for 3 minutes, or until the cheese melts completely.
- Make a salad using the green vegetable as a side dish with the chicken.
- Serve hot.

360: BBQ Chicken Lasagna

Yields: 10 servings— Prep time: 10 minutes (not including the time to cook chicken) — Cook time: 45 minutes
Nutrition value per serving: Calories: 345 net— Fats: 21 g net— Proteins: 31 g net— Carbs: 8 g net

Ingredients

- 4 cups tomato sauce
- 2 teaspoons liquid smoke
- ¼ cup Swerve confectioners' style sweetener or equivalent amount of liquid or powdered sweetener
- 16 thin slices deli roasted chicken breast
- 2 cups shredded cheddar cheese
- 3 cups shredded cooked chicken thighs (see below)
- 1-pound button mushrooms, sliced and sautéed in butter
- 1 green bell pepper, chopped and sautéed in butter
- ½ cup diced onions, sautéed in butter
- 2-pounds bone-in, skin-on chicken thighs
- 2 cups chicken bone broth, homemade
- ¼ cup diced onions
- 2 teaspoons minced garlic
- 1 teaspoon fine sea salt
- ½ teaspoon ground black pepper

Directions

- Preheat the oven to 375 degrees °F, and grease a baking dish.
- To make the sauce, put the tomato sauce in a bowl. Then, add the liquid smoke and sweetener, and mix thoroughly. Set aside.
- To make shredded chicken thighs, put all the ingredients in a slow cooker and cover. Let the chicken cook for 6 hours, until it becomes tender.
- Once tender, take out the chicken from the cooker. Remove the skin and save it to make cracklings. Shred the meat using a fork and set aside.
- To make lasagna, pour one cup sauce on the greased baking dish, then layer with half of the deli chicken noodles, then half amounts of cheese, shredded chicken and any other optional fillings of your choice.
- Finally, layer with the remaining sauce, deli chicken noodles, shredded chicken and cheese on top. You can also top it with any ingredient of your choice apart from the cheese.
- Bake the lasagna for 45 minutes until the sauce starts bubbling, the cheese melts completely and turns golden brown.
- Take out the lasagna and let it rest for 10 minutes before serving.

361: Herb Roasted Chicken

Yields: 12 servings— Prep time: 5 minutes — Cook time: 1 hour 15 minutes.
Nutrition value per serving: Calories: 320 net— Fats: 23 g net— Proteins: 25 g net— Carbs: 2 g net

Ingredients

- 1 (3 to 4-pound) chicken
- Fine sea salt and ground black pepper
- 3 tablespoons lard or coconut oil (or unsalted butter if not dairy-sensitive), softened
- 1 tablespoon chopped fresh thyme
- 2 teaspoons chopped fresh rosemary
- 1 lemon, sliced
- 1 onion, quartered
- 3 cloves garlic, whacked with the side of a knife

Directions

- Preheat the oven to 420 degrees °F.
- Season the chicken skin and inside cavity with salt and pepper generously. Then, refrigerate for 4 hours until the skin dries out completely. Before roasting, let it sit at room temperature for half an hour.
- Mash the lard in a bowl, add thyme and rosemary and mix thoroughly.
- Softly slip your fingers under the chicken skin on the breasts and legs to loosen it. Take some of the herbs and butter mixture in a spoon and slide it under the loosen chicken skin. Grip the skin in place while you remove back the spoon. Smooth out the chicken skin to distribute the butter evenly. Repeat with the remaining butter and coat the whole skin with it.
- Slide the lemon slices, onion, and garlic cloves into the cavity of the chicken. Squeeze some lemon juice inside too.
- Place a rack in a large roasting pan and roast the chicken on the rack for 1 hour and 15 minutes, or until the skin turns golden brown.
- Transfer the chicken on a platter and let it rest for 10 minutes. Toss out the lemon, onions and garlic before carving. Serve hot.

362: Chicken pot pie

Yields: 4 servings— Prep time: 10 minutes, 1 hour extra if the dough needs chilling — Cook time: 15 minutes
Nutrition value per serving Calories: 631 net— Fats: 50 g net— Proteins: 38 g net— Carbs: 9 g net

Ingredients

- 1¾ cups shredded mozzarella cheese
- 2 tablespoons unsalted butter
- 1 large egg, beaten
- ¾ cup blanched almond flour
- ⅛ teaspoon fine sea salt
- 2 tablespoons unsalted butter
- ¼ cup diced celery
- ¼ cup diced onions
- ¼ teaspoon minced fresh oregano
- ¼ teaspoon minced fresh thyme
- ¼ teaspoon fine sea salt
- 3 boneless, skinless chicken thighs, cut into ¼-inch pieces
- 4-ounces cream cheese (½ cup), softened
- ½ cup of chicken bone broth

Directions

- Preheat the oven to 425 degrees °F.
- In a microwave-safe bowl, mix butter and cheese, then melt in a microwave for 2 minutes. Once melted, add an egg and mix thoroughly.
- Mix the almond flour and salt in the above mixture. Knead the dough using your hands for 3 to 4 minutes. If the dough is gluey, chill the dough in the refrigerator for 1 hour.
- Melt the butter in a pan; add celery, onions, herbs and salt; and sauté until all the vegetables become soft, or for 3 to 4 minutes.
- Add in the chicken and sauté for another 4 minutes. Remove from the heat.
- Mix in the cream cheese, then gradually pour the broth while stirring continuously. Stir until combined well. Divide the mixture into 4 large ramekins.
- Divide the dough into 4 parts. Take out ¼ of the dough on a greased surface and flatten it out in a circle using your hands. Ensure the diameter of the circle is slightly larger than the diameter of the ramekin to ensure secure closing of the pie. Repeat the step with the remaining 3 parts of the dough.
- Place the circular dough in the top of the ramekins with the mixture and seal the edges using your fingers. Repeat the process for the remaining ramekins.
- Place all the ramekins on a baking sheet and bake for 15 to 25 minutes in the preheated oven, or until the dough colour turns golden brown.
- Take out and garnish the pie with thyme. Serve hot.

363: Slow cooker delightful balsamic chicken

Yields: 4 servings — Prep time: 5 minutes — Cook time: 4 hours.
Nutrition value per serving Calories: 190 net— Fat: 6 g net— Protein: 26 g net— Carbohydrates: 6 g net

Ingredients

- 6 pieces of boneless, skinless chicken
- 2 cans of diced tomatoes,
- 1 large onion, thinly sliced
- 4 cloves of garlic
- 1/2 teaspoon dried oregano
- ½ cup of balsamic vinegar
- 1 tablespoon of olive oil
- 1 tablespoon of dried rosemary
- 1 teaspoon of dried basil
- ½ teaspoon of thyme
- Salt and Pepper to taste

Directions

- In a bowl, combine and mix all the ingredients except for chicken. Set aside;
- Place the chicken in a slow cooker and pour the mixture of the ingredients over the top of the chicken.
- Cover the cooker and let it cook for 4 hours on a medium to high flame.
- Take out, garnish with oregano and basil if desired and serve hot.

364: Simple Chicken Salad

Yields: 6 servings— Prep time: 10 minutes — Cook time: 1 hour.
Nutrition value per serving Calories: 413 net— Fats: 25 g net— Proteins: 43 g net— Carbs: 2 g net

Ingredients

- 4 Chicken Breasts
- 105 g of Green Peppers
- 125 g of Celery
- 20 g of Green Onions
- 3/4 Cup of Mayo
- 3/4 Cup of Sugar-Free Sweet Relish
- 3 Large Hardboiled Eggs

Directions

- Preheat the oven to 350 degrees °F.
- Place the chicken in a baking dish and bake for 45 to 60 minutes until thoroughly cooked.
- Meanwhile, chop the onions and celery and peppers.
- Smash the boiled eggs and mix in the Mayo and sugar-free Sweet Relish. Then, add the chopped vegetables in the mixture, combine well.
- Once the chicken is cooked, shred it and combine it with the veggies and eggs mixture in a larger bowl and serve.

365: Chicken Cordon Bleu

Yields: 8 servings — Prep time: 5 minutes — Cook time: 30 minutes.

Nutrition value per serving: Calories: 592 net— Fats: 45 g net— Proteins: 45 g net — Carbs: 3 g net

Ingredients

- ½ cup (1 stick) unsalted butter
- ½ cup beef or chicken bone broth
- 1-ounce cream cheese (2 tablespoons)
- 10-ounces Swiss cheese, shredded
- Fine sea salt
- 8 boneless, skinless chicken thighs
- ½ teaspoon ground black pepper
- 8 slices Swiss cheese
- 8 slices cooked deli ham
- 1 cup powdered Parmesan cheese
- 2 teaspoons Italian seasoning
- 1 tablespoon ghee or coconut oil, for frying
- Chopped fresh parsley, for garnish

Directions

- For making the sauce, heat the butter in a pan and whisk until it turns brown. Ensure it does not go black. Then, gradually pour broth, cream cheese, and shredded cheese to the pan, and cook until the cheese melts and everything is well combined. Add salt and pepper to taste and mix well. Remove from heat and transfer it to the blender or food processor to blend well. Set aside
- Preheat the oven to 350 degrees °F and grease a baking dish.
- Place the chicken thighs between 2 pieces of parchment paper and gently pound them to ¼-inch thickness, then season with salt and pepper.
- Put a slice of Swiss cheese and ham on each thigh, then roll and secure with a toothpick. Repeat the process until all 8 thighs are done in the same way.
- Coat the chicken thighs in parmesan cheese and Italian seasoning thoroughly.
- Heat the ghee in a large skillet over medium-high heat, and fry the prepared chicken thighs for 4 minutes, or until it turns brown.
- Take out the fried chicken thighs on a baking pan and bake for 5 minutes.
- Take out of the oven and remove the toothpick.
- Garnish with chopped parsley, slice and serve hot.

366: Sunday Supper Pot Roast with fauxtatoes

Yields: 8 servings— Prep time: 15 minutes (not including time to make fauxtatoes) — Cook time: 6 hours

Nutrition value per serving Calories: 597 g net— Fats: 40 g net — Proteins: 51 g net — Carbs: 4 g net

Ingredients

- 1 (5-pound) bone-in beef chuck roast
- Fine sea salt and ground black pepper
- 3 tablespoons ghee (or coconut oil if dairy-free), divided
- 2 stalks celery, cut into ½-inch pieces
- 2 sprigs fresh thyme
- 1 sprig fresh rosemary
- 8 ounces sliced mushrooms
- 1 cup chopped onions
- 2 cloves garlic, minced
- 2 tablespoons tomato paste
- 2½ cups beef bone broth
- 1 batch Mashed Fauxtatoes, for serving.

Directions

- Generously rub salt and pepper on both sides of the roast, then sear in hot oil in a skillet for 5 minutes, each side.
- Put the celery in a slow cooker. Put the roast on top of the celery and pour in any juices from the skillet. Then, add in the thyme and rosemary sprigs. Set aside.
- Sauté the mushrooms for 3 to 4 minutes in a skillet on medium flame, then add onions and continue to sauté for 5 minutes more. Add in the garlic and sauté for another minute. Add tomato sauce and cook for 1 to 2 minutes. Finally, mix in the beef broth and let it simmer for 1 minute.
- Pour this mixture over the top of the roast in the slow cooker, and let it cook for 5 to 6 hours on high flame, until the meat pulls off the bones easily.
- Pull the meat off the bones and serve on fauxtatoes.

367: Spicy Italian meatballs

Yields: 3 servings — Prep time: 5 minutes — Cook time: 10 minutes.

Nutrition value per serving Calories: 458 net— Fats: 35.8 g net— Proteins: 28.2 g net— Carbs: 4.3 g net

Ingredients

- 3 ounces Asiago cheese, grated
- 1/4 cup mayonnaise
- 1 chilli pepper, minced
- 1 teaspoon yellow mustard
- 1 teaspoon Italian parsley
- 1/2 teaspoon red pepper flakes, crushed
- 1/2 teaspoon sea salt
- 1/2 teaspoon ground black pepper
- 1/2-pound ground beef
- 1 egg
- 1 tablespoon olive oil

Directions

- Take a medium bowl, and add in the cheese, chilli, mayo, mustard, parsley, salt, black pepper, and red pepper, mix well until thoroughly combined.
- Then, mix in the ground beef and egg thoroughly. Make meatballs of this prepared mixture.
- Heat olive oil in a skillet or deep pan over a medium flame, and cook the meatballs for 2 to 3 minutes on each side. Serve hot and enjoy!

368: Philly Cheesesteak Cupcakes

Yields: 6 jumbo or 12 regular servings — Prep time: 10 minutes — Cook time: 16 minutes.
Nutrition value per serving Calories: 504 net— Fats: 39 g net— Proteins: 33 g net

Ingredients
- 2 tablespoons coconut oil or unsalted butter
- 1½ cups diced green bell peppers
- ¾ cup chopped onions
- 1 clove garlic, smashed to a paste
- 1½ pounds ground beef or lamb
- 1 large egg, beaten
- ½ cup powdered Parmesan cheese
- ½ teaspoon fine sea salt
- ½ teaspoon ground black
- Black pepper
- ½ teaspoon dried basil
- ⅓ teaspoon chilli powder
- ½ teaspoon dried ground marjoram
- ½ teaspoon paprika
- ½ teaspoon dried thyme leaves
- 1½ cups cubed provolone or fontina cheese

Directions
- Preheat oven to 350 degrees °F.
- Place paper liners on large 6 muffin tray or a medium size 12 muffin tray.
- Heat the oil in a skillet over medium-high flame, add bell peppers and onion, and sauté until soft for about 3 minutes. Then, put in garlic and sauté for another minute. Remove from the heat and take out the vegetable mix in a large bowl.
- In the same bowl, mix in the ground beef, beaten egg, and Parmesan cheese, salt, other spices and cheese cubes; mix well to combine.
- Shape out the mixture into six 2½-inch balls or twelve 1½-inch balls depending in the muffin tray.
- Place a ball in each lined muffin cup, and bake for about 12 to 15 minutes for large cupcakes or 9 to 12 minutes for regular-sized cupcakes.
- Take out from the oven and serve warm.

Note: If you left with extra cupcakes, then store it in an airtight container or zip-lock bag and keep in the refrigerator for up to 3 days. Before serving, reheat the cupcakes in a baking pan in a preheated oven at 350 degrees °F for 5 minutes, or until warmed thoroughly.

369: Gyro Loaf with Tzatziki Sauce

Yields: 6 servings — Prep time: 10 minutes, plus at least 1 hour to chill Tzatziki sauce— Cook time: 55 minutes
Nutrition value per serving Calories: 539 net— Fats: 41 g net— Proteins: 33 g net— Carbs: 6 g net

Ingredients
- 1 cup sour cream
- 1 medium cucumber, peeled, seeded, and finely chopped or shredded and squeezed dry
- ½ teaspoon garlic powder
- ½ teaspoon fine sea salt
- 1 tablespoon finely chopped fresh parsley
- 1½ pounds ground lamb or beef
- ¾ cup finely chopped mushrooms
- ½ cup diced red onions
- ¼ cup diced black olives
- 8-ounces feta cheese, cut into ¼-inch dice, plus extra for garnish
- ½ cup powdered Parmesan cheese
- ¼ cup tomato sauce
- 1 large egg
- 1 teaspoon Greek seasoning
- 1 teaspoon dried oregano leaves
- 1 clove garlic, smashed to a paste
- Diced red onions
- Diced tomatoes

Directions
- To make the sauce, mix sour cream, peeled and squeezed cucumber, garlic powder, fine sea salt and chopped parsley together in a small bowl. Whisk well to combine. Then, chill in the refrigerator for 2 hours.
- Preheat the oven to 350 degrees °F.
- To make the loaf, mix together the ground lamb or beef with chopped mushrooms, diced red onions, diced black olives, feta cheese, powdered Parmesan cheese. Use your hands to mix well. Then, add in the tomato sauce, egg, Greek seasoning, garlic paste, and dried oregano leaves. Combine well and press the mixture into a loaf pan evenly.
- Bake for 55 minutes. Take it out and put on a cake rack for ten minutes.
- Before slicing, ensure the meatloaf is cool enough. Garnish with red onions, tomatoes and feta cheese. Serve with tzatziki sauce. Enjoy!

370: Meatloaf Cordon Bleu

Yields: 8 servings — Prep time: 7 minutes — Cook time: 1 hour.
Nutrition value per serving: Calories: 437 net — Fats: 32 g net— Proteins: 31 g net— Carbs: 3 g net

Ingredients
- 2 pounds ground beef
- 2 large eggs, beaten
- 1 small onion, chopped
- ½ cup chopped mushrooms
- ½ cup grated Parmesan cheese
- 1 clove garlic, smashed to a paste
- 1 teaspoon fine sea salt
- 1 teaspoon ground black pepper
- 4 ounces thinly sliced cooked ham
- 4 ounces thinly sliced provolone cheese

Directions
- Preheat the oven to 350 °F.
- Mix the ground beef, beaten eggs, onion, mushrooms, and Parmesan cheese in a bowl. Then, add in the garlic, salt, and pepper. Mix thoroughly to combine well.
- Put the meat on a greased parchment paper and flatten it into ½ inch thickness. Then, top it with ham and provolone cheese. Roll the meat into a loaf and seal the ends.
- Place the meatloaf in a loaf pan, then bake it for 1 hour 15 minutes.
- Let the loaf cool thoroughly before slicing. Serve.

371. Steak Fries with Béarnaise Sauce

Yields: 1 serving— Prep time: 6 minutes (not including time to make béarnaise) — Cook time: 30 minutes
Nutrition value per serving: Calories: 655 net— Fats: 61 g net— Proteins: 24 g net— Carbs: 6 g net

Ingredients

- 1 cauliflower stem
- 2 teaspoons melted unsalted butter (or melted coconut oil, lard, or avocado oil if dairy-free)
- ½ teaspoon fine sea salt
- ¼ teaspoon ground black pepper
- 1 (4-ounce) boneless rib-eye steak, about ¾ inch thick
- 1 teaspoon fine sea salt
- ½ teaspoon ground black pepper
- 2 tablespoons unsalted butter (or coconut oil, lard, or avocado oil if dairy-free)
- 3 tablespoons Béarnaise Sauce or 2 tablespoons beef bone broth for a dairy-free, egg-free pan sauce
- Fresh thyme leaves (optional)

Directions

- Preheat the oven to 425 degrees °F and grease a rimmed baking sheet.
- Slice the cauliflower stem into French fries' shapes.
- In a small bowl, mix ½ tsp salt and ¼ tsp pepper in melted butter.
- Then, coat cauliflower French fries with this melted butter mixture.
- After coating well, put them on the greased baking sheet, and bake for 25 minutes, or until it turns golden brown.
- For making the steak, season the boneless rib-eye steak from with 1 teaspoon of salt and ½ teaspoon of pepper from all sides.
- Heat oil in a skillet at high flame, then toast the steak for 1 to 2 minute from each side.
- Lower the heat to normal, and cook for another 5 to 6 minutes, or until thoroughly cooked. Take out the steak and let it rest for 12 to 15 minutes before slicing it.
- If Béarnaise is not available, you can use the beef broth to make the pan sauce. For it, pour the bone broth in the same skillet. Whisk to scrape the bottom of the skillet and mix the steak drippings with the broth.
- Place the steak on a serving plate, top it with cauliflower fries, and drizzle with the béarnaise sauce or pan sauce. Decorate it with fresh thyme leaves and serve hot.

372: Meat and Goat Cheese Stuffed Mushrooms

Yields: 5 servings — Prep time: 10 minutes— Cook time: 25 minutes.
Nutrition value per serving Calories: 148 net— Fats: 8.4 g net— Proteins: 14.1 g net — Carbs: 4.8 g net

Ingredients

- 4 ounces ground beef
- 2 ounces ground pork
- Kosher salt and ground black pepper, to taste
- 1/4 cup goat cheese, crumbled
- 2 tablespoons Romano cheese, grated
- 2 tablespoons shallot, minced
- 1 garlic clove, minced
- 1 teaspoon dried basil
- ½ teaspoon dried oregano
- ½ teaspoon dried rosemary
- 20 button mushrooms, stems removed

Directions

- Preheat the oven at 370 degrees °F and grease a baking pan.
- Mix grounded beef, grounded pork together. Then, season with salt and black pepper.
- Add in crumbled goat cheese, minced shallot, grated Romano cheese, minced garlic, and all herbs. Mix all the ingredients well by using your hands.
- Stuff the button mushrooms with this mixture and place them on the baking pan.
- Bake for approximately 18 minutes.
- Serve hot or cold, as you desire.

373: Filet Mignons Florentine

Yields 2 servings — Prep time: 5 minutes (not including time to make hollandaise) — Cook time: 10 minutes
Nutrition value per serving Calories: 497 net— Fats: 43 g net— Proteins: 20 g net— Carbs: 6 g net

Ingredients

- 1 tablespoon Keto fat, for frying
- 2 (3-ounce) filet mignons, about 1¼ inches thick (Grass-Fed Beef Tenderloin Steaks)
- 1½ teaspoons fine sea salt
- ½ teaspoon ground black pepper
- 1 large tomato, thinly sliced
- 2 tablespoons minced shallots
- 2 cups fresh spinach
- ¼ cup Easy Basil Hollandaise

Directions

- Pat dry the steaks and season it thoroughly with salt and pepper.
- Heat Keto fat in a cast-iron skillet, and toast the steak in the heated oil. Cook from 3 minutes on each side.
- Remove the steak from the skillet, and set aside for 10 minutes.
- Sauté shallots in the same skillet for 1 to 2 minutes on medium heat. Then add spinach and sauté for another 2 minutes or until floppy. Add salt according to your taste.
- Place 3 slices of tomatoes on a plate. Top the tomatoes with the shallots and spinach mixture.
- Then, put the cooked steak on the greens, and drizzle with 2 tablespoons of hollandaise sauce. Serve.

374: Meatballs with Brown Gravy

Yields: 4 servings— Prep time: 5 minutes — Cook time: 35 minutes.
Nutrition value per serving Calories: 550— Fats: 44 g net— Proteins: 36 g net— Carbs: 1 g net

Ingredients
- 1 tablespoon coconut oil (or unsalted butter if not dairy-sensitive)
- ¼ cup chopped onions
- 1 teaspoon fine sea salt
- 2 pounds ground beef
- 1 cup finely chopped mushrooms
- 1 cup grated Parmesan cheese (omit for dairy-free)
- 1 large egg
- 2 tablespoons bacon fat or lard (or unsalted butter if not dairy-sensitive)
- 1 cup beef bone broth, homemade
- 1 teaspoon coconut aminos or wheat-free tamari
- ¼ teaspoon fine sea salt
- ¼ teaspoon ground black pepper
- 1 teaspoon fish sauce (optional, for umami flavour)

Directions
- Preheat the oven to 350 degrees °F.
- Heat the coconut oil in a skillet, put in the onions and sauté for about 4 to 5 minutes, or until the onions turn soft. Add salt to taste. Take out the onions in a bowl and let it cool.
- Mix the ground beef, mushrooms, Parmesan cheese, and egg in a medium mixing bowl. Then, add in the onion mixture. Mix thoroughly to combine well.
- Shape the meat mixture into 2-inch balls and place on a baking sheet.
- Bake for 30 minutes, or until the meat is thoroughly cooked. Take the meatballs out on a serving bowl or dish.
- For making gravy, combine bacon fat, beef bone broth, coconut aminos, sea salt and black pepper in a saucepan. You can also add fish sauce if you like. Whisk it well.
- Then, boil this mixture while constantly stirring for 10 minutes, or until the gravy reduces to the preferred thickness.
- Serve the meatballs with this hot gravy and enjoy!

375: Steak with Blue Cheese Whip

Yields: 2 servings — Prep time: 5 minutes — Cook time: 20 minutes.
Nutrition value per serving Calories: 566 net— Fats: 48 g net— Proteins 33 g net— Carbs 1 g net

Ingredients
- 1 (12-ounce) T-bone steak, about ¾ inch thick
- 1¼ teaspoons fine sea salt
- ½ teaspoon ground black pepper
- 1 tablespoon Keto fat, for frying
- ¼ cup heavy cream
- ¼ ounce blue cheese, finely crumbled
- ⅛ teaspoon fine sea salt

Directions
- Preheat the oven to 400 degrees °F.
- Thoroughly season the steak from all sides with the salt and pepper.
- Heat oil in a skillet and cook the steak for 3 minutes from each side.
- Put the steak in a baking dish and cook it in the oven until it becomes tender.
- Take the steak out and let it rest for 10 minutes before slicing it into desired portion size and then serving it.
- For making blue whip cheese, put the heavy cream in a stand mixer or blender, and whip until it becomes stiff and firm. Then, mix in the blue cheese and salt to taste.
- Place each portion of the steak on a plate and serve it with 2 to 3 tablespoons of the blue cheese whip.

376: Perfect Prime Rib with Tiger Sauce

Yields: 16 servings — Prep time: 8 minutes, plus 8 hours to marinate— Cook time: 3½ - 5½ hours, depending on— the lowest available oven temperature.
Nutrition value per serving Calories: 703 net— Fats: 49 g net— Proteins: 60 g net— Carbs: 2 g net

Ingredients
- 1 (8-pound) boneless prime rib roast
- 2½ tablespoons fine sea salt
- 1½ tablespoons ground black pepper
- ½ cup softened ghee or unsalted butter
- 2 tablespoons chopped fresh rosemary
- 2 tablespoons chopped fresh thyme
- 1 cup sour cream
- ¼ cup prepared horseradish
- 2 tablespoons chopped fresh dill or 2 teaspoons dried dill
- Fine sea salt (optional)

Directions
- Season the rib roast with the salt and pepper thoroughly and generously. Then, put it in an airtight box or zip-lock bag and keep in the refrigerator for at least 8 hours, so that all the flavours incorporate well
- Take the roast out from the fridge at least two hours before baking, and let it rest at room temperature to thaw.
- Place the roast in a greased baking pan, and rub ghee on the roast. Then, put chopped herbs on the roast.
- Bake the roast for 3½ to 5½ hours depending on the lowest available temperature, until it is thoroughly cooked.
- When you were about to serve, before ten minutes, increase the oven temperature to 500 degrees °F, and cook the roast for 8 to 10 minutes, or until it turns golden brown and crispy.
- For the tiger sauce, mix the sour cream, horseradish, and dill in a small mixing bowl together. Then, add sea salt and stir well to combine.
- Serve the crispy hot roast with the tiger sauce and the baking pan juices.

377: Greek Burgers with Feta Dressing

Yields: 3 servings — Prep time: 15 minutes — Cook time: 6 minutes.
Nutrition value per serving Calories 556 net— Fats 46 g net— Proteins 28 g net— Carbs 6 g net

Ingredients
- 1 tablespoon ghee, lard, or coconut oil, for frying
- 1-pound ground lamb
- 1½ teaspoons fine sea salt
- 1 teaspoon ground black pepper
- 6 leaves lettuce
- ½ cup thinly sliced red onions
- ¼ cup thickly sliced cucumbers
- 6 cherry tomatoes, sliced
- ½ cup Greek dressing

Directions
- Shape the ground meat into 3 patties using your hands, and season each side with salt and pepper.
- Heat the ghee in a skillet on medium heat, and fry the patties from each side for 5 to 6 minutes, until it is cooked through.
- Place each burger petty on 2 lettuce leaves, then top it with sliced onions, tomatoes, cucumbers. Finally, drizzle 2½ tablespoons of the Greek dressing on it and serve.

378: Country-Fried Steak and Gravy

Yields: 4 servings — Prep time: 10 minutes, (not including time to make fauxtatoes or rice) — Cook time: 10 minutes
Nutrition value per serving: Calories 775 net— Fats 58 g net— Proteins 50 g net— Carbs 12 g net

Ingredients
- 4 (4-ounce) bottom round steaks
- 2 teaspoons fine sea salt
- 1 teaspoon ground black pepper
- 1 large egg
- 1 cup powdered Parmesan cheese (or pork dust if dairy-free)
- ½ teaspoon paprika
- ¼ teaspoon cayenne pepper
- 1 tablespoon ghee (or coconut oil if dairy-free)
- 2 tablespoons minced onions
- 1 clove garlic, minced
- 4-ounces cream cheese (½ cup) (Kite Hill brand cream cheese style spread if dairy-free), softened
- ½ cup beef or chicken bone broth
- Fine sea salt and ground black pepper
- 1 batch Mashed Fauxtatoes (or Cauliflower Rice if dairy-free)
- Chopped fresh parsley (optional)
- Melted ghee (or avocado oil if dairy-free), for drizzling

Directions
- Pound the steaks to ¼ inch thickness with a meat tenderiser or meat pounder. Generously season it from all sides with salt and pepper.
- Whisk an egg in a medium bowl.
- Take another bowl, and mix in the Parmesan cheese, paprika, and cayenne pepper. Mix well to combine. Then, divide this Parmesan mixture between 2 bowls.
- Dip steak into the first bowl of Parmesan mixture, then into the egg wash, and finally into the second bowl of Parmesan mixture. Coat thoroughly by pressing the cheese mixture on each side using your hands. Repeat the steps with all other steaks.
- Heat ¼ cup of ghee in a skillet, then fry the well-coated steaks for 2 to 3 minutes from each side, or until the steak's colour turns golden brown. Take out the steak in a serving dish. Set aside.
- For making gravy, heat 1 tablespoon of ghee in a skillet, and sauté onions and garlic for 2 to 3 minutes, or until the onions turn soft.
- Then, add in the cream cheese to the skillet and whisk vigorously to avoid any lumps. Then, slowly mix in the broth while stirring continuously. Let it simmer on medium heat until the mixture reduces to the desired thickens. Remove from the heat. Then, add salt and black pepper in the gravy. Stir well.
- Pour the gravy on to the steaks. Garnish with chopped parsley and drizzle some melted ghee on top. Serve hot with mashed fauxtatoes or cauliflower rice.

379: Garlic and Rosemary Rack of Lamb

Yields: 4 servings (2 ribs per serving) — Prep time: 10 minutes — Cook time: 25 minutes.
Nutrition value per serving Calories 344 net— Fats 27 g net— Proteins 17 g net— Carbs 4 g net

Ingredients
- 2 (4-rib) racks of lamb, trimmed and frenched at the tips
- 1 teaspoon fine sea salt
- ½ teaspoon ground black pepper
- 2 teaspoons ghee (or coconut oil if dairy-free)
- 2 cloves garlic, minced
- 1 tablespoon finely chopped fresh rosemary
- 2 teaspoons finely chopped fresh thyme
- 2 tablespoons avocado oil
- Melted ghee or avocado oil, for drizzling
- Greek olives, for garnish
- Lemon slices, for garnish
- Fresh herbs of choice, for garnish

Directions
- Preheat the oven to 350 degrees °F.
- Heat oil in a pan or skillet and fry the rack of lamb from each side for 2 minutes. Set aside to cool.
- Mix the garlic, rosemary, thyme, and avocado oil in a bowl and coat the rack of lamb in this mixture.
- Then, roast the rack of lamb in the oven for 18 to 20 minutes until cooked through. Take out and let it rest for 10 minutes.
- Slice the rack of lamb into chops. Drizzle ghee on top and garnish the chops with lemon slices, olives and the fresh herbs of your choice. Serve hot.

380: Classic Duck à l'orange

Yields: 8 servings— Prep time: 7 minutes — Cook time: 2 hours 15 minutes.
Nutrition value per serving: Calories: 478 net— Fats: 41 g net— Proteins: 20 g net— Carbs: 7 g net

Ingredients

- 1 (5-pound) duck
- 1 tablespoon fine sea salt
- 1 teaspoon ground black pepper
- Rind from 1 orange
- 4 sprigs fresh thyme
- 4 sprigs fresh marjoram
- Unsalted butter, softened
- 1 onion, sliced thin
- 1 stalk celery, chopped
- 1 cup duck or chicken bone broth
- 2 cups duck or chicken bone broth
- ½ cup (1 stick) unsalted butter or duck fat
- ¼ cup Swerve confectioners' style sweetener or equivalent amount of liquid or powdered sweetener, or more to taste
- Salt to taste (optional)
- 2 tablespoons coconut vinegar or sherry wine vinegar
- 2 tablespoons minced shallots
- Grated zest of 2 oranges, plus extra for garnish (optional)
- Juice of 3 lemons
- 6 drops food-grade orange oil, or more to taste
- Fresh thyme leaves, for garnish
- Orange slices, for garnish

Directions

- Set the oven temperature at 475 degrees °F for preheating.
- Thoroughly season the duck from all sides (inside the cavity and outside skin) with the salt and pepper.
- Stuff the duck with the orange rind, thyme, and fresh marjoram, and rub butter on the outside of the duck.
- Place the duck on a roasting pan. Then, add in the broth, onion slices along with chopped celery. Bake for 30 minutes. Meanwhile, prepare your sauce.
- To make orange sauce, mix all the ingredients of the sauce in a small to a medium saucepan. Whisk to combine well. Put the saucepan over medium heat, and let the mixture simmer for about 30 to 45 minutes. Season it with salt if desired. Then, strain the sauce and discard the zest.
- After 30 minutes of baking, reduce the temperature of the oven to 350 degrees °F. Then, add the prepared sauce on the duck in the roasting pan, and bake for another 80 to 90 minutes, until thoroughly cooked.
- Turn on the oven broiler to broil the duck for 4 to 5 minutes, or until the skin is crisp and golden brown.
- Take out the duck from the oven, and set it aside for 10 to 15 minutes. Then, serve it with orange sauce and garnish with thyme leaves, orange zest and orange slices.

381: Braised Duck Legs with Mushrooms

Yields: 4 serving — Prep time: 10 minutes — Cook time: 1 ½ hour.
Nutrition value per serving Calories: 393 net— Fats: 33 g net— Proteins: 19 g net— Carbs: 6 g net

Ingredients

- 2 tablespoons ghee or unsalted butter, for frying
- 4 duck leg quarters (legs and thighs)
- Fine sea salt and ground black pepper
- ½ cup diced onions
- 1 leek, cleaned and diced
- 2 bay leaves
- 2 sprigs fresh rosemary
- 2 sprigs fresh thyme
- 4 cups duck or chicken broth
- 2 strips bacon, diced
- 8-ounces mushrooms, sliced

Directions

- Season the duck's legs with salt and pepper thoroughly.
- Heat 1 tablespoon ghee in a pan over a high flame, and fry each side of the duck's legs for 3 to 4 minutes. Remove from the heat and set aside.
- Heat 1 tablespoon ghee in a pot, and sauté onions and leek for 2 to 3 minutes, or until soft. Then, add in the broth, rosemary, bay leaves and thyme.
- Put in the fried duck legs in the pot, and simmer for 75 to 80 minutes, or until the duck is thoroughly cooked and tender.
- Remove the duck legs from the pot and set aside. Keep cooking the sauce until reduced to the desired thickness, then put the duck back into the sauce. Stir and remove from the heat.
- Place the diced bacon and mushrooms in a preheated skillet and sauté until it turns golden brown.
- Serve the duck hot along with sauce and onion mixture, and top it with the sautéed bacon and mushrooms.

382. Peanut powder salad dressing

NUTRITIONAL VALUE PER SERVING Calories: 50 kals; Carbohydrates grams: 7; Sodium: 0.563 grams; Fat: 2 grams; — Protein:3 grams ; Dietary Fiber: 1.21 grams ; Sugar: 5 grams — Preparation time: 20 minutes

Ingredients

- 1/2 tablespoon of soy sauce
- 1/2 tablespoon of water
- 1 tablespoon of peanut powder
- 1/4 teaspoon of garlic powder
- 1/2 teaspoon of ground pepper
- 1/2 teaspoon of Szechuan chili sauce
- 2 teaspoons of brown sugar blend
- 1/2 teaspoon of sesame oil

Directions

- Pour all the ingredients into a blender or food processor and blend until a smoothie like consistency is gotten. This should take 10 approximately 10 minutes.
- Serve and refrigerate any remaining sauce.

383. Egg chilada

NUTRITIONAL VALUE PER SERVING Calories: 171kals; Sugar: 3 grams; Carbohydrate:3 grams; Protein: 23 grams , — Fat:8 grams

Ingredients:
- 1 full egg
- 1 egg white
- 1 ounce of chicken
- 2 tablespoons of Salsa
- Black pepper
- 2 tablespoons Mexican cheese (shredded)
- 3 tablespoons of plain fat-free Greek yoghurt
- Salt to taste

Directions
- Defreeze chicken
- Place both egg and egg white in a bowl and whisk briskly
- Pour your whisked eggs into a preheated pan. Let the circumference cover the whole pan evenly
- Sprinkle your salt and pepper as the eggs begin to harden
- Flip the eggs (Use a spatula to help if it is stuck the pan) to enable the other side cook as well
- Take out the eggs and lay flat
- Fill the eggs with spoonfuls of chicken and Mexican cheese.
- Roll up the eggs
- Top with Greek yogurt and salsa

384. Moist chicken

NUTRITIONAL VALUE PER SERVING Calories: 233 kal; Sugar 0g; Carbohydrate: 8g; Fat: 5g; Protein: 37g; Sodium: 268mg— Preparation time: 55 minutes

Ingredients:
- 3 ½ pounds skinned chicken breasts (boneless)
- 1 and 1/3 Italian bread crumbs (whole wheat)
- 1½ jar of light mayonnaise dressing

Directions
- Preheat your oven to a temperature of about 420 °
- Apply mayonnaise over the total surface of the pieces of chicken breasts
- Place your breadcrumbs in a large and flat tray and roll the soaked chicken parts through it
- Place foil on a pan and bake the crumb covered chicken for 45-50 minutes

385. Creamy tarragon dressing

NUTRITIONAL VALUE PER SERVING Per half cup serving: Calories: 189kal; protein 11.17g; Carbohydrate: 19.166g; Fat 7.25g. — Preparation time: 15 minutes

Ingredients
- 1 Tablespoon fresh minced tarragon
- 1 tablespoon of spicy mustard (brown)
- ½ cup of plain yogurt (fat free)
- ¼ cup no fat sour cream
- ¼ cup of apple juice concentrate (unsweetened)

Directions
- In a bowl, put in tarragon and yoghurt
- Pour in mustard and mix
- Put in sour cream and mix
- Then put in apple juice and mix
- Serve

386. Steam fish and yogurt sauce

NUTRITIONAL VALUE PER SERVING Calories: 270 kals; Fat: 6 g; saturated fat:1 g; cholesterol: 95 mg; protein: 46 g; calcium: 20mg; sugars: 9g— Preparation time: 15 minutes

Ingredients:
- ½ cup low-fat, plain yogurt
- 1 diced scallion include the green part
- 1 large lemon, thinly sliced
- ½ cup of chicken broth
- 2 tablespoons canola oil
- 1 teaspoon finely chopped fresh basil
- 1 ½ pounds of firm-fleshed salmon
- 1 tablespoon of divided fresh dill
- 1 tablespoon finely chopped fresh chives
- Salt to taste
- Pepper to taste

Directions
- Put oil, salt, basil, chives and half of the dill
- Mix together and rub the fish with it
- Pour yogurt in a bowl and put in dill. Cover and set aside
- Mix remaining dill with yogurt and set sauce aside.
- Place scallions in large rimmed dish
- Place fish on scallions
- Place lemon in slices on the fish
- Pour in broth
- Microwave till soft and serve with yoghurt

387. Refried kidney beans

NUTRITIONAL VALUE PER SERVING Calories: 253 kals; Fat: 11 g; saturated fat:1 g; cholesterol: 45 mg; protein: 56 g; calcium: 36mg; — Preparation time: 15 minutes

Ingredients:
- 1 can kidney beans

Directions
- Dice onions
- Set a saucepan on medium heat
- Open up can of beans and pour in with the water
- Add onions, garlic, cumin, salt and pepper
- Cook until it boils well
- Take off and leave to cool
- Mash and reheat
- If it is too thick, you can put in vegetable stock

388.Black bean soup

NUTRITIONAL VALUE PER SERVING Calories: 273 kals; Fat: 13 g; saturated fat:1 g; cholesterol: 48.5 mg; protein: 65 g; calcium: 36mg; — Preparation time: 15 minutes

Ingredients

- 1 can of black beans
- ½ teaspoon chili powder
- 1 teaspoon cumin
- 1 minced garlic clove
- 1 teaspoon minced jalapeños
- 1 teaspoon tomato paste
- Kosher salt
- Black pepper
- 8 ounces of vegetable stock
- 1 bay leaf
- Sour cream
- 1 tablespoon canola oil

Directions

- Heat oil in saucepan over medium heat
- Put in onions and fry till soft
- Add jalapeños and then garlic
- Stir fry for 2-3 minutes
- Put in tomato paste
- Add salt, pepper, chili and cumin
- Stir well
- Open can and pour in beans with the water in them
- Add bay leaf and leave to boil on low heat for 15-20 minutes
- Take off heat and allow to cool
- Using blender or food processor, blend food till it is as smooth as you want

389: Turkey Goulash Over Mashed Fauxtatoes

Yields: 8 servings Prep time: 10 minutes (not including time to make fauxtatoes) — Cook time: 1 hour
Nutrition value per serving Calories: 342 net— Fats: 18 g net— Proteins: 32 g net— Carbs: 12 g net

Ingredients

- 2 tablespoons ghee or coconut oil
- 1 green bell pepper, diced
- ½ cup diced onions
- 2 cloves garlic, smashed to a paste
- 8 ounces Mexican-style fresh (raw) chorizo, removed from casings
- 4 cups leftover cooked turkey, ¾ inch cubed
- 3 tablespoons chilli powder
- 1 tablespoon ground cumin
- 1 tablespoon dried oregano leaves
- 1 tablespoon paprika
- ½ teaspoon ground black pepper
- 1 teaspoon fine sea salt
- 1 (24-ounce) jar fire-roasted diced tomatoes
- 2 cups turkey or chicken bone broth
- 1 lime, halved
- 1 batch Mashed Fauxtatoes, for serving
- Sour cream, for garnish
- Chopped fresh chives, for garnish

Directions

- Heat the ghee or coconut oil in a pan, and add in the bell pepper and onions and cook, while stirring continuously, until the onions turned soft, for about 5 minutes. Then, add in the garlic and cook for another 1 to 2 minutes.
- Add in the chorizo and sauté it for a minute, then add the turkey cubes, chilli powder, ground cumin, paprika, oregano along with tomatoes and broth. Keep stirring and let it simmer for an hour, or until the mixture reduces to the desired thickness. Remove from the heat.
- Squeeze in the lime juice, then season it with the salt and pepper to taste, and stir well.
- Serve in bowls over fauxtatoes and garnish with sour cream and chopped chives on top.

390: Braised Turkey Legs with Creamy Gravy

Yields: 4 servings — Prep time: 15 minutes (not including time to make fauxtatoes) — Cook time: about 2 hours.
Nutrition value per serving Calories: 650 net— Fats: 30 g net— Proteins: 80 g net— Carbs: 10 g net

Ingredients

- 2 tablespoons ghee or coconut oil
- 4 turkey legs
- Fine sea salt and ground black pepper
- ¼ cup diced onions
- ¼ cup diced celery
- 2 sprigs thyme, plus extra for garnish
- 1½ cups turkey or chicken bone broth, or water, or more as needed
- Mashed Fauxtatoes for serving
- 1-ounce mascarpone or cream cheese (2 tablespoons), softened
- Chopped fresh herbs, such as thyme, for garnish
- Melted ghee or extra-virgin olive oil, for drizzling

Directions

- Preheat the oven to 300 degrees °F.
- Season the turkey legs with salt and pepper on all sides generously.
- Heat ghee in a skillet, and fry the seasoned turkey legs for 4 to 5 minutes, or until they turn golden brown.
- Remove the turkey legs from the skillet, and put on a roasting pan.
- Then, add in the onions, celery, and thyme sprigs in the same skillet, and fry for 7 to 8 minutes, or until the onions become soft. Then, put these veggies on the roasting pan with the turkey legs.
- Then, add in the broth to the roasting pan.
- Place the roasting pan in the oven uncovered, and roast for about 1 hour 40 minutes.
- Place the mashed fauxtatoes on 4 plates. And top each with the turkey leg.
- Take all the veggies from the roasting pan and put it in a food processor or blender. Then, add in the mascarpone. Blend it well until pureed.
- Top each turkey leg with the puree, and garnish with herbs, and finally drizzle with melted ghee.

391: Lemon Pepper Roast Turkey with Bacon Gravy

Yields: 14 servings — prep time: 15 minutes (not including time to make fauxtatoes) — cook time: 3 hours.
Nutrition value per serving: Calories: 349 net— Fats: 19 g net— Proteins: 39 g net— Carbs: 3 g net

Ingredients

- 1 (12-pound) turkey
- 3 lemons, plus extra for garnish
- 2 tablespoons ground black pepper
- 1 tablespoon fine sea salt
- 1 cup diced onions
- 2 cloves garlic, minced
- 1 large stalk celery, diced
- 4 small sprigs fresh thyme
- 10 strips bacon, diced
- ½ cup ghee or unsalted butter
- ⅛ teaspoon guar gum (a natural thickener), or 1-ounce cream cheese (2 tablespoons)

Directions

- Preheat the oven to 350 degrees °F.
- Remove the neck and giblets from the turkey and pat it dry.
- Grate the zest of the lemons into a small bowl, then add in the salt and pepper.
- Season the inside cavity of the turkey with a little amount of lemon zest, then rub all the remaining lemon zest on the outside of the turkey.
- Stuff the inside cavity of the turkey with half-cut lemons along with onions, garlic, celery and thyme sprigs. Then, tie up turkey legs with kitchen twine.
- Place the turkey on a large roasting pan.
- Cook the diced bacon in a skillet for about 5 minutes. Take out the bacon and set aside.
- In the same skillet, add the ghee to the drippings and let it melt.
- Pour the skillet drippings in a bowl, and add in the lemon juice. Then, pour this mixture on the turkey and rub well.
- Put the turkey in the oven and bake for 3 hours.
- While baking, keep basting the turkey with the drippings after every 30 minutes with the help of a spoon.
- Once cooked, let the turkey rest for 20 to 25 minutes before carving.
- Meanwhile, pour the drippings from the roasting pan into a saucepan, and place it over medium heat. Then, whisk in the cream cheese and mix vigorously to avoid any lumps. Cook for 4 to 6 minutes, or until the gravy becomes thick, then add in the sautéed bacon.
- Serve the turkey with the sauce and garnish with lemons. Enjoy!

392: Catfish and Cauliflower Casserole

Yields: 4 servings — Prep time: 10 minutes — Cook time: 20 minutes.
Nutrition value per serving: Calories: 510 net— Fats: 40 g net— Proteins: 31.3 g net— Carbs: 5.5 g net

Ingredients

- 1 tablespoon sesame oil
- 11-ounces cauliflower
- 4 scallions
- 1 garlic clove, minced
- 1 teaspoon fresh ginger, grated
- Salt and ground black pepper, to taste
- Cayenne pepper, to taste
- 2 sprigs dried thyme, crushed
- 1 sprig rosemary, crushed
- 24-ounces catfish, cut into pieces
- ½ cup cream cheese
- ½ cup double cream
- 1 egg
- 2-ounces butter, cold

Directions

- Preheat the oven to 390 degrees °F, and lightly grease a casserole dish with a nonstick cooking spray.
- Heat sesame oil in a pan or skillet over medium flame, and cook the cauliflower and scallions for 4 to 7 minutes, or until soft. Then, put in the garlic and ginger, and sauté for 1 to 2 minutes more.
- Place these sautéed vegetables to the greased casserole dish. Top it with the seasonings. Then, add catfish pieces on the top.
- In a small mixing bowl, mix in the cream cheese, double cream, and egg thoroughly. Top the casserole with this cream and egg mixture.
- Finally, top it with the slices of butter and bake for 15 to 25 minutes, or when the fish is thoroughly cooked and tender.
- Serve hot and enjoy!

393: Walleye Simmered in Basil Cream

Yields: 4 servings — Prep time: 5 minutes — Cook time: 10 minutes.
Nutrition value per serving Calories: 210 net— Fats: 11 g net — Proteins: 23 g net— Carbs: 3 g net

Ingredients:

- ¼ cup heavy cream (or full-fat coconut milk if dairy-free)
- ¼ cup fresh basil leaves, plus extra for garnish
- 2 tablespoons ghee or unsalted butter (or coconut oil if dairy-free), divided
- ½ cup chopped onions
- 1 clove garlic, smashed to a paste
- 1-pound walleye fillets, skinned and cut crosswise into 1-inch-wide pieces
- 1 teaspoon fine sea salt
- ¼ teaspoon ground black pepper
- ¼ cup fish or chicken bone broth
- Cherry tomatoes, cut in half, for garnish.

Directions

- Put cream and basil in a food processor or blender and blend well until smooth puree.
- Heat ghee in a skillet, then add onions and garlic and sauté for 2 minutes, or until the onions turn soft.
- Season the fish pieces with the salt and pepper. Then, add the seasoned fish to the skillet along with the basil and cream puree and bone broth. Stir well and let it cook for 5 to 7 minutes, or until the fish is thoroughly cooked.
- Serve the fish with the sauce. Garnish the fish with basil leaves and halved cherry tomatoes. Enjoy!

394. Pineapple meatballs

NUTRITIONAL VALUE PER SERVING— Serving size: 24(2 each) meatballs; Calories: 91 kals; Protein: 6.43 grams; Carbohydrates: 13.37 grams; Fat: 1.3 grams. — Preparation time: 30 minutes

Ingredients:

- 2cans of pineapple chunks
- 1 cup of chopped bell pepper
- 2 tablespoons light soy sauce
- 24 pairs of turkey meatballs
- 4 tablespoons of corn starch
- 4 beef bouillon cubes

Directions:

- Place all ingredients (except the corn starch) together in a pot.
- Boil gently for 17 minutes
- Pour some water into the cornstarch
- Stir until it's even, thick and clear.
- Place the meatballs into it
- Boil gently for 12 minutes
- Serve warm

395. Baked tomatoes

NUTRITIONAL VALUE PER SERVING— Calories: 73kals; Sugar: 3 grams; Carbohydrate: 6 grams; Protein: 3 grams ; Fat:5 grams; Dietary fiber: 2 grams— Preparation time: 1 ½ hours

Ingredients
- 8 small fresh tomatoes
- Extra virgin olive oil cooking spray
- ½ cups of shredded low fat parmesan cheese
- Greek Seasoning
- Salt

Directions
- Oven must be preheated to 177º c.
- Wash and half each tomato
- Place each half face down on a non-stick frying pan
- Rub the outer covering of each tomato with the extra virgin olive oil
- Coat with pine nuts and cheese (The oil will help it stick)
- Sprinkle a pinch of salt
- Place in the preheated oven and let it bake for 50 minutes.

396. High protein cheesecake

NUTRITIONAL VALUE PER SERVING— Calories: 152 kal; Sugar 2g; Carbohydrate: 610g; Unsaturated Fat: 7g; Protein: 13g; Sodium: 385 mg. — Preparation time: 50 minutes

Ingredients:
- ½ teaspoons of baking soda
- 1/3 teaspoons of olive oil
- 1 cup low-fat cottage cheese
- 1 teaspoons of peppermint extract
- 3 large eggs

Directions
- Beat eggs
- Mix your flour and baking powder together in a small bowl
- In a bigger bowl, mix your cottage cheese, eggs, peppermint extract, and olive oil
- Pour the flour mixture into the bigger bowl containing the cheese
- Stir with a spoon until they are thoroughly mixed together
- Set fire to medium heat and place a pan on
- Pour the batter into the pan and cook until bubbles begin to escape. Wait until it hardens a bit
- Flip the batter and repeat the process until both sides have a brownish shade
- May be served with syrup (low calorie)

397. Cake o' watermelon

NUTRITIONAL VALUE PER SERVING— (per one inch slice): Calories: 106kal; protein 3.2g; Carbohydrate: 13.15g; Fat 5.1g. — Preparation time: 30 minutes

Ingredients:
- 1 watermelon (approximately 6 cups)
- 1 packet of vanilla pudding (sugar free)
- 1 container of whipped cream (sugar free)
- 5 inch long bamboo skewers
- 1 cup of slivered pecans(toasted)
- Sliced mixed fruits (berries)
- 1 teaspoon almond flavoring (optional)

Directions
- Slice the watermelon into three equal parts.
- Peel away the outer covering
- Mix the vanilla pudding with the almond flavor (this is optional)
- Top a round of the watermelon with half of the mixed fruit and half of the (flavored) vanilla pudding.
- Repeat the process with the remainder of the mixed fruit and pudding on another watermelon piece
- Keep the pudding in place by passing bamboo skewers through the cake. Cut them to the appropriate size if they exceed the length required.
- Coat the whole cake with whipped cream, sprinkling it with toasted pecans for added flavoring and aesthetics.

398. Chicken salad

NUTRITIONAL VALUE PER SERVING— (per half cup serving): Calories: 169kal; protein 19.88g; Carbohydrate: 11.39g; Fat 4.39g. — Preparation time: 15 minutes

Ingredients:
- 6 ounces of boiled and crumbled chicken
- Half an onion (preferably diced)
- 1 package mixed salad greens
- 3 large hardboiled eggs
- ½ cap full of vinegar
- Light mayonnaise
- Salt and pepper
- One half head of lettuce

Directions
- Chop the lettuce
- Place the chicken in a bowl, then the eggs, salad greens, diced onions, vinegar and lettuce.
- Add mayonnaise to your taste
- Stir together
- Season with salt and pepper to taste

399.Asparagus Soup

Preparation Time: 5 minutes— Cook Time: 25 minutes— Serving: 2

Ingredients
- Leek: 1 medium
- Asparagus: 500 gm
- Onion: 1 chopped
- Lemon juice: 1 tbsp
- Garlic: 4 cloves (crushed) + 1 clove
- Vegetable stock: 1 liter
- Soya cream
- Olive oil
- Bread: for making croutons
- Salt & pepper: as per your taste

Directions
- Take a large saucepan and add olive oil to it
- Fry onion and garlic till it turns golden brown
- Chop asparagus and leek and reserve asparagus tips separately
- Add asparagus, leek, and vegetable stock in the pan having onion
- Let it boil and then cook on low heat for 20 minutes
- When ready, add lemon juice and salt and pepper as per your taste
- In the meantime, boil water with the salt and add asparagus tips for two minutes
- Drain the asparagus and set aside
- Turn the oven grill on and cut bread into pieces and roast with olive oil till croutons are done
- Scrub the remaining garlic clove all over the croutons to give flavor
- Serve the hot soup with a bit of cream, croutons, and asparagus tip present on top

400.Red Lentils Tomato Soup

Preparation Time: 5 minutes— Cook Time: 25 minutes— Servings: 6

Ingredients

- Red lentils: 1 cup
- Tomato paste: 1 tbsp
- Onion: 1
- Garlic: 2 cloves
- Ground cumin: 1 tsp
- Vegetable oil: 2 tbsp
- Sumac: 1 tbsp
- Vegetable stock: 1 liter
- Chickpeas: 400 gm can
- Chopped tomatoes: 400 gm can
- Water: 2 cup
- Lemon juice: as per your taste
- Red chili: 1 sliced
- Parsley leaves: for garnishing

Directions

- In a large saucepan, heat some oil and add chopped garlic and onion
- Fry till it becomes soft and add tomato paste, ground cumin, and sumac
- In this pan, add lentils, vegetable stock, and chopped tomatoes
- Bring the mixture to boil and cover for 20 minutes and cook till lentils are done
- Now add half chickpeas and start adding water till your desired consistency is achieved
- Season with salt, pepper and lemon juice
- Pour the soup in the bowl and top with the remaining chickpeas, parsley leaves, and red chilies
- Serve hot

401.Cashew Carrot Soup

Preparation Time: 10 minutes— Cook Time: 35 minutes— Servings: 6 people

Ingredients

- Apple: 1 medium
- Carrots: 800 gm
- Onion: 1 medium
- Cashew nuts: ¾ cup or 75 gm
- Freshly grated ginger: 2 tbsp
- Curry powder: 1 tbsp mild
- Vegetable stock: 1 liter
- Olive oil: 2 tbsp
- Lemon juice: as per your taste
- Garlic: 3 cloves
- Water: 500 ml
- Fresh coriander: 30 gm

Directions

- In a large pan, heat the olive oil
- Add onion and chopped garlic and fry for a minute
- Then add curry powder and ginger
- Continue frying for 5 minutes or till onion turns soft
- Cut carrots and apple in the meanwhile and make medium pieces
- Add them into the pan with onions along with the vegetable stock, cashews, and water
- Bring to boil on high heat
- Lower the flame and then cook on low heat till carrots become soft for 30 minutes
- Whizz them till smooth
- Serve with lemon juice and fresh coriander on top

402.Spring Onion Potato Soup

Preparation Time: 10 minutes— Cook Time: 25 minutes— Servings: 6 people

Ingredients

- Spring onion: 400 gm
- Potatoes: 500 gm
- Watercress: 80 gm
- Vegetable oil 2 tbsp
- Vegetable stock: 1 liter
- Onion: 1 medium
- Garlic: 2 cloves
- Almond milk: 125 ml
- Salt & pepper: as per your taste

Directions

- In a large pan, heat the oil and fry the chopped onion till it becomes soft
- Chop potatoes, spring onion, and garlic, and add to the oil
- Cook for a few minutes
- Pour vegetable stock now and watercress and bring to boil
- Now lower the heat and cook for 20 minutes
- Blend the soup to give it a smooth texture
- Top with almond milk and sprinkle salt and pepper at the end

403.Roasted Cauliflower and Brussels Sprouts Soup

Preparation Time: 5 minutes— Cook Time: 50 minutes— Servings: 6 people

Ingredients

- Cauliflower: 800 gm
- Fresh rosemary: 2 branches
- Brussels sprouts: 500 gm
- Olive oil: 3 tbsp
- Onion: 1 small
- Garlic: 5 cloves
- Vegetable stock: 1 liter
- Lemon juice: As per your taste
- Water: 250 ml or 1 cup

Directions

- Preheat the oven to 200 C
- Cut Brussels sprout in half and separate cauliflower florets
- Spread them both on an oven tray along with garlic cloves and brush with oil
- Roast for 30 minutes till they cook
- When vegetables are ready, take a large pan and 2 tbsp oil to it
- Add chopped onion to the oil and cook on low heat till they become soft
- Now add roasted vegetables, vegetable stock, rosemary, and water and bring to boil
- Let them cook for 20 minutes in medium flame
- Whiz the soup when done
- Season with salt and pepper and add lemon juice

404.Creamy Tomato Soup

Preparation Time: 10 minutes— Cook Time: 20 minutes— Servings: 4 person

Ingredients

- Tomatoes: 400g can chop
- Tomatoes: 500 gm chunks
- Tomato paste: 2 tbsp
- Fresh basil: 1 small bunch
- Oregano: 2 tbsp dried
- Onion: 1 (finely chopped)
- Garlic: 3 cloves (crushed)
- Cannellini beans: 400 g can
- Sugar: 2 tbsp (optional)
- Vegetable stock: 1 liter
- Olive oil
- Salt & pepper: as per your taste

Directions

- In a large saucepan, heat olive oil
- Fry onion and garlic in it
- Add tomato chunks, chopped tomatoes, and tomato paste and mix them all together
- Now add oregano, vegetable stock, and fresh basil
- Bring them to boil and then cook on medium flame for 15 minutes
- Rinse the cannellini beans and dry them and roast in a pan
- Blend the soup together and sprinkle salt, pepper, and sugar
- Add the beans on top and serve hot

405.Spinach, Watercress and Leek Soup

Preparation Time: 10 minutes— Cook Time: 25 minutes— Servings: 4

Ingredients

- Watercress: 100 gm
- Spinach: 65 gm
- Leek: 200 gm
- Potatoes: 450 gm
- Garlic: 2 cloves (crushed)
- Vegetable stock: 1 liter
- Olive oil: 2 tbsp
- Nutmeg: a dash
- Cream: Optional

Directions

- Take a large saucepan and heat olive oil
- Add crushed garlic and chopped leek and cook for 3 minutes
- Now add diced potatoes, spinach, and watercress and add vegetable stock
- Bring the mixture to boil and then heat on a medium flame for 20 minutes
- Blend the soup and serve with nutmeg and dollop of cream on top

406.Curried Root Vegetable Soup

Preparation Time: 20 minutes— Cook Time: 25 minutes— Servings: 4 person

Ingredients

- Carrots: 300 gm
- Potatoes: 300 gm
- Parsnips 300 gm
- Onion: 1 large
- Grated ginger: 2 tbsp
- Curry powder: 1 tbsp mild
- Tomato paste: 1 tbsp
- Garlic: 3 cloves (crushed)
- Turmeric: 1 tsp
- Vegetable stock 1.5 liter
- Ground coriander: 1 tsp
- Ground cumin: 1 tsp
- Lemon juice: of one lemon
- Cannellini Beans: 400 gm can
- Coconut milk: 400 ml can
- Fresh coriander: 50 gm
- Olive oil
- Salt & pepper: as per your taste

Directions

- Take a large saucepan and add olive oil to it
- Add the chopped onion, curry powder, garlic, ground cumin, ground coriander, turmeric, grated ginger, and tomato paste
- Fry till they all become soft
- Peel all the vegetables and make them into chunks
- Add the vegetables and the stock to the pan
- Bring the mixture to boil and cover and heat for 20 minutes
- Blend the soup
- Rinse and drain the cannellini beans and serve with the soup on top
- Add fresh coriander, coconut milk, and lemon juice and serve hot

407.Kale Miso Mushroom Soup

Preparation Time: 3 minutes— Cook Time: 17 minutes— Servings: 4 person

Ingredients

- Dried shiitake mushrooms: 40 gm
- Mixed mushrooms: 150 gm
- Spring onions: 5
- Miso paste: 2 tbsp
- Garlic: 2 cloves crushed
- Sesame oil: 1 tbsp
- Ginger root: 2 tbsp crushed
- Sheet nori: 1
- Tamari sauce: 1 tsp
- Kale leaves: 1 handful
- Water: 1 liter

Directions

- Chop spring onion and reserve its green part
- Cut shiitake mushrooms in half
- Chop fresh mushrooms
- Take a large saucepan and add sesame oil and fry white part of the spring onion
- Fry for a minute and add ginger and garlic and fry again for a minute
- Add water, dry shiitake, miso paste, and fresh mushrooms
- Cook for 10 minutes on medium flame
- Add kale, torn nori, and tamari sauce and boil for two minutes
- Serve hot with spring onion's green part on top

408.Green Spinach Broccoli Soup

Preparation Time: 15 minutes— Cook Time: 30 minutes— Servings:6 person

Ingredients
- Broccoli: 300 gm
- Potato: 500 gm f
- Spinach: 200 gm
- Garlic: 4 cloves
- Mustard seeds: 1 tsp
- Spring onion: 1 bunch
- Ground coriander: 1 tsp
- Ground cumin: 1 tsp
- Turmeric: 1 tsp
- Vegetable stock: 1.5 liters
- Ginger root: 1 tbsp grated
- Chickpeas: 400 gm can
- Lemon juice: of two lemons
- Coriander: 1 large bunch
- Salt & pepper: as per your taste
- Extra virgin olive oil: 2 tbsp

Directions
- Take a large saucepan and heat olive oil
- Crush garlic and chop spring onion white part and add to the pan and fry
- Add mustard seeds, coriander, cumin, ginger and turmeric to the pan and fry
- Wash spinach, peel and dice potatoes, and separate broccoli florets and fry and stir for 5 minutes with other ingredients in the pan
- Add vegetable stock, boil, and heat on low flame for 20 minutes
- Blend the soup and serve with lemon juice, chickpeas, and chopped coriander leaves on top

409.Tomato Courgettes Soup

Preparation Time: 15 minutes— Cook Time: 25 minutes— Servings: 4

Ingredients
- Tomatoes: 400 gm
- Courgettes: 500 gm
- Potato: 250 gm
- Coconut oil: 1 tbsp
- Onion: 1 medium
- Ground cumin: 1 tsp
- Red chili: ½
- Grated ginger root: 1 tbsp
- Garlic: 3 cloves
- Chickpeas: 400 g can
- Ground coriander: 1 tsp
- Lemongrass stalks: 2
- Light coconut milk: 400 g can
- Vegetable stock: 1 liter
- Coriander leaves: a small bunch
- Lime juice: of 1 lime
- Salt & pepper: As per your taste

Directions
- Take a large saucepan and heat coconut oil in it
- Fry onion for a minute and add garlic, cumin, ground coriander, finely chopped lemongrass, ginger, and chopped chili until they turn golden brown
- Peel and cut potatoes in medium-size and make medium slices of tomatoes and courgettes
- Add the vegetables into the pan and stir well
- Pour the vegetable stock in the pan and allow to boil
- Lower the heat and let it cook for 20 minutes
- Add coconut milk
- Blend the soup and add rinsed and drained chickpeas to it
- Serve with lime juice, salt, and pepper
- Place coriander leaves on top

410.Easy Detox Soup

Preparation Time: 15 minutes— Cook Time: 25 minutes— Servings: 4

Ingredients
- Asparagus: 350 gm
- Broccoli: 350 gm
- Watercress: 100 gm
- Onion: 1 medium (finely chopped)
- Extra virgin olive oil: 1 tbsp
- Fresh rosemary leaves: 1 tbsp (chopped)
- Garlic: 3 cloves (crushed)
- Fresh lemon thyme leaves: 2 tbsp (chopped)
- Vegetable stock: 1 liter
- Lemon: 1
- Salt & pepper: as per your taste
- Nutmeg: 1 tbsp grated

Directions
- Heat a large saucepan and add olive oil
- Add chopped onion to it along with garlic for a minute
- Add rosemary and lemon thyme and stir fry till they become golden brown
- Make small chunks of asparagus and cut broccoli with its stems
- Add them to the saucepan along with the vegetable stock and watercress
- Bring the mixture to boil
- Lower the heat and cover and cook for 20 minutes
- Blend the soup and sprinkle grate nutmeg, salt, pepper, and lemon juice on top

411.Cauliflower and Butternut Spicy Soup

Preparation Time: 20 minutes— Cook Time: 30 minutes— Servings: 4

Ingredients
- Cauliflower: 300 gm
- Butternut squash: 900 gm
- Onion: 1 (chopped)
- Potatoes: 2 medium
- Ground cumin: 1 tsp
- Garlic: 3 cloves (crushed)
- Ground ginger
- Chipotle: 1
- Vegetable stock: 1.5 liter
- Cinnamon: 1 tsp
- Soya cream
- Fresh coriander: a small bunch
- Lemon juice: 2 tbsp
- Olive oil
- Salt & pepper: as per your taste

Directions
- Take a large saucepan and heat olive oil
- Add onion and garlic and fry for a minute
- Sprinkle ginger, cumin, and cinnamon on top
- Peel potatoes and butternut and make their small chunks
- Divide cauliflower into small florets
- Add all the vegetable to the saucepan and add vegetable stock and chipotle
- Cover and cook for 20 minutes
- Blend the soup and season as per your taste
- Serve with lemon juice, and top with cream and chopped coriander leaves

412.Corn salad

NUTRITIONAL VALUE PER SERVING Calories: 47kal; protein 1.80g; Carbohydrate: 10.6g; Fat 3g. — Preparation time: 20 minutes

Ingredients:
- 5 ears of fresh corn
- Extra virgin olive oil
- 1 teaspoon Jalapeño pepper
- ½ cup of chopped Jicama
- ¼ teaspoon of salt
- 1 teaspoon Stevia
- ½ teaspoon ground cumin
- ½ cup of red bell pepper (chopped)
- ½ finely chopped red onion
- 8 thinly sliced green onions

Directions
- Place a non- stick skillet over medium heat
- Place chopped jicama and jalapeño in the pan with olive oil
- Stir frequently as it sauté's for 2 minutes
- Add onions into the mix and stir until they mix and the onions lose their redness and become clear in color
- Toss in the red bell pepper and cook till tender
- Finally, add corn, ground cumin and green onions. Sauté for an additional 2 minutes and add Stevia if it is not as sweet as you would like.

413.Mussels and coconut milk

NUTRITIONAL VALUE PER SERVING Calories: 49kal; protein 60g; Carbohydrate: 27g; Fat 15g; sat fat: 5g; sugar 1g— Preparation time: 20 minutes

Ingredients:
- 500g mussels of mussels be sure to have your fishmonger de-bearded it
- 250ml coconut milk
- 1 small red chili pepper
- Handful coriander
- 2 limes, juiced

Directions
- Chop the coriander and chili separately
- Place sauce pan and heat at medium heat

- Put in mussels and coconut milk simultaneously
- Cook for 2 minutes
- The mussels should have opened and if they haven't, leave for a minute more
- Put in lime juice and coriander
- Leave to boil for 1 minute
- Serve warm

414.Salmon and canola noodles

NUTRITIONAL VALUE PER SERVING Calories: 344 kal; protein 32g; Carbohydrate: 27g; Fat 10g; sat fat: 2g; sugar 4g— Preparation time: 20 minutes

Ingredients:
- 1 salmon fillet
- 1 tablespoon canola oil
- 1 tablespoon of soy sauce
- 1 garlic clove crushed
- 70g of buckwheat soba noodles
- 1 small red chili
- 2 spring onions

Directions:
- Soak noodles in hot water
- Slice onions
- Slice chili

- Preheat the oven to 200C
- Line a baking tray and spray with low fat baking spray
- Place in the fillets and rub with oil and garlic
- Bake for 8 minutes
- Cook noodles with red chili and spring onions
- Let noodles be soft and transparent
- Serve fish with noodles

415.Green salad

NUTRITIONAL VALUE Calories: 301 kal; protein 22 g; Carbohydrate: 48 g; Fat 5 g; sat fat:3 g; sugar 6g— Preparation time: 10 minutes

Ingredients:
- 250 grams of puy lentils
- 2 carrots
- 1 tablespoon vinegar
- 1 shallot
- 1 bag kale
- 1 tablespoon of canola coconut oil
- 1 handful parsley
- 3 tablespoons of chopped spring onions
- 1 tablespoon mustard
- 1 small bunch dill
- 2 firm tomatoes

Directions:
- Cook the puy lentils
- Chop the shallot, carrot, kale, parsley, dill, and tomatoes separately
- In a salad bowl, put in a teaspoon of oil and rub the bowl
- Put in the lentils followed by the shallot, carrot, kale, parsley, dill, and tomatoes
- Toss the salad
- Pour in the remaining oil

416.Lentil curry soup

NUTRITIONAL VALUE PER SERVING Calories: 199 kal; protein 9 g; Carbohydrate: 25g; Fat 7g; sat fat: 5 g; sugar 6g— Preparation time: 20 minutes

Ingredients
- 500 grams of red lentils
- 400ml low fat coconut milk
- 400g of firm tomatoes
- 150 grams of spinach
- 1 tbsp olive oil
- 1 medium sized onion
- 1 ½ tablespoons of grated ginger
- 1 tablespoon curry powder
- 1 tablespoon of red pepper
- Salt and pepper to taste

Directions
- Chop the onions
- Grate ginger
- Dice tomatoes
- Heat saucepan at medium heat level

- Put in olive oil and onions
- Put in ginger, salt, curry, and pepper to taste
- Stir fry till onions are almost transparent
- Coconut milk
- Close for a minute on low heat and then pour in tomatoes
- Close and let almost boil then put in a cup of water
- Put in lentils and allow to simmer for 35 minutes
- Put in spinach and leave to boil for 2-4 minutes

417.Chicken and salmon casserole

NUTRITIONAL VALUE PER SERVING Calories: 515 kal; protein 54g; Carbohydrate: 22 g; Fat 10g; sat fat: 18 g; sugar 12g—
Preparation time: 20 minutes

Ingredients:
- 1 tablespoon of canola oil
- 2 chicken breasts
- 50g smoked salmon
- 1 medium onion
- 1 green peppers
- 1 cloves ginger, crushed
- ½ teaspoon of curry
- 1 basil leaf
- 150ml passata

Directions:
- Remove skin on chicken and chop into pieces
- Chop salmon into pieces
- Chop onions and peppers
- Preheat the oven to 160C

- Pour canola oil in pan and heat on medium heat
- Put in onions, peppers, ginger, and chopped salmon
- Stir fry for 8-10 minutes
- Pour in passata
- After 10 seconds put in chicken breasts
- Stir the fish and chicken in the sauce
- Take off heat, put basil leaf in and cover pot
- Place in oven to bake for 1 hour
- Open and stir to the other side and let bake for another hour

418.Mexican baked turkey

NUTRITIONAL VALUE PER SERVING Calories: 600 kal; protein 43 g; Carbohydrate: 32 g; Fat 37 g; sat fat: 9 g; sugar 5g—
Preparation time: 20 minutes

Ingredients
- 200g chopped turkey
- 1 serving cooked brown rice
- 2 tablespoons of chopped cauliflower
- 5 firm tomatoes
- 1 jar chipotle paste
- 60ml red wine vinegar
- 3 garlic cloves, peeled
- 1 tablespoon of minced ginger
- Salt
- 1 stock cube

Directions
- Preheat the oven to 180C
- In a saucepan that can survive oven heat pour in the paste and vinegar
- Put on high heat and when it begins to boil, put in turkey
- Then put in garlic and tomatoes
- Put in garlic, ginger and stir
- Put in salt and stock cube
- Stir again
- Cover pan and place in oven for 2 hours
- When ready, serve with rice

419.Cream soup

NUTRITIONAL VALUE PER SERVING Calories: 225.7 kal; protein 4.6 g; Carbohydrate: 39 g; Fat 5.7 g; sat fat: 3 g; sugar
4.4g— Preparation time: 25 minutes

Ingredients
- 1 cup strained cream soup
- 1 cup smooth mashed potatoes
- A pinch of salt
- ¼ teaspoon of canola oil

Directions
- In a skillet, pour in cream soup
- Pour in mashed potatoes
- Heat on low heat till it simmers
- Serve warm

420.Cauliflower soup

NUTRITIONAL VALUE PER SERVING Calories: 214 kal; protein 32g; Carbohydrate: 19g; Fat 12.5g; sat fat: 2g; sugar 3g—
Preparation time: 45 minutes

Ingredients
- 1 small cooked cauliflower
- 1 medium sized onion
- 3 teaspoons canola oil
- 4 teaspoons of protein powder
- 2 cups skimmed milk
- 1 teaspoon salt
- 1 egg yolk
- 2 tablespoons of grated low fat mozzarella cheese
- ½ cup of spicy sausage, cooked

Directions
- Shred cauliflower
- Mix cauliflower in milk and set aside
- Heat oil in large skillet
- Pour in onions and stir fry
- Put in protein powder and stir
- Pour in milk and cauliflower
- Allow to simmer
- Take off fire and blend well

421.Borscht yogurt

NUTRITIONAL VALUE PER SERVING 261 calories, 5g total fat, 1g saturated fat, 1mg cholesterol, 581mg sodium, 48g
carbohydrate, 10g fiber, 17g sugar, 8g protein, — Preparation time: 20 minutes

Ingredients:
- 2 ½ cups plain low-fat yogurt
- ¾ cups sour cream
- 1/4 tablespoons of salt
- 1/4 tablespoons of celery salt
- 1/4 tablespoons of onion salt
- 1 cup of beetroots

Directions
- Dice and cook the beetroots
- Pour the sour cream, yoghurt, celery salt, onion salt, beets and salt in blender.
- Switch on the blender and blend till mixture is smooth
- Add ice cubes or chill to enjoy.

422.Cheesy Tuna Casserole

Yields: 6 servings — Prep time: 10 minutes — Cook time: 20 minutes.
Nutrition value per serving Calories: 344 net— Fats: 22 g net— Proteins: 31 g net — Carbs: 3 g net

Ingredients

- 1 tablespoon ghee or unsalted butter (or coconut oil or lard if dairy-free), plus extra for greasing the dish
- 1 tablespoon diced celery
- 1 tablespoon diced onions
- 1 clove garlic, smashed to a paste
- 3 (6-ounce) cans tuna, drained
- 2 cups cauliflower florets, cut into ½-inch pieces
- 1 cup chopped dill pickles
- ⅓ cup softened cream cheese
- 2 tablespoons mayonnaise
- ½ teaspoon fine sea salt
- ¼ teaspoon ground black pepper
- 1 cup shredded sharp cheddar cheese (omit for dairy-free)
- Sliced green onions, for garnish
- Chopped fresh parsley, for garnish
- Cherry tomatoes, cut in halved or quartered, for garnish.

Directions

- Preheat the oven to 375 degrees °F, and grease a baking dish with non-stick cooking spray.
- Heat oil in a skillet, then add onions and celery and sauté for 2 to 3 minute, or until the onions turn soft. Then, add in the garlic and continue to sauté for another 1 minute.
- In a large mixing bowl, mix the tuna, cauliflower, pickles, cream cheese, mayonnaise, salt, and pepper. Then, add in the sautéed veggies. Mix well to combine.
- Place the mixture in the greased dish, then top it with cheddar cheese evenly.
- Then, put it in the oven and bake for 20 to 25 minutes. Take out from the oven and let it rest for 4 to 5 minutes.
- Place the fish on a serving plate. Then, garnish it with green onions, cherry tomatoes and parsley. Serve hot!

423.Charleston Shrimp 'n' Gravy Over Grits

Yields: 4 servings — Prep time: 5 minutes (not including time to make grits) — Cook time: 15 minutes.
Nutrition value per serving Calories: 500 net— Fats: 34 g net— Proteins: 41 g net— Carbs: 5 g net

Ingredients

- 3 strips bacon
- 2 tablespoons ghee or unsalted butter
- 1 green bell pepper, chopped
- ½ cup diced onions
- 1 clove garlic, minced
- 1-pound jumbo shrimp (about 30), peeled and deveined
- 2 teaspoons fine sea salt
- ½ teaspoon ground black pepper
- ½ cup of chicken bone broth
- Double batch Keto Grits for serving.

Directions

- Fry the bacon in a skillet for 4 minutes, or until it turns golden brown. Then, set the bacon aside, leaving the drippings in the skillet.
- Add ghee to the drippings in the skillet. Add in the bell peppers and onions and

sauté for 4 to 5 minutes. Then, add in the garlic and continue to sauté for one more minute.

- Season the shrimps with salt and pepper thoroughly. Add the seasoned jumbo shrimps into the skillet and continue to cook for 4 to 5 minutes, or until the shrimps are no longer translucent.
- Remove the shrimp from the skillet. Add in the broth in the same skillet with veggies, and let it simmer until reduced to the desired thickness. Remove from the heat.
- Once thickened, add the shrimps back into the skillet, and combine the shrimps well in the sauce.
- Place the shrimps on Keto grit, and top it with crushed bacon. Serve hot.

424.Crawfish Étouffée

Yields: 4 servings — Prep time: 10 minutes (not including time to make cauliflower rice) — Cook time: 25 minutes
Nutrition value per serving Calories: 327 net— Fats: 21 g net— Proteins: 36 g net— Carbs: 7 g net

Ingredients

- 3 tablespoons ghee or unsalted butter (or coconut oil if dairy-free)
- 3 strips bacon, chopped
- ½ cup chopped onions
- ½ green or red bell pepper, chopped
- 3 cloves garlic, smashed to a paste or minced
- ¼ cup diced tomatoes
- 2 bay leaves
- 1 teaspoon chopped fresh thyme leaves
- 1 teaspoon paprika
- ¼ teaspoon cayenne pepper
- ¼ teaspoon fine sea salt
- ¼ teaspoon ground black pepper
- 1 cup of chicken bone broth
- 1½ pounds peeled frozen crawfish tails, defrosted
- 1 to 2 tablespoons sour cream (or Kite Hill brand cream cheese style spread if dairy-free), it helps thicken the sauce
- 2 teaspoons hot sauce, or more to taste
- Chopped fresh parsley leaves, for garnish

- Sliced green onions, for garnish
- ½ batch Cauliflower Rice, for serving
- Lemon wedges, for serving (optional)

Directions

- Heat ghee in a skillet, and fry the bacon until crisp. Then, add in the onions and bell pepper and sauté for 4 to 5 minutes. Then, add in the garlic and sauté for another 1 minute.
- Mix in the tomatoes, thyme, bay leaves, paprika, cayenne pepper, salt, and black pepper; and cook for 2 to 3 minutes.
- Then, add in the broth, and let it simmer for 10 minutes, or until it starts to thicken.
- Then, combine the crawfish into the broth. Stir and let it cook for 10 to 12 minutes, or until the fish is thoroughly cooked. Then, mix in the hot sauce and sour cream while stirring continuously.
- Transfer the Étouffée to a serving dish or plate. Garnish it with green onions and parsley along with lemon wedges. Serve hot with cauliflower rice.

106

425.Halibut with Creamy Sauce

Yields: 4 servings — Prep time: 5 minutes — Cook time: 15 minutes.
Nutrition value per serving Calories: 270 net— Fats: 17 g net— Proteins: 24 g net— Carbs: 4 g net

Ingredients

- 4 (4-ounce) halibut fillets
- 1 teaspoon fine sea salt
- ¼ teaspoon ground black pepper
- 2 tablespoons ghee or unsalted butter (or coconut oil if dairy-free), divided
- ½ cup finely diced red onions
- 1 clove garlic, smashed to a paste
- 2 to 3 sprigs fresh dill, plus extra for garnish
- ¼ cup fish or chicken bone broth
- ¼ cup heavy cream (or full-fat coconut milk if dairy-free)
- 2 outer leaves of red cabbage, for colour (optional)
- ½ teaspoon lemon juice
- Lemon wedges, for garnish
- Purple salt, for garnish (optional)

Directions

- Heat ghee in a pan over normal heat, and add in the onions and garlic. Sauté for 2 to 3 minutes, until onions become soft.
- Season the fish with salt and pepper thoroughly, and add to the pan along with red cabbage, broth and heavy cream. Cook the fish until it is no more translucent, and mix in the lemon juice.
- Take out the fish from the pan and discard the cabbage.
- Cook the sauce in the skillet until it reduces to the desired thickness.
- Gently put the cooked fish on a serving plate and top it with the sauce. Garnish with lemon wedges, fresh dill, and purple salt. Serve hot.

426.Sole Meunière

Yields: 4 servings — Prep time: 5 minutes — Cook time: 6 minutes.
Nutrition value per serving Calories: 383 net— Fats: 31 g net— Proteins: 28 g net — Carbs: 1 g net

Ingredients

- 4 (4-ounce) sole fillets
- Ground black pepper
- ½ cup powdered Parmesan cheese
- 2 tablespoons ghee or avocado oil
- ¼ cup plus 2 tablespoons unsalted butter, divided
- 1 tablespoon lemon juice
- 2 tablespoons chopped fresh parsley leaves
- Lemon wedges or slices, for serving

Directions

- Gently rinse the fish and pat it dry before seasoning.
- Season the fish with ground black pepper thoroughly from all sides. Then, coat the fish well into the parmesan cheese. Set aside.
- Add ghee in a skillet or pan and heat it over medium flame, then add 2 tablespoons of butter in it.
- Once heated, add the coated fish in the skillet, and fry each side for 2 minutes or until it turns golden brown.
- Take out the fish and pour some of the skillet's drippings on the fish.
- Add the remaining butter to the skillet, and heat it until it turns brown. Then, add in the lemon juice and parsley. Stir and pour this mixture on the fish.
- Garnish the fish plater as you desire or with some lemon wedges or slices and serve hot.

427.Baked Mackerel Fillets

Yields: 3 servings — Prep time: 5 minutes — Cook time: 10 minutes.
Nutrition value per serving Calories: 275 net— Fats: 68 g net— Proteins: 38 g net— Carbs: 1 g net

Ingredients

- 2 to 3 tablespoons melted butter + extra to grease
- 1-pound mackerel fillets
- Salt and Pepper to taste
- ½ teaspoon salt

Directions

- Preheat the baking oven at 350 degrees ° F. Lightly grease a baking dish with non-stick cooking oil or butter.
- Season the mackerel fillets with salt and pepper thoroughly.
- Place the fillets in the baking dish and trickle 2 to 3 tablespoons of melted butter over the fillets evenly.
- Put the baking dish in the oven and bake for about 20 to 25 minutes, or until the fish shred with ease with the help of a fork.
- Take out the fish on serving dish and serve hot.

428.Lobster bisque

NUTRITIONAL VALUE PER SERVING— Calories 310, calories from fat 210, total fat 24g, saturated fat 15g, trans fat 1g, cholesterol 115mg, total carbohydrate 13g, sugars 1g, protein 12g, calcium 10%, iron 4%. — Preparation time: 20 minutes

Ingredients

- 2 ½ cups of skimmed milk
- 1 tablespoon of protein powder
- 1 tablespoon of canola oil
- 2/3 cup of cooked lobster meat
- 1 tablespoon of salt
- 1/4 tablespoon of paprika
- Dash pepper

Directions

- Blend the protein powder, skimmed milk, pepper, salts, oil, paprika and lobster meat together.
- Over low heat, bring to a boil while stirring.
- Strain of excess moisture.

429.Curried fish bisque

NUTRITIONAL VALUE PER SERVING— Calories: 459 kal; protein 32g; Carbohydrate: 24g; Fat 25; — Preparation time: 25 minutes

Ingredients

- 1 tablespoon of salt
- Dash of paprika
- Dash of pepper
- 1 tablespoon of protein powder
- 2 ½ cups of skimmed milk
- 1 tablespoon of olive oil
- ¼ tablespoon of curry

- 1 cup of cooked lean white meat fish (NO BONES)

Directions

- Blend protein powder, oil, milk and spices together.
- Put in fish and blend
- Pour the mixture in saucepan
- Heat on low heat for 15-20 minutes

107

430.Poached eggs salad

NUTRITIONAL VALUE PER SERVING— 72 calories; 4.7 g total fat; 1.6 g saturated fat; 185 mg cholesterol; 149 mg sodium. 69 mg potassium; 0.3 g carbohydrates; 6.3 g protein; 28 mg calcium; 1 mg iron; 6 mg magnesium— Preparation time: 15 minutes

Ingredients:
- 1 egg
- 1 ½ teaspoons of vinegar

Directions
- Crack eggs without piercing yolk
- Boil a little water to about 1.5 to 2 inches height of the pot
- Put in vinegar
- Gently pour the eggs into the boiling water from the bowl
- Cook for 5 minutes
- Serve warm

431.Egg salad

NUTRITIONAL VALUE PER SERVING— Per Serving: 100 calories; 5.8 g fat; 3.1 g carbohydrates; 8.1 g protein; 212 mg cholesterol; 388 mg sodium — Preparation time: 25 minutes

Ingredients:
- 6 hard boiled eggs
- 1/3 cup low-fat mayonnaise
- 1/3 cup chopped fresh chives
- ½ teaspoon paprika
- ½ teaspoon pepper
- ½ teaspoon Dijon mustard
- ¼ teaspoon pink salt

Directions:
- Cut up 4 or the eggs into chunks
- Take out the eggs of the remaining 2 eggs and cut up only the whites
- Mix all ingredients together
- Serve

432.Turkey salad

NUTRITIONAL VALUE PER SERVING— 417 calories; 19.8 g total fat; 3.2 g saturated fat; 70 mg cholesterol; 467 mg sodium. 892 mg potassium; 29.7 g carbohydrates; 2.6 g fiber; 13 g sugar; 31.5 g protein; 34 mg vitamin c; 168 mcg folate; 124 mg calcium; 3 mg iron; 91 mg magnesium; 7 g added sugar; — Preparation time: 25 minutes

Ingredients
- 6 cups mixed salad greens
- 3 tablespoons dried cranberries
- 3 cups chopped cooked turkey
- 3 tablespoons olive oil
- ½ cup leftover wheat bread stuffing
- ⅓ cup of protein powder
- ¼ cup cranberry sauce
- 1 tablespoon cider vinegar
- 1 teaspoon grated orange zest
- 1 cup roasted Brussels sprouts
- ¼ teaspoon salt
- ¼ teaspoon black pepper

Directions
- Place skillet with olive oil on medium heat
- Pour in wheat bread stuffing and stir
- Pour in protein powder
- Stir for 3-5 minutes
- Pour in cranberry sauce
- Our in orange zest and stir for a minute
- Put in vinegar and stir
- Put in salt and pepper to taste
- Put in turkey, vegetables and cranberries
- Stir and serve warm

433.Tuna salad

NUTRITIONAL VALUE PER SERVING— Calories: 404 kal; protein 49g; Carbohydrate: 12.5g; Fat 17.5; — Preparation time: 25 minutes

Ingredients:
- 2 cans of tuna
- 1/8 teaspoon mustard
- 1 tablespoon parsley
- Salt and pepper to taste
- 1 minced garlic clove
- 1 small onion
- ½ celery stick
- 1 tablespoon lemon juice

Directions:
- Pour tuna in sieve and drain
- Use a spoon to mash it
- Pour in bowl and put all ingredients except mayonnaise and Dijon
- Mix very well
- Mayonnaise and Dijon mix again and serve

434.Beef stew

NUTRITIONAL VALUE — 317 calories; 9 g total fat; 3.2 g saturated fat; 92 mg cholesterol; 396 mg sodium. 1205 mg potassium; 22.4 g carbohydrates; 4.2 g fiber; 5 g sugar; 35.3 g protein; 7046 IU vitamin a iu; 20 mg vitamin c; 38 mcg folate; 92 mg calcium; 5 mg iron; 65 mg magnesium; — Preparation time:8 hours minutes

Ingredients:
- 3 ounces of red potatoes
- 1 carrot
- 1 small red onion, cut into wedges
- ¼ pound of beef
- 3 ounces of condensed cream of mushroom soup
- 1 cup beef broth
- 1/3 teaspoon of thyme
- 1/3 teaspoon of curry
- 2 ounces of package frozen cut green beans
- 1 stock cube
- ¼ teaspoon salt

Directions
- Quarter the potatoes
- Cut onion into cubes
- Dice carrots
- In a soup pot, pour in potatoes, carrots, onion, beef, mushroom soup, broth, thyme, and curry
- Stir and add stock cube and salt
- Cook on medium heat for 7 hours
- Add green beans
- Cook for 15 minutes
- Serve hot

435.Meatloaf

NUTRITIONAL VALUE Per Serving.Calories: 69 calories; 2.3 g total fat; 0.4 g saturated fat; 19 mg cholesterol; 283 mg sodium. 157 mg potassium; 10.3 g carbohydrates; 1.6 g fiber; 4 g sugar; 2.1 g protein; 420 IU vitamin a iu; 15 mg vitamin c; 13 mcg folate; 20 mg calcium; 1 mg iron; 8 mg magnesium; 1 g added sugar — Preparation time: 1 ½ hours

Ingredients
- 2 pounds lean ground beef
- ¾ cup dry whole-wheat breadcrumbs
- 2 stalks celery
- 1 onion
- 1 green bell pepper
- 1 tablespoon canola oil
- 4 tablespoons ketchup
- 3 tablespoons Worcestershire sauce
- 1 tablespoon whole-grain mustard
- 1 tablespoon paprika
- 1 teaspoon crushed garlic
- Salt to taste
- Pepper to taste
- 1 egg

Directions
- Chop onions
- Chop celery
- Chop pepper
- Beat egg lightly
- Preheat oven to 375 degrees F
- Spray baking tray with low fat baking spray
- Put oil in skillet on medium heat
- Take out and let cool
- Add Worcestershire, mustard, garlic, paprika, salt, pepper and half of the ketchup.
- Mix bread an egg crumbs
- Pour in mix
- Put in ground beef
- With your hands mix the mixture
- Spread out the mixture on baking pan
- Pour left over ketchup
- Bake for 45 minutes at 165 degrees F
- Take out and let cool for 15 minutes divide into six servings

436.Tuna burger

NUTRITIONAL VALUE — 307 calories; 11.8 g total fat; 1.8 g saturated fat; 22 mg cholesterol; 669 mg sodium. 334 mg potassium; 39.1 g carbohydrates; 5.3 g fiber; 7 g sugar; 14.1 g protein; 1315 IU vitamin a iu; 19 mg vitamin c; 34 mcg folate; 67 mg calcium; 2 mg iron; 53 mg magnesium; 5 g added sugar; — Preparation time: 30 minutes

Ingredients:
- 6 ounces light tuna
- 2 slices tomato
- ¼ of cup whole wheat breadcrumbs
- 1/3 cup of low-fat mayonnaise
- 3 tablespoons of roasted red peppers
- ½ stalk of chopped celery
- 3 tablespoons finely chopped onion
- 2 teaspoons extra-virgin olive oil
- 2 whole-wheat hamburger buns or English muffins, toasted
- 2 lettuce leaves
- ½ stock cube

Directions:
- In a large bowl, put in drained tuna
- Pour half of mayonnaise, pepper, and celery
- Sprinkle stock cube and mix well
- The form is to hold together
- Form two patties
- Put in the other half of the mayonnaise and peppers
- Heat oil
- Place molded patties and fry for two minutes on each side
- Spread the mayonnaise and peppers on the top side of each bun.
- Arrange the patty, onions, lettuce and tomato in the bun
- Serve

437.Carnivore Meatloaf

Yields: 2 to 4 servings — Prep time: 10 minutes— Cook time: 40 minutes.
Nutrition value per serving Calories: 645 net — Fats: 47 g net— Proteins: 45 g net Carbs: 5 g net

Ingredients
- 2 pounds ground pork
- 4 pounds ground beef
- Salt to taste

Directions
- Heat the baking oven at 350 degrees ° F. Lightly grease a rectangular baking dish or loaf pan with a non-stick cooking spray and line it with parchment paper.
- Add ground beef into a mixing bowl. Then, add in the salt and mix well with your hands, until thoroughly combined.
- Add in the ground pork, and knead with your hands, until thoroughly combined and mixed.
- Transfer the mixture into the prepared rectangular baking dish or loaf pan. Press it thoroughly and evenly on to the baking dish or loaf pan.
- Put it in the oven and bake for about 30 - 40 minutes, or until the meat juices are released in the centre and it seems cooked from the edges. One way to ensure is to note the edges; the edges will shrink and start to leave the dish's sides.
- Remove from the oven and let it rest at room temperature for a while before slicing.
- Then, cut into desirable slices and serve.

438.Carnivore Schnitzel

Yields: 4 servings — Prep time: 7 minutes — Cook time: 12 minutes.
Nutrition value per serving Calories: 464 net— Fats: 36 g net— Proteins: 37 g net— Carbs: 2 g net

Ingredients
- 4 boneless pork chops or veal cutlets
- Fine sea salt and ground black pepper
- 2 large eggs
- ¾ cup powdered Parmesan cheese (or pork dust if dairy-free)
- ¼ cup coconut oil or avocado oil, for frying, plus more if needed
- 1 lemon, sliced into wedges
- Chopped fresh parsley

Directions
- Pound the meat to ¼ inch thickness with a meat tenderiser to make schnitzels. Season the schnitzels with salt and pepper generously. Set aside.
- Divide the parmesan into 2 separate bowls.
- In another bowl, whisk an egg.
- Dip the meat in the first bowl of parmesan cheese; then in the egg wash; and finally into the second bowl of parmesan cheese. Ensure even coating by pressing the cheese well with your hands.
- Heat oil in a skillet over medium heat. Then, cook each schnitzel for 2 to 3 minutes from each side.
- Once cooked, take out in a dish lined with a paper towel to drain the excess oil.
- Place the schnitzels on a serving dish and garnish with parsley and lemon wedges. Serve hot.

KETO BREAD

439.Collagen Keto Bread

Ingredients
- Half cup Unflavored Grass-Fed Collagen Protein
- Six tablespoons of almond flour
- Six pastured eggs
- Half tablespoon of unflavored liquid coconut oil
- One teaspoon aluminum-free baking powder o
- One teaspoon of xanthan gum
- One or two pinches of Himalayan pink salt
- Pinch of Stevia

Directions
- Oven preheats to 325 degrees F.
- Generously oil with the help of coconut oil (or ghee or butter) only the lower part of a regular size (one and a have quarter) ceramic loaf dish or glass. You can also use a cut piece of baking paper to match the lower part of your sheet. Not lining or oiling your platter's sides will allow the bread to stick to the edges and remain elevated while cooling.
- Beat the egg white in a large bowl till the time stiff peaks are formed and then set it aside.
- Stir together the dry ingredients in a separate, little bowl and after that set it aside. If you do not like eggs then apply the optional pinch of stevia. Without the addition of sweetness to your bread, it will help to offset the sweetness.
- Stir the wet ingredients— liquid coconut oil and egg yolks — all together in a separate bowl and then set it aside.
- In the egg whites, add the wet and dry ingredients both and blend until well integrated. Your mixture is going to be a bit gooey and thick.
- In the lined or oiled dish, spill the mixture and position it in the oven.
- Bake for about forty-five minutes. The loaf in the oven must increase dramatically.
- Take it out from the oven and allow to cool for about one to two hours. The bread is going to sink a few and that is all right.
- Drag the sharp edge of a knife around the sides of the platter once the bread is cooled to remove the loaf.
- Slice evenly into twelve slices.

440.Almond keto flour bread

Ingredients
- Take two hundred grams of almond flour/meal
- Take two tablespoons of baking powder
- Take one tablespoon of salt or quantity according to your taste
- Take twenty grams of psyllium husk
- Take four to five eggs - medium
- Take fifty grams of coconut oil which are melted
- At last but not least, take one twenty-five ml hot/cozy water.

Directions
- In a small bowl, break two to three eggs and add two more eggs white. If the eggs are room temp, then the method works the best. Stir the whites and eggs until foamy mixture is formed for about a minute.
- Mix the remaining ingredients, namely almond flour, psyllium husks, melted butter, xanthan gum, baking powder, warm water, and salt.
- Mix until the dough is soft. Don't mix too much.
- Fill the dough with baking paper in a tin of loaf. If you do not use a silicone loaf line all edges with parchment paper for easy release of the bread.
- Soften the top side, but do not overpress— keep as much air as possible in the dough. Bake for about forty-five minutes at a temperature of 180 Celsius/350 Fahrenheit or until the implanted knife comes out clean and neat.

441.Easy cloud dread

Ingredients
- Take three large eggs, at room temperature
- Take a half tablespoon of cream of tartar
- Take one pinch of kosher salt
- Take two ounces of cream cheese which are softened

Directions
- Segregate the egg whites and the eggs and place them in separate bowls.
- Mix tartar cream to egg whites and stir until the stiff peaks are formed.
- In addition to egg yolks, add salt, cream cheese, and garlic powder. Mix well with each other.
- Gradually add a combination of egg yolk to whipped egg whites and softly fold in.
- Scoop the mixture in the form of circles, on prepared plates.
- Bake until golden on top of the crust.
- Entirely cool.

442.Macadamia nut bread:

Ingredients
- Take one cup macadamia nuts
- Take half cup almond flour
- Take two scoops whey protein powder
- Take two tablespoon flax meal
- Take one tablespoon baking powder
- Take four to five large eggs
- Take two large egg whites
- Take half cup melted butter
- Take one tablespoon lemon juice

Directions
- The oven is preheated to 350F.
- Grease with a bit of butter a baking dish or loaf pan.
- Pulse the macadamia nuts in a food processor for about thirty to forty-five seconds or until the flour consistency is reached.
- Add flax meal, whey protein and baking powder to the almond flour. Continue to pulse until all is well balanced.

443.Low-Czgb garlic and herb foccacia

Ingredients
- Take one cup of Almond Flour
- Take half cup of Coconut Flour
- Take half tablespoon of Xanthan Gum
- Take one tablespoon of Garlic Powder
- Take one tablespoon of Flaky Salt
- Take a half tablespoon of Baking Soda
- Take a half tablespoon of Baking Powder
- Take Falk Salt which is optional to garnish
- Take two eggs
- Take one tablespoon of Lemon Juice
- Take two tablespoons of Olive oil and 2 tablespoons of Olive Oil to drizzle

Directions
- Preheat the oven at 350 ° F.
- Place the mozzarella and cream cheese in a bowl and mix. Put the bowl in the microwave for a few seconds, then stir to mix well
- Replace the bowl with the potato, garlic powder, and almond meal, Cut until the dough has formed.
- To create 5 inches circle crust split the dough into two pieces. Attach a divergence into the dough to make a few gaps.

444.Grain free tortillass

Ingredients
- Take two tablespoons of tapioca flour
- Take two tablespoons coconut flour
- Take one pinch of fine sea salt
- Take one or two large eggs
- Take seven tablespoons unsweetened almond milk, (or milk of choice, if nut-free)

Directions
- Sift and set aside your dry ingredients (, coconut flour, tapioca starch, and salt).
- Heat a casserole over variable-low heat. If possible, very gently spray or grease it (it is safer to use a well-seasoned cast-iron skillet that does not need greasing).
- Stir together the combination of almond milk and egg.
- Add the dry combination and whisk gently until mixed.
- Add into the pan around three Tablespoons of the mixture. If required, shift the pan across a bit to distribute it in a circular pattern, but otherwise, do not touch it for three to four minutes.
- Turn it over and cook for another one to two minutes or until soft.
- Take away and transfer with the rest of the mixture to a cooling rack and repeat the same process over again.
- Serve quickly or keep the container fully packed at room temperature for around two days in an airtight container with one edge open (if the space is fairly dry; if it is wet).

445.Coconut Flour Flat

Ingredients:
- Take one and a half tablespoons Coconut Flour
- Take one Tablespoon Coconut Oil which is in melted form
- Take one egg
- Take half teaspoon of Sea Salt
- Take half teaspoon of Baking Powder preferably homemade grain-free baking pow

Directions
- Preheat the oven to 350 ° C.
- Combine sea salt, coconut flour, and baking powder.
- Remove coconut oil (melted) and egg and mix properly.
- To allow the flour to absorb the water, let the mixture sit for a few mins.
- On a baking pan, pour half the mixture and make use of a spatula to spread the mixture into a bun circle.
- Use the rest of the mixture to repeat the process. Bake the mixture until the color turns golden brown for ten minutes.

446.Cauliflower Tortillas:

Ingredients:
- Take a cauliflower head which is sliced and the steams are removed
- Take two large eggs
- Take one and a half cup Oregano dried
- Take a half tablespoon of Paprika
- Take the salt from the sea and black pepper from fresh soil

Directions
- Preheat your oven to 375 F.
- Using a liquidizer or a kitchen appliance, pulse the cauliflower until you get a texture finer than rice.
- Steam the riced cauliflower over boiling water for five minutes.
- Place the steamed cauliflower in a very towel and squeeze out the maximum amount of excess water as you'll. You would possibly wish to let it cool for some minutes initial, thus you don't burn yourself. You must be able to get out a great deal of water; be extremely aggressive concerning comp ression it, or you'll find yourself with soggy tortillas later.
- Transfer the cauliflower to a bowl. Add within the eggs, oregano, and paprika, and season to style (You will use any spices you like).
- Separate the mixture into half dozen balls of equal size, and unfold every ball out on a parchment-lined baking sheet to form six little circles.
- Place within the kitchen appliance and bake for eight to ten minutes; then flip and cook for an additional five minutes.
- Reheat in an exceedingly pan placed over low heat once able to serve.Makes concerning half a dozen tortillas.

447.Buttery And Soft Skilled Flatbread:

Ingredients:
- Take one cup of Almond Flour
- Take two tablespoons of Coconut Flour
- Take two tablespoons Xanthan Gum
- Take half tablespoon of Baking Powder
- Take half tablespoon of Falk Salt
- Take one Whole Egg plus one Egg White
- Take one tablespoon of Water
- Take one tablespoon of oil for frying
- Take one tablespoon of melted Butter-for brushing

Directions
- Stir collectively the dry elements (flours, baking powder, xanthan gum, salt) till nicely united.
- Add the egg white and egg and stir smoothly into the flour to incorporate. The dough will start to form.
- Add the tablespoon of water and commence to work the dough to enable the xanthan gum and flour to soak up the moisture.
- Slice the dough in four equal components and press every part out with hold wrap.
- Heat a giant skillet over medium warmth and add oil.
- Fry each flatbread for about one minute on each side.
- Slather with butter (while hot) and decorate with chopped parsley and salt.

448.Fluffy Keto Buns:

Ingredients:
- Take a half cup of coconut flour
- Take two tablespoons of ground psyllium husks
- Take four egg whites
- Take two egg yolks
- Take one teaspoon paleo baking powder
- Take half tablespoon apple cider vinegar
- Take one cup of water
- Take one teaspoon dried oregano which is optional
- Take one teaspoon dried thyme which is also optional
- At last but not the least take Salt and pepper according to your taste

Directions
- Preheat the oven to 350 degrees. Line a sheet of parchment paper for baking.
- Beat the egg whites with a hand mixer or brush until a foam with steep peaks is formed. After that set aside.
- In a separate bowl, combine the remaining ingredients. Fold gently in the whites of the egg.
- From your dough, form four, evenly sized, thick rolls and place them on the baking sheet. (Thickness is important to prevent buns from flattening.)
- Bake for about forty minutes or until all the way through it is fried. When you slice one open and it is still hot, put it back into the oven for a couple of more minutes (even the one you've cut open).
- Remove and serve immediately from the oven.

449.Keto Drop Biscuits:

Ingredients:
- Take one and a half cups of Almond Flour
- Take two nicely beaten eggs
- Take half a cup of Sour Cream
- Take four Tablespoons of Grass-Fed Butter which is melted.
- Take one and a half Cup of Shredded Cheddar Cheese
- Take one teaspoon of swerving confectioners or powdered erythritol
- Take one Tablespoon of Baking Powder
- Take half teaspoon of baking soda
- Take a Pinch of Salt

Directions
- Preheat the oven to 450 C.
- Add the baking powder, almond flour, salt, and baking soda to a separate bowl and stir using a fork or hand whisk.
- Add the swerve, eggs, melted butter and sour cream in another bowl and whisk until blended. In the wet ingredients, add the cheese and start to blend.
- In the hot, add the dry ingredients and blend.
- For silicone muffin pan liners, pour the biscuit mixture (or spray a non-stick muffin pan with non-stick spray) and bake for ten to twelve minutes.
- It was exactly ten minutes that mine took. Place the remaining in the refrigerator.

450.Keto Breakfast Pizza:

Ingredients:
- Take two ounces of cream cheese
- Take two cups of shredded mozzarella cheese
- Take two nicely beaten eggs
- Take one cup of almond flour
- Take a pinch of salt and pepper
- Take two beaten eggs
- Take six strips of cooked bacon
- Take four sausage links, cooked and diced
- Take two diced deli ham slices
- Take half cup of mozzarella cheese
- Take half a cup of shredded cheddar

Directions
- Preheat oven to 400, grease a solid iron pan.
- Mix cream cheese and mozzarella collectively in a bowl and microwave for 1 minute. Stir and heat additional 20 seconds till melted and combining smoothly.
- Add overwhelmed eggs to almond flour, blend well. Combine with the cheese mixture and paintings until dough is fashioned.
- Push dough into the forged iron skillet (like you will for a deep-dish pizza). Poke holes to keep away from air bubbles. Bake for 10 minutes.
- Pour beaten eggs over the dough, top with all meats and cheeses.
- Go back to the oven to bake for an extra ten to fifteen minutes or until installation and golden.
- Cut into eight identical pieces. The serving length is two.
- Net carbs are around three consistent with a serving (at the excessive aspect).

451.Coconut Flour Pizza Crust:

Ingredients:
- Take Olive oil spray to use it to grease the pizza pans.
- Take four large eggs.
- Take one cup of water to make the mixture thin.
- Take one teaspoon of garlic powder, dried oregano, and onion powder.
- Take one-fourth cup of coconut flour which is 1 ounce.
- Take half a cup of Grated parmesan cheese: Make sure you make use of perfectly grated cheese and not coarsely shredded.
- Take Marinara sauce and shredded mozzarella for topping.

Directions
- Line 2 kitchen appliance and broiler-safe dishpans with parchment paper circles and spray them with vegetable oil. You'll be able to conjointly build these pizzas aspect by side on one, massive baking sheet. Or simply build one massive rectangular pizza!
- In an exceedingly massive bowl, combine the crust ingredients within the order listed. Enable the mixture to rest and thicken for a handful of minutes. This may enable the coconut flour to absorb the liquid.
- Employing a rubber spatula, transfer 1/2 the mixture into each of the ready pans. Use a spatula to unfold it out equally into associate degree 8-inch circle.
- Bake the coconut flour dish crusts till set and therefore the edges are setting out to brown, regarding quarter-hour at 400°F.
- Take away the pizzas from the kitchen appliance and switch the oven to broil. Position the highest kitchen appliance rack half-dozen inches below the constituent (not directly below). Unfold every dish with 0.5 the pizza sauce, sprinkle with 0.5 the cut cheese, and add the other toppings you prefer. Broil every dish till the cheese is liquefied and therefore the crust is golden brown, 2-3 minutes.

452.Turmeric Cauliflower Flatbread:

Ingredients:
- Take one cup of coconut flour (I used Bob's, Red Mill)
- Take one-third cup Swerve Sweetener or another erythritol
- Take one tablespoon of baking powder
- Take half tablespoon of salt
- Take seven large eggs which are lightly beaten
- Take one cup of unsweetened almond milk
- Talk half cup butter and melted OR avocado oil
- Take half tablespoon of vanilla
- Take one cup fresh cranberries which are cut in half
- Take three tablespoon minced jalapeño peppers
- Take one jalapeño with seeds removed and sliced into twelve slices for garnish

Direction
- Preheat the oven to 325F and use paper liners to grease a muffin tin well or side.
- Whisk flour, sweetener, baking powder and salt together in a medium bowl. Split some clumps with a fork's back.
- Add the butter, eggs and almond milk and stir vigorously. Add the vanilla extract and stir until the solution is smooth and well mixed. Stir in minced jalapeños and cranberries.

453.Mini Paleo Pizza Crust:

Ingredients:
- Take one cup of almond flour or almond meal
- Take one egg
- Take one tablespoon of preferred fat, for example, extra virgin olive oil/extra virgin coconut oil, etc.
- A pinch of salt and pepper
- Plus any other seasoning you like in your pizza crust
- Take about a half cup of tomato sauce
- Add pizza toppings

Directions
- Preheat your kitchen appliance to 350 F.
- In a bowl combine all the ingredients along.
- Make three to four little balls of dough.
- Lay an oversized sheet of parchment paper on your operating surface. Massive enough to hide the pan you're baking the dish in. Place the balls of dough on the parchment paper with enough area between them. Place paper or parchment paper on high of the dough.
- Using a kitchen utensil, roll the dough to the desired thickness. Don't go too skinny or it would not be durable.
- Move the parchment paper with the dough on that to your dish receptacle.
- Remove the highest piece and paper or parchment paper.
- Bake for ten minutes or till the dough is crisp.
- Take out of the kitchen appliance and place your pasta sauce and toppings on the grilled dough. If you are employing a ton of toppings it's best to make them.
- Bake once more for ten to fifteen minutes.

454.Keto Zucchini Bread With Walnuts:

Ingredients:
- Take three large eggs
- Take half a cup of olive oil
- Take one teaspoon of vanilla extract
- Take two and a half cups of almond flour
- Take one and a half cups of erythritol
- Take half teaspoon salt
- Take one and a half teaspoons baking powder
- Take half teaspoon nutmeg
- Take one teaspoon of ground cinnamon
- Take one-fourth teaspoon of ground ginger
- Take one cup of grated zucchini
- Take half cup chopped walnuts

Directions
- Preheat kitchen appliances to 350°F. Whisk along the eggs, oil, and flavoring. Set to the facet.
- In another bowl, combine along with the almond flour, salt, erythritol, leaven, nutmeg, ginger, and cinnamon. Set to the facet.
- Using gauze or towel, take the zucchini and squeeze out the surplus water.
- Then, whisk the zucchini into the bowl with the eggs.
- Slowly add the dry ingredients into the egg mixture employing a hand mixer till amalgamated.
- Lightly spray a 9×5 loaf pan, and spoon within the zucchini bread mixture.
- Then, spoon within the shredded walnuts on high of the zucchini bread. Press walnuts into the batter employing a spatula.
- Bake for 60-70 minutes at 350ºF or till the walnuts on high look bronzed.
- This makes a complete of sixteen servings of Keto Zucchini Bread with Walnut Crust. Every slice comes bent to be two hundred.13 Calories, 18.83g Fats, 2.6g web Carbs, and 5.59g macromolecule

455.Keto Pumpkin Bread

Ingredients:
- Take one cup of creamy unsweetened almond butter
- Take two large eggs
- Take two and a half cup of erythritol
- Take two and a half cup of canned pumpkin puree
- Take one tablespoon of baking powder
- Take half tablespoon of ground cinnamon
- Take half tablespoon of ground nutmeg
- Take a one-eight tablespoon of ginger
- Take a one-eight tablespoon of ground cloves

Directions
- Preheat kitchen appliances to 350°F. Line associate eight x four in. baking loaf pan with parchment paper.
- Add almond butter and eggs into an outsized bowl. Whisk smartly with an outsized whisk till swish. Add in erythritol and whisk till swish. Add in pumpkin and leaven and whisk to mix. Add in cinnamon, nutmeg, ginger, cloves and whisk till equally combined.
- Pour batter into ready loaf pan. Rap bottom of the loaf pan against counter some times to interrupt up air bubbles. Bake regarding 45-55 minutes or till done. To visualize if the bread is finished, apply mild pressure to the surface and it ought to retrieve. A pick inserted ought to solely have some crumbs clinging.
- Bread can sink slightly whereas cooling. Let bread cool utterly before slicing and serving. Keep any cooked-over bread sealed tightly to stop it from drying.

456.Low Carb Blueberry English Muffin Bread Loaf:

Ingredients:
- Take half cup of almond butter or peanut butter or cashew
- Take one-fourth cup of coconut oil or butter ghee
- Take half a cup of almond flour
- Take half tablespoon of salt
- Take two tablespoons of baking powder
- Take half a cup of almond milk (unsweetened)
- Take half eggs beaten
- Take cup blueberries

Directions
- Preheat kitchen appliances to 350 degrees F.
- In a microwavable bowl soften paste and butter along for thirty seconds, stir till combined well.
- In a massive bowl, whisk almond flour, salt, and leavening along. Pour the paste mixture into the big bowl and stir to mix.
- Whisk the almond milk and eggs along then pour into the bowl and stir well.
- Drop-in contemporary blueberries or break apart frozen blueberries and gently stir into the batter.
- Line a loaf pan with parchment paper and gently grease the parchment paper further.
- Pour the batter into the loaf pan and bake forty-five minutes or till a strip in center comes out clean.
- Cool for regarding half-hour then take away from the pan.
- Slice and toast every slice before serving.

457.Paleo Coconut Bread:

Ingredients:
- Take half a cup of coconut flour
- Take one-fourth tablespoon of salt
- Take a one-fourth tablespoon of baking soda
- Take six eggs
- Take one-fourth cup of coconut oil which is melted
- Take one-fourth unsweetened almond milk

Directions
- Preheat kitchen appliances to 350°F.
- Line associate degree 8×4 in. loaf pan with parchment paper.
- In a bowl mix the coconut flour, salt, and saleratus.
- In another bowl mix the eggs, milk, and oil.
- Slowly add the wet ingredients into the dry ingredients and blend till combined.
- Pour the mixture into the ready loaf pan.
- Bake for forty to fifty minutes, or till a strip, inserted within the middle comes out clean.

458.Cinnamon Almond Flour Bread:

Ingredients:

- Take two cups of fine blanched almond flour(I use Bob's, Red Mill)
- Take two tablespoons of coconut flour
- Take half tablespoon of sea salt
- Take one tablespoon of baking soda
- Take half cup of Flaxseed meal or chia meal (ground chia or flaxseed)
- Take five eggs and one egg white whisked together
- Take half tablespoon of Apple cider vinegar or lemon juice
- Take half tablespoon of maple syrup or honey
- Take two to three tablespoon of clarified butter (melted) or Coconut oil; divided. Vegan butter will also work
- Take one tablespoon of cinnamon plus extra for topping
- Optional chia seed to sprinkle on top before baking

Directions

- Preheat kitchen appliances to 350F. Line Associate in Nursing 8×4 bread pan with parchment paper at all-time low and grease the edges.
- In a massive bowl, combine along with your almond flour, coconut flour, salt, sodium hydrogen carbonate, oilseed meal or chia meal, and half tablespoon of cinnamon.
- In another little bowl, whisk along your eggs and ovalbumin. Then add in your syrup (or honey), apple vinegar, and melted butter (one and a half to two tablespoons).
- Mix wet ingredients into dry. Make certain to get rid of any clumps that may have occurred from the coconut flour or almond flour.
- Pour mixture into your lubricated loaf pan.
- Bake at 350º for thirty to thirty-five minutes, till a strip inserted into the center of the loaf, comes out clean. Mine too around thirty-five minutes, however, I am at altitude.
- Remove from and kitchen appliances.
- Next, whisk along the opposite one to two tablespoons of melted butter (or oil) and blend it with half tablespoon of cinnamon. Brush this on prime of your cinnamon almond flour bread.
- Cool and serve or store for later.

459.Paleo Chocolate Zucchini Bread:

Ingredients:

- Take one cup of zucchini
- Take two nicely beaten eggs
- Take half a cup of sour cream (I used Daisy brand)
- Take one teaspoon of vanilla extract
- Take half a cup of almond flour
- Take one teaspoon baking powder
- Take half teaspoon salt
- Take one cup of Swerve powdered sugar
- Take one-fourth cup of cup cocoa powder
- Take sixty low carb mini chocolate chips

Directions

- Preheat kitchen appliances to 350°F.
- Chop zucchini into giant chunks and increase a mixer. Mix on an all-time low setting till the zucchini sounds like rice or has to be grated.
- Take out the zucchini and place it in a very variety of paper towels. Pull out the surplus water and put aside.
- Add cream, eggs, and vanilla added to the mixer and mix on medium for twenty seconds.
- Then add within the almond flour, leavening, sweetener, chocolate, and salt. Mix on medium for twenty seconds.
- Add within the zucchini and mix on an all-time low setting for a couple of seconds to urge it well integrated into the mixture.
- Spoon mixture into a lubricated bread loaf pan and sprinkle chocolate chips on prime.
- Bake for fifty to sixty minutes till a strip pulls out clean. Mine took an hour. Let cool fully before cutting.

460.Keto Bread Rolls:

Ingredients:

- Take four to five large eggs
- Take half tablespoon of cream of tartar
- Take half cup of cream cheese
- Take half tablespoon of salt

Directions

- Break the eggs and then remove the egg whites from the yolks.
- Shift the separated egg whites in a mixing bowl and blend it for a duration of two to three minutes with an electric mixer.
- Mix the Tartar Cream into this mixture and stir it with electric mixture for another one minute. The mixture will begin to make softened peaks.
- Mix the cream cheese and yolks in a separate container and blend it until it is uniformly mixed.
- Smoothly transfer this batter in another into the bowl containing the egg whites.
- Take a tray or any big baking container and place the layer of obtained batter on this tray. The batter rise up significantly when placed in the oven so it gives significant room for breathing.
- Place in the oven for fifteen to twenty minutes at 180 ° Centigrade (375 ° F) till it turns a little bit golden brown. Serve the rolls fresh and cherish your cravings with low carbs in ketogenic diet.

461.Low-Carb Eggplant Pizza:

Ingredients:

- Take one large eggplant
- Take one Tablespoon of olive oil
- Talk half or one cup no sugar added pizza sauce
- Take two minced garlic cloves
- Take a half sliced yellow onion
- Take one cup of fresh baby spinach
- Take sea salt, to taste
- Take ground pepper, to taste
- Take half a cup of shredded mozzarella cheese
- Take one-fourth cup of chopped fresh oregano
- Take crushed red pepper which is optional

Directions:

- Preheat to 400 ° F the oven.
- Lengthwise cut the eggplant, about 1/4-1/3 inches thick. Brush or rub on each side of the eggplant slices a little olive oil and place it on a baking sheet lined with parchment or baking stone. Sprinkle with pepper and salt. Put seven to ten minutes in the oven or until the eggplant is warm and start cooking.
- Add half tablespoon of olive oil and sauté the garlic and onion until soft (about three to four minutes). Salt and pepper season. Add the skillet with pizza sauce and spinach and cook for one to two more minutes until the mixture is warm and the spinach is wilted.
- Take the slices of the eggplant from the oven, cover each with the mixture of onions and spinach. Sprinkle with minced orégano and cheese. Put in the oven for about five minutes or until the cheese melts. Serve with fresh oregano and crushed red pepper immediately.

462.Keto Sesame Bread:

Ingredients:

- Take seven large Eggs
- Take two cups of Almond flour
- Take half a cup of unsalted butter
- Take one-fourth cup of Coconut flour
- Take three tablespoons of Psyllium husk
- Take three tablespoons of Sesame seeds
- Take one tablespoon of Baking powder
- Take half tablespoon of Xanthan gum
- Take one-fourth tablespoon of Salt
- Take half cup of Water

Directions

- Preheat the oven to 180C
- Use the hand mixer to whisk the eggs.
- Then add the butter and water that has been warmed, blend well.
- Add almond flour, psyllium husk, coconut flour, cinnamon, xanthan gum, sesame seeds, and baking powder.
- Use a spatula to mix everything well.
- Then pour the mixture into a butter-grassed loaf tin.
- Shine the dough with some sesame seeds.
- Bake for forty minutes afterward.
- Leave the cooling bread, then cut and serve.

463.Stove Top Pizza Crust:

Ingredients:

- Take ninety-six grams of almond flour
- Take twenty-four grams of coconut flour
- Take two teaspoons of xanthan gum
- Take two teaspoons of baking powder
- Take one-fourth teaspoon of kosher salt depending on whether savory or sweet.
- Take two teaspoons of apple cider vinegar
- Take one egg lightly beaten
- Take five teaspoons of water as required
- Keto marinara sauce
- Mozzarella cheese
- Pepperoni or salami
- Fresh basil

Directions

- Attach to the food processor almond meal, coconut meal, xanthan gum, baking powder, and salt. Pulse when combined thoroughly.
- Running the food processor, pour in apple cider vinegar. Once it has been evenly distributed, pour in the shell. Followed by the heat, adding enough to make it into a ball together. The dough is going to be sticky but still strong to touch from the xanthan gum.
- Wrap the dough in plastic wrap and knead for a minute or two through the plastic. Speak of it a little like a ball of pressure. The dough should be smooth and not broken substantially (a few are perfect here and there). In this scenario, return it to the food processor and substitute one teaspoon at a time in more liquid. Enable dough to rest at room temperature for ten minutes (and in the fridge for up to five days).
- Cooking on top of the stove: Heat the skillet or saucepan over medium/high heat while the dough is resting (you want the saucepan to be hot!). When using the oven: heat up in the oven at 350 ° F/180 ° C a pizza plate, skillet or baking tray. The premise is that first on both sides you must blind cook / bake the crust without toppings on a very hot surface.
- Roll out the dough with a rolling pin between two sheets of parchment paper. Here you can play with thickness, but we like to roll it out nice and thin (about twelve inches in diameter) and fold over the edges (wet fingertips press down).
- Cook the pizza crust, top-side down first, in your pre-heated skillet or oven, until blistered (about two minutes depending on your skillet and heat). Lower to medium / low heat, turn over the pizza crust, add range toppings and cover with a lid. Instead, to finish off the pizza, you can always pass it to your grill oven.
- Serve as soon as possible. Note that the dough can be stored in the refrigerator for about five days. Throughout the week, you can make individual mini pizzettes.

464.Low Carb Keto Garlic Breadsticks:

Ingredients:

- Take one and a half cups of part-skim low moisture shredded mozzarella cheese
- Take two ounces of full-fat cream cheese
- Take one and a half cups of super-fine almond flour
- Take two tablespoons of coconut flour
- Take one and a half tablespoon of aluminum-free baking powder
- Take one tablespoon of garlic powder
- Take one-fourth tablespoon of onion powder
- Take three large eggs one egg is reserved for egg wash
- Take two cloves of garlic minced
- Take one tablespoon of butter
- Take one tablespoon of olive oil
- Take one and a half tablespoon of grated parmesan cheese
- Take one tablespoon of parsley finely chopped

Directions

- Preheat kitchen appliances to 350°F. Line a baking sheet with parchment paper.
- In a tiny bowl, whisk along almond flour, coconut flour, leavening, garlic powder, and onion powder. Set aside.
- Add cheese and cheese to an oversized microwave-safe bowl. Cowl the cheese with cheese (this can stop the cream cheese from warming and creating a large number in your microwave). Soften within the microwave at thirty second intervals. Once every thirty seconds, stir cheese till cheese is liquefied and uniform and resembles a dough in look (see ikon for reference). This could solely take around one minute total preparation time. Don't attempt to microwave the complete time quickly as a result of a number of the cheese can cook. You'll additionally soften the cheeses over the stove in a very saucepan.
- Allow cheese dough to chill slightly (only many minutes) so that it still takes the bit however not too hot. If the cheese is just too hot it'll cook the eggs. however, don't let the cheese quiet down fully as a result of then it'll flip arduous and you may not be able to mix it with the opposite dough ingredients.
- Add cheese, two eggs (remember the third egg is for the egg wash end at the top only), and almond flour mixture into a kitchen appliance with a dough blade attachment. Pulse on high speed till the dough is uniform. The dough is going to be quite sticky, which is traditional.
- Scoop out dough with a spatula and place onto an oversized sheet of wrapping. Cowl the dough in wrapping and knead many times with the dough within the plastic wrap till you've got a homogenous dough ball.
- Wrap your pastry board with wrapping till the plastic wrap is taut. You must have the wrapping running across all-time low of the board so that the load of the board can facilitate keep the plastic wrap in situ. The wrapping ought to keep your dough from jutting to the board. Gently coat your hands with oil and divide the dough into eight equal components. Roll every dough into sleek one in. thick sticks.
- Add the ultimate egg to a tiny low bowl and whisk. Liberally brush the surface of rolls with egg wash.
- Bake rolls for regarding quarter-hour within the middle rack of your kitchen appliance, or till breadsticks are simply fried and just commencing to brown.
- While breadsticks are baking, create the spread topping. Add garlic, butter, and oil in a very tiny cooking pan. Bring back low-medium heat and stir till butter is liquefied and garlic is gently brunette.
- When breadsticks are simply done baking however still pale, take away from a kitchen appliance. Quickly brush them liberally with the spread topping (You don't wish to interrupt the preparation of the breadsticks for too long.) Sprinkle cheese and parsley over the breadsticks.
- Place breadsticks back to the kitchen appliance and bake for an extra three minutes or till breadsticks flip a golden brown.
- If desired, sprinkle additional cheese and parsley over breadsticks before serving. You will serve breadsticks plain or with low carb pasta sauce.

465.Keto Chocolate Chip Cookies:

Ingredients:

- Take 3.5 ounces of Salted Butter (3.5 ounces to half cup)
- Take 4.5 ounces of Erythritol (So Nourished) (4.5 ounces to three-fourth cup)
- Take one tablespoon of Vanilla Extract
- Take one large Egg (fifty gram / 1.7 ounce)
- Take six ounces of Almond Flour (six-ounce – one and a half cups)
- Take one and a half tablespoon of baking powder
- Take half tablespoon of xanthan gum (optional)
- Take one-fourth tablespoon of Salt
- Take three ounces of Sugar-Free Chocolate Chips (thirty grams – Three-fourth cup)

Directions

- Preheat the kitchen appliance to one hundred eighty C (355 F). Microwave the butter for thirty seconds to soften, however, ensure it's not hot.
- Place the butter and erythritol in an exceedingly bowl and beat till combine. Add the vanilla and egg, and beat on low for one more fifteen seconds precisely.
- Add the almond flour, leavening, xanthan gum, and salt. Beat till well combined.
- Press the dough along and take away from the bowl. Knead within the chocolate chips together with your hands.
- Divide and form the dough into twelve balls (or use a little frozen dessert scoop) and place it on a baking receptacle. Bake for ten minutes.
- Allow chilling before serving. Confine AN airtight instrumentation for up to seven days.

466.Keto Peanut Butter Bread:

Ingredients:

- Take 250 grams of Peanut Butter (Natural and with no added sugar) Cook it at your home.
- Take three large Eggs
- Take one tablespoon of Vinegar
- Take one tablespoon of Baking Soda
- Take Stevia Powder to taste, you can also use the liquid one.
- Take a pinch of salt
- Take Butter for greasing

Directions

- Whisk all the ingredients together with Butter. Then
- Pour in the batter and bake at 170C/350F for 25 minutes or until the toothpick is clean and allow to cool and then remove Slice and Serve from the loaf tin

467.Keto Low Carb Banana Bread:

Ingredients:
- Take two cups of Blanched almond flour
- Take one-fourth cup of Coconut flour
- Take half cup of Walnuts (chopped, and more for topping if required)
- Take two tablespoons of Gluten-free baking powder
- Take two tablespoons of Cinnamon
- Take a pinch of Sea salt which is optional
- Take six tablespoons of Butter (softened; can use coconut oil for dairy-free, but texture and flavor will be different)
- Take half cup of Erythritol
- Take four large Eggs
- Take one-fourth cup of Unsweetened almond milk
- Take two tablespoons of Banana extract

Directions
- Preheat the kitchen appliance to 350 degrees F. Line a 9x5 in (23x13 cm) loaf pan with parchment paper, so the paper hangs over 2 opposite sides (for simple removal later).
- In a massive bowl, combine along with the almond flour, coconut flour, leaven, cinnamon, and ocean salt (if using).
- In another massive bowl, use a hand mixer to butter and erythritol till soft. Drill the eggs (use the low setting to avoid splashing). Stir within the banana extract and almond milk.
- Pour the dry ingredients into the wet. Beat on low setting till a dough/batter forms.
- Stir within the sliced walnuts.
- Transfer the batter into the lined loaf pan and press equally to create a sleek prime. If desired, sprinkle the highest with extra sliced walnuts and press them gently into the surface.
- Bake for 50-60 minutes, till Associate in the nursing inserted pick, comes out clean.
- Cool fully before removing from the pan and slicing. (The longer you let it sit before slicing, the higher it'll hold along. subsequent day is right if potential.)

468.Low-Carb Blueberry Muffins:

Ingredients:
- Take one cup of fine almond flour
- Take two tablespoons of powdered erythritol or one tablespoon of sugar or stevia equivalent
- Take one-fourth cup of milk of choice
- Take one large egg or one whole flax egg
- Take half tablespoon of baking powder
- Take one-fourth tablespoon of salt
- Take two and a half cup of blueberries
- Take optional pinch cinnamon

Directions
- Preheat kitchen appliances to 350 F.
- Line or grease a mini quick bread tin fine.
- Stir all dry ingredients fine, then add all remaining ingredients except berries.
- Scoop into the quick bread cups – I added a touch batter, placed many berries per quick bread on prime, then lined with additional batter. You'll additionally simply press many berries into the highest of every quick bread when filling with batter.
- Bake thirteen minutes on the middle rack (or 17-18 for regular-size muffins).
- Take away from the kitchen appliance and let cool a further ten minutes, throughout which period they still arrange.
- Rigorously go round the sides of every quick bread with a knife and take off. Or if you've used liners, they peel off simply when sitting for daily

469.Cranberry Walnut Cookies:

Ingredients:
- Take two and a half cup of all-purpose flour
- Take one teaspoon of baking soda
- Take half teaspoon of baking powder
- Take three-fourth of teaspoon salt
- Take one cup of butter which is softened to room temperature
- Take half a cup of sugar
- Take one cup of brown sugar
- Take two eggs
- Take two teaspoons of vanilla
- Take one bag of semi-sweet chocolate chunks
- Take one and a half cups dried cranberries
- Take one and a half cups of chopped walnuts

Directions
- Preheat kitchen appliances to 375 degrees F (190 degrees C). Grease a baking sheet.
- Cream white sugar, sugar, and butter along in an exceedingly massive bowl. Beat milk, fruit crush, and egg into the creamed mixture.
- Sift flour, leaven, cinnamon, salt, and bicarbonate of soda along in an exceedingly separate bowl; mix into the wet ingredients within the bowl to create cookie dough. Stir cranberries and walnuts into the dough.
- Drop the dough onto the ready baking sheet by the teaspoon.
- Bake within the preheated kitchen appliance till the sides are golden, ten to fifteen minutes. Enable the cookies to cool down on the baking sheet for one minute before removing to a wire rack to cool fully. Sprinkle confectioners' sugar over the cookies to serve.
- You might additionally like

470.Paleo Hot Cross Buns:

Ingredients:
- Take two cups of almond meal
- Take half a cup of coconut flour
- Take one-fourth cup of hundred percent maple syrup or honey
- Take six whole eggs
- Take 250 grams of grass-fed butter melted (or ghee or coconut oil)
- Take two apples peeled and grated (we used granny smiths)
- Take a three-fourth cup of unsweetened sultanas (or raisins, ensure to check for nasties!).
- Take two tablespoons of nutmeg
- Take three tablespoons of cinnamon

Directions:
- Heat the oven to 350 ° F (180 ° C).
- Label 12 tins of muffins with large cases of muffins.
- Mix the almond meal, coconut meal, nutmeg and cinnamon in a mix in a large bowl.
- Add the butter and eggs of the maple syrup and blend well.
- Now add the sultanas and apple. Mix again until a dough is shaped.
- Once all of the water is mixed, even the balls roll into 12.
- Place them in the cases of the muffin and press a little down.

471.Brown Butter Coconut Cookies:

Ingredients:

- Take two cups of sweetened flaked coconut
- Take one cup of (8 oz.) unsalted butter
- Take two and a half cups (about 10 5/8 oz.) of all-purpose flour
- Take one teaspoon of baking soda
- Take one teaspoon of baking powder
- Take one teaspoon of kosher salt
- Take a three-fourth cup of packed light brown sugar
- Take a three-fourth cup of granulated sugar
- Take two large eggs
- Take two teaspoons of vanilla extract
- Take two cups of white chocolate chips

Directions

- Preheat kitchen appliances to 375°F. Line three baking sheets with parchment paper. Unfold flaked coconut in a fair layer on a separate red-rimmed massive baking sheet. Bake in preheated kitchen appliance till gently cooked, half dozen to eight minutes, stirring once when four minutes. Take away from oven; let cool fully, regarding quarter-hour. (Do not put off kitchen appliances.)
- Melt butter during a little cooking pan over medium, stirring perpetually, till

butter begins to show golden brown and smells nutty, half dozen to eight minutes. Take away from heat; at once pour into a tiny low heatproof bowl (to stop burning); let cool five minutes.

- Sift along with flour, sodium bicarbonate, leaven, and salt during a bowl. Beat cooled butter, refined sugar, and sugar during an industrial stand mixer fitted with a paddle attachment on medium speed till well combined, two to three minutes. Add eggs one at a time, beating till simply incorporated when every addition. Add vanilla; beat till simply incorporated. Bit by bit add flour mixture, beating on low speed till incorporated, regarding two minutes, stopping to scrape downsides of the bowl as required. Stir in cooked coconut and chocolate. Let dough rest at temperature twenty minutes.
- Using a one 1/2-inch cookie scoop, scoop cookies two inches apart onto ready baking sheets. Bake at three75°F in 3 batches till golden, eight to ten minutes per batch. Transfer baking sheets to wire racks; let cookies cool on baking sheets five minutes. Transfer cookies on to wire racks; let cool fully, regarding half-hour.

472.Maria's Almond Psyllium Bread:

Ingredients:

- Take one and a half (five ounces) cup of blanched almond flour (or half cup coconut flour or 2.5 oz.)
- Take five tablespoons (forty-five grams) of psyllium husk (must be a fine powder, not whole husks)
- Take two teaspoons of baking powder
- Take one teaspoon of sea salt
- Take two and a half (one ounce) tablespoons apple cider vinegar
- Take three egg whites (six egg whites if using coconut flour)
- Take seven and a Half cup (seven ounces, a little less than a cup) of boiling water

Directions

- Preheat the kitchen appliance to 350 degrees F (176C). In an exceedingly medium-sized bowl, mix the flour, plantain powder (no substitutes: oilseed meal won't work), leaven and salt. Use an

electric hand-held mixer, combine till dry ingredients are well combined.

- Add the eggs and vinegar and blend till the dough is thick. Add boiling water to the bowl. Combine till well combined and also the dough has firmed up.
- Place dough into a lubricated 5x7 loaf pan, bake for fifty-five minutes or till a picket skewer perforated within the center of the bread comes out clean.
- Remove from the kitchen appliance and permit the bread to chill utterly. Cut open with a toothed knife. Fill with desired fillings.
- Alternatively, the kind dough into four to five mini subs (the dough can rise regarding two to three times thus I begin mine as a one in. disk) and place onto a lubricated baking sheet. Bake forty-five to fifty minutes for smaller shapes like buns.

473.Cinnamon Scrolls:

Ingredients:

- The base of Scroll:
- Take one and a half cups of mozzarella cheese
- Take two tablespoons of cream cheese
- Take one or two large eggs
- Take three and a half cups of almond flour
- Take one tablespoon of erythritol
- Inside:
- Take one tablespoon of erythritol
- Take one tablespoon of cinnamon
- Take one tablespoon of warm water
- Icing:
- Take one tablespoon of cream cheese
- Take one tablespoon of heavy cream
- Take one tablespoon of erythritol

Directions

- Mix the cheese in a safe microwave bowl and heat up in thirty-second increments

until the mixture is melted enough to fully bind.

- Add egg and almond flour to stevia for approximately one and a half minutes. Put two sheets of parchment paper in between and roll into a rectangle.
- In a small cup, mix stevia, cinnamon, and water and spread over the mixture of rolled out cheese.
- Start from one side and roll the scrolls into a long roll. Cut into two lengths of your finger and put on a baking tray. Put in the oven for ten minutes at 375F (180C).
- In a plastic bag, mix the cream cheese, cream, and stevia together. Cut off the corner and pipe over the scrolls of cinnamon.

Snacks

474. Keto Raspberry Cake And White Chocolate Sauce

Serves: 5 — Preparation time: 45 minutes — Meal Type: Snack.
Nutritional Value Per Serving. Calories: 325 kcal— Total Fat: 12g — Total Carbs: 3g— Protein: 40g

Ingredients:
- 5 ounces cacao butter, melted
- 4 teaspoons of pure vanilla extract. You can replace with vanilla powder.
- 4 eggs
- 3 cup raspberries
- 2½ ounces grass-fed ghee
- 1 teaspoon baking powder
- 1 tablespoon of apple cider vinegar
- 1 cup green banana flour
- ¾ cup coconut cream
- ¾ cup of granulated sweetener
- 4 ounces cacao butter
- 2 teaspoons pure vanilla extract
- ¾ cup of coconut cream
- Pinch of salt

Directions
- Mix the butter and the sweetener together till they are completely mixed. You can make use mixer for this.
- Pour in your grass-fed ghee into the mix, blend.
- In a separate bowl, whisk the eggs together.
- Take 2 ½ cups of the raspberries and slice them into halves.
- Preheat your oven to 350 degrees F.
- Get out a baking pan, and rub in the butter or spray it with cooking spray.
- Pour in your mixed eggs to the butter and sweetener mixture. Mix well, until the sweetener disclosed wholly.
- Pour in your banana flour and mix very well with a wooden spoon.
- When mixed, mix in vanilla extract, apple cider, coconut cream, baking powder, and mix the mixture very well until batter form.
- Spoon around the sliced berries lightly. Then, sprinkle just a little flour in your oiled or buttered baking pan
- Hit the pan around, so the flour is absorbed by the oil or butter, dust out any extra flour.
- Pour batter into the pan, and level it by smacking lightly on the counter.
- Place in the oven, and bake for 45 minutes to an hour.
- If you doubt its readiness, stick in a knife in the cake, and pull it out. If it comes out with any moistened, then it is not ready. We recommend you to run the cake test after 45 minutes. Not before.
- When done take out, and leave it on a cake rack to cool.
- For the sauce
- Mix your cacao butter with 2 teaspoons pure vanilla extract.
- Add coconut cream and beat the mixture very well.
- Put in a pinch of salt to taste and beat again.
- Chop up your remaining berries into tiny cubes and throw it in the mix.
- Pour the mix on your cake and spread evenly.
- Serve cold.

475. Keto Chocolate Chip Cookies

Serves: 4 — Preparation time: 40 minutes — Meal Type: Snacks.
Nutritional Value Per Serving. Calories: 287 kcal— Total Fat: 19g — Total Carbs: 6.5g— Protein: 6.8g

Ingredients:
- 7 spoons of unsweetened coconut powder
- 7 tablespoons of Keto chocolate chips
- 5 tablespoons of butter
- 2 flat tablespoon of baking powder
- 2 eggs
- 2/3 confectioners swerve
- 1 1/3 cups of almond flour
- A teaspoon of vanilla extract

Directions
- Preheat oven to 325˚.
- Put in half of the chocolate chips and all the butter, and heat in the oven till it melts slightly.
- Mix the melted chocolate and butter completely.
- Crack and mix the eggs, and pour eggs in chocolate and butter mixture.
- Mix in the vanilla extract, coconut powder, confectioners swerve, and almond flour. Mix well.
- Add chocolate chip cookies. Remember to leave some chocolate chips to top the dough. Then, add baking powder, and mix until dough forms.
- Spread out and cut out cookies, top with the rest of your chocolate chips.
- Bake for 8 to 10 minutes. They will come out very soft.
- Set them down and let them cool so they can harden. Enjoy.

476. Keto Beef And Sausage Balls

Serves: 3 — Preparation time: 30 minutes — Meal Type: Snacks.
Nutritional Value Per Serving. Calories: 592 kcal— Total Fat: 53.9g — Total Carbs: 1.3g— Protein: 25.4g

Ingredients:
- MEAT
- 2 pounds of ground beef
- 2 pounds of ground sausage
- 2 eggs
- ½ cup of Keto mayonnaise
- 1/3 of cup ground pork rinds
- ½ cup of Parmesan cheese
- Salt
- Pepper
- 2 tablespoons of butter
- 3 tablespoons of oil
- SAUCE
- 3 large diced onions
- 2 pounds of mushrooms sliced
- 5 sliced cloves of garlic
- 3 cups of beef broth
- 1 cup of sour cream
- 2 tablespoons of mustard
- Worcestershire sauce
- Salt
- Pepper
- Parsley
- 1 tablespoon of Arrowroot powder

Directions
- Put your meat, egg, and onions in a bowl. Mix with a spoon.
- Put beef, parmesan, egg, mayonnaise, sausage, pork rind in a bowl.
- Add salt and pepper to taste.
- Heat oil or butter in a skillet.
- Take the beef mix and mould into balls, place the balls in the oil and fry for 7-10 minutes.
- When cooked, remove the balls from the pan and set aside.
- Your skillet should still have oil, and so, you will put in your diced onions and fry till they brown a little.
- Then, add the garlic and mushrooms, and sauté for 3 minutes. Then, add the broth.
- Mix in mustard, sour cream and Worcestershire sauce well.
- Boil for a minute or two then adds in the meatballs.
- Add salt and pepper to your taste, let it simmer.
- The arrowroot powder is to make the sauce thick. If the sauce is already thick, you may ignore it.
- Serve hot.

477. Keto Coconut Flake Balls

Serves: 2 — Preparation time: 15 minutes — Meal Type: Snacks
Nutritional Value Per Serving. Calories: 204 kcal— Total Fat: 11g — Total Carbs: 4.2g— Protein: 1.5g

Ingredients:

- 1 Vanilla Shortbread Collagen Protein Bar
- 1 tablespoon of lemon or coconut flavoured FAT water [In the absence, regular filter water is fine]
- ¼ teaspoon ground ginger
- ½ cup unsweetened coconut flakes,
- ¼ teaspoon ground turmeric

Directions

- Put protein bar, ginger, turmeric, and ¾ of the total flakes into a food processor, and process, until crumble. Avoid smoothing it.
- Take out and add a spoon of water and roll till dough forms. If the spoonful is not enough, add a little more.
- Roll into balls, and sprinkle the rest of your flakes on it or roll the balls in it.
- Serve as it is or refrigerates it for a cold snack.

478. Keto Chocolate Greek Yoghurt Cookies

Serves: 3 — Preparation time: 1 hour — Meal Type: Snacks.
Nutritional Value Per Serving. Calories: 287 kcal— Total Fat: 19g — Total Carbs: 6.5g— Protein: 6.8g

Ingredients:

- 3 eggs
- 1/8 teaspoon of tartar
- 5 tablespoons of softened Greek yoghurt

Directions

- Separate egg whites from the yolk and beat the whites until fluffy.
- In the egg whites, pour the tartar, and mix well.
- In the yolk, put in the Greek yoghurt, and mix well.
- Combine both bowls' contents and mix thoroughly until thick.
- With a spoon, line out scoops on the baking tray. Be sure to have parchment on the tray.
- Lightly spread out the scoops, so they are like cookies. They will be very light, so apply no pressure.
- Bake for 25-30 minutes, then take out and leave to cool for two hours.

479. Keto coconut flavoured ice cream

Serves: 4 — Preparation time: 20 minutes — Meal Type: Snacks.
NUTRITIONAL VALUE PER SERVING. Calories: 244 kcal— Total Fat: 48g — Total Carbs: 6g— Protein: 15g

Ingredients:

- 4 cups of coconut milk
- 2/3 cup of xylitol or erythritol
- ¼ teaspoon of salt
- 2 teaspoons of vanilla extract
- 1 teaspoon of coconut extract

Directions

- Add the coconut milk in a bowl, with the sweetener, extracts, and salt. Stir well.
- Pour this mixture in the ice cube trays, and put it in freezer.
- When frozen, blend it at highest speed in a strong blender.
- Freeze a little and consume same day.

480. Chocolate-coconut cookies

Serves: 4 — Preparation time: 15 minutes — Meal Type: Snacks.
NUTRITIONAL VALUE PER SERVING Calories: 260 kcal— Total Fat: 26g — Total Carbs: 4.5g— Protein: 1g

Ingredients:

- 2 eggs
- ½ cup of cocoa powder
- ½ cup of flour
- ½ cup of coconut oil
- ¼ cup of grated coconut
- Stevia

Directions

- Preheat oven to 350 °F.
- Crack eggs and separate whites and yolks, mix well separately.
- Add a pinch of salt to the yolks.
- Heat oil in a skillet, and add cocoa, egg whites, stirring continuously, add in the salted yolks. Mix thoroughly. Then, add stevia to your taste.
- Add in coconut flour, and mix until dough forms.
- On a clean flat surface, sprinkle grated coconut.
- Roll the dough around in the coconut, so they mix well. Now, your dough is ready to be molded in cookies.
- Bake for 15 minutes, let it cool to set.

481. Keto Buffalo Chicken Meatballs

Serves: 3 — Preparation time: 30 minutes — Meal Type: Snacks
Nutritional Value Per Serving Calories: 360 kcal— Total Fat: 26g — Total Carbs: 4.5g— Protein: 1g

Ingredients:

- 1 pound of ground chicken
- 1 large
- 2/3 cup of hot sauce
- ½ cup of almond flour
- ½ teaspoon of salt
- ¼ teaspoon of pepper
- ½ cup of melted butter
- 1 large chopped onion
- 1 teaspoon of minced garlic
- Cooking spray or butter

Directions

- Combine meat, egg, and onions in a bowl, mix well with a spoon.
- Pour in almond flour, garlic, salt, and pepper in, and mix well.
- Preheat oven to 350°F, and prepare a baking tray by lining it with foil, then spray with cooking spray or rub butter thinly on it.
- Mold the egg mixture into balls.
- Set on the tray and bake for 18-20 minutes.
- While it is done baking, place butter in microwave for few seconds to melt lightly.
- Mix the melted butter and hot sauce in another bowl.
- When the meatballs are slightly cooled, rub in this sauce.
- Serve warm.

Drinks

482. Tangerine Avocado Smoothie

Serves: 3 — Preparation time: 5 minutes — Meal Type: Drink
Nutritional Value Per Serving. Calories: 546 kcal— Total Fat: 93g — Total Carbs: 44g— Protein: 32g

Ingredients:
- 8 scoops of vanilla collagen protein powder
- 7 tangerines, peeled and separated
- 4 scoops of whey protein
- 4 frozen steamed cauliflower florets
- 1 cup full-fat coconut milk
- 1 cup water
- 1 cup of ice
- 1 frozen avocado

Directions
- Add tangerines, whey protein, frozen steamed cauliflower florets, full-fat coconut milk, and the frozen avocado with a cup water in the blender, blend well for 4 to 6 minutes, or until smooth.
- Add vanilla collagen protein powder and blend for 5 seconds more.
- Add ice and serve cold.

483. Coffee and egg latte

Serves: 2 — Preparation time: 15 minutes — Meal Type: Drinks.
Nutritional Value Per Serving. Calories: 112 kcal— Total Fat: 12g — Total Carbs: 5.2g— Protein: 9.5g

Ingredients:
- 15 ounces of black coffee
- 3 large pasture-raised eggs
- 2 tablespoons of grass-fed butter
- 2 scoop Vanilla Collagen Protein
- 1 tablespoon Brain Octane Oil
- ½ teaspoon of cinnamon

Directions
- Put in oil, butter, eggs and cinnamon, black coffee in the blender, and blend for 50 seconds.
- Then, add collagen protein, and blend for 5 seconds more.
- Pour out in a glass, and sprinkle cinnamon.

484. Keto lemonade slushies

Serves: 4 — Preparation time: 20 minutes — Meal Type: Drinks.
Nutritional Value Per Serving Calories: 68 kcal— Total Fat: 6g — Total Carbs: 7g— Protein: 1g

Ingredients:
- 8 ounces of lemon juice [get this from juicing 7 medium-sized lemons]
- 2 ½ ounces unsweetened almond milk
- 1 tablespoon of birch xylitol
- ¼ a teaspoon of lemon stevia
- 1 teaspoon Brain Octane Oil

Directions
- Add lemon juice in a blender and cover. Do not blend yet.

- Mix the almond milk with the octane oil, then pour in birch xylitol and lemon stevia.
- Pour it into the blender with lemon juice, and blend until smooth.
- You can add ice, if you desire.
- You can shred the ice or simply place it in the drink.

485. Coconut vanilla milkshake

Serves: 2 — Preparation time: 20 minutes — Meal Type: Drinks.
Nutritional Value Per Serving Calories: 246 kcal— Total Fat: 93g — Total Carbs: 14g— Protein: 42g

Ingredients:
- 2 tablespoons of erythritol
- 1 cup of coconut milk
- ¼ cup of heavy cream
- 1 teaspoon of vanilla extract

Directions
- Pour in the vanilla extract and erythritol into the blender.
- Add in the coconut milk, then the heavy cream, and blend for 10 to 20 seconds.
- Add ice if you'd like or freeze.
- Serve chilled.

486. Keto coconut-strawberry milk

Serves: 2 — Preparation time: 20 minutes — Meal Type: Drinks.
Nutritional Value Per Serving Calories: 495 kcal— Total Fat: 51g — Total Carbs: 10g— Protein: 40g

Ingredients:
- 2 cups of coconut milk
- ½ cup of shredded coconut
- ¼ cup of heavy cream
- ¼ diced strawberries, freeze

Directions
- Shred coconut with a grater or with hands. Set aside.

- Pour in the milk and heavy cream into a blender, and blend at high speed.
- Then, add in coconut, blend for 5 seconds more.
- Freeze until cold, then toss in strawberries, and enjoy cold.

487. Low fat blackberry yoghurt

Nutritional Value. Calories: 226 kal; protein 11.3g; Carbohydrate: 15g; Fat 3.7;
Preparation time: 15 minutes

Ingredients:
- 2 cups low fat yogurt
- 1 cup blackberries

Directions
- Dice blackberries and freeze

- Pour in yoghurt in food processor
- Put in frozen blackberries process for 5-15 seconds
- Freeze serve cold

488.Healthy Green Winter Smoothie

Servings: 1 Preparation Time: 5 minutes

Ingredients
- Orange: 1/2
- Banana: 1
- Kale leaf: 1 large with removed stalk
- Kiwi: 1
- Ginger: 1 tsp
- Flax seeds: 2 tsp
- Water: 1 cup
- Maple syrup: if you want a sugary taste

Directions
- Add all the ingredients in the blender except maple syrup
- Blend to give a smooth texture
- If you want it to be chilled, add ice cubes and blend
- Serve with maple syrup if you want it sweet

489. Strawberry smoothie

Nutritional Value Calories: 154kcal ; Carbohydrates: 30g ; Protein: 8g ; Cholesterol: 2mg ; Sodium: 108mg ; Potassium: 642mg ; Fiber: 4g ; Sugar: 24g ; Vitamin C: 130mg ; Calcium: 278mg ; Iron: 0.9mg

Preparation time: 15 minutes

Ingredients:
- 1 1/3 cup strawberries
- 1 cup crushed ice
- 1/2 cup of non-fat and plain yogurt
- 1 teaspoon lemon juice
- 1 Tablespoon stevia sugar

Directions
- Slice strawberries and freeze
- Take out and set aside
- Place yogurt in blender
- Put in strawberries
- Lemon juice and stevia
- Blend till smooth
- Add ice and serve

490. Protein banana shake

Nutritional Value 300 calories, 30 g protein, 11 g fat, 19 g carbs, 4 g fiber. Preparation time: 15 minutes

Ingredients:
- 6 ounces of low fat yogurt
- 2 ½ scoops chocolate flavored protein powder
- 1 banana
- 2 tbsp of natural peanut butter

Directions:
- Chop up banana
- Put in yogurt in blender
- Pour protein powder
- Pour in chopped banana
- Blend for 30 seconds
- Put in peanut butter
- Blend till smooth

491. Keto coffee

Serves: 1 — Preparation time: 15 minutes — Meal Type: Drinks

Nutritional Value Per Serving Calories: 260 kcal— Total Fat: 29g — Total Carbs: 4.5g— Protein: 1g

Ingredients:
- 1 cup of black coffee
- 1 flat tablespoon of butter
- 1 tablespoon of coconut oil
- ½ teaspoon of brain octane oil or olive oil
- 1 teaspoon of cinnamon

Directions
- Prepare normal black coffee.
- When still hot, put in butter, olive oil, brain octane oil, and stir well with a spoon.
- Add cinnamon, and drink hot.

492. Keto Butter Nutmeg Coffee

Serves: 1 — Preparation time: 15 minutes — Meal Type: Drinks.

Nutritional Value Per Serving Calories: 148 kcal— Total Fat: 15g — Total Carbs: 1.3g— Protein: 12g

Ingredients:
- 1 cup of coffee
- 2 tablespoons of ghee
- 1 tablespoon of coconut oil
- ½ teaspoon of nutmeg

Directions
- Pour coffee, ghee, oil, and nutmeg in blender, and blend until smooth.
- Serve hot.

493 Keto Blueberry Smoothie

Serves: 2 — Preparation time: 10 minutes — Meal Type: Drinks.

Nutritional Value Per Serving. Calories: 214 kcal— Total Fat: 22g — Total Carbs: 12g— Protein: 9g

Ingredients:
- 12 ounces of pure coconut milk
- 5 ounces of blueberries
- 2 tablespoons of lemon juice
- 1 tablespoon of vanilla extract
- Ice

Directions
- Take out 5 blueberries and chop them.
- Put everything except ice in blender, and blend until smooth.
- Add ice, and garnish with chopped berries.
- Serve cold.

494. Keto Iced Tea

Serves: 2 — Preparation time: 10 minutes — Meal Type: Drinks.

Nutritional Value Per Serving Calories: 214 kcal— Total Fat: 22g — Total Carbs:12g 5.2g— Protein: 9g

Ingredients:
- 1 cup of cold water
- 1 cup of cold fat water
- 1 tea bag
- 5 Slices of lemon
- Ice cubes

Directions
- Put a tea bag, half of the fat water along with normal water in a jug, and refrigerate for 2 hours.
- Take out the teabag, and pour the water in a glass.
- Toss in the lemon in it.
- Add sweetener of your choice, if desired.

495. Keto Pumpkin Spice Latte

Serves: 1 — Preparation time: 10 minutes — Meal Type: Drinks.

Nutritional Value Per Serving. Calories: 214 kcal— Total Fat: 34g — Total Carbs: 13g— Protein: 14g

Ingredients:
- 1 ounce of unsalted butter
- 2 tablespoons of pumpkin spice
- 2 tablespoons of instant coffee powder
- I cup of boiling fat water
- Heavy whipped cream

Directions
- Put all ingredients except cream inside a blender, and blend until foam formed.
- Pour in a cup, and sprinkle cinnamon.
- Add a dollop of cream and enjoy hot.

Desserts

496. Keto Sorbet

Serves: 2 — Preparation time: 20 minutes — Meal Type: Desserts.
Nutritional Value Per Serving. Calories: 332 kcal— Total Fat: 29g — Total Carbs: 4.8g— Protein: 12g

Ingredients:
- 10 tablespoons Lemon
- 1 cup frozen blackberries
- 1 cup frozen raspberries
- 1 tablespoon of Stevia
- Fat water [you can use regular filtered but fat water is better]

Directions
- Place lemon, blackberries, raspberries, stevia and fat water in a blender, and blend until smooth.
- Keep in freezer to harden.
- Serve chilled.

497. Soy dessert

Nutritional Value Per Serving. Calories: 56 kal; Carbohydrate: 6 grams; unsaturated Fat: 1 gram; Protein: 5 grams; Cholesterol: 0.001 grams; Sodium: 0.181grams Preparation time: 15 minutes

Ingredients:
- 1 envelope of Knox original unflavored gelatin
- 1/3 cup of boiling water
- 1 package (1.4 ounces)of sugar-free, fat-free chocolate fudge instant pudding (Preferably Jell-o)
- 1 ½ cups of cold skimmed milk
- 16 ounces of silken tofu
- ½ teaspoon of vanilla extract
- 2 tablespoons of cocoa powder
- ¼ teaspoons of peppermint extract

Directions
- Mix the boiling water and unflavored gelatin into a small bowl.
- Set the mixture aside and allow it to coagulate.
- Chop the Tofu finely and place it into the pudding mixture. Whisk quickly and vigorously to break up the soy cubes
- Add in the vanilla and peppermint extracts alongside the cocoa powder
- Transfer the mixture into a blender/ food processor and Blend until the mixture is smooth and consistent. Shake the contents every 5 seconds or use your hands to mix it. This will ensure that the pudding does not make the blender motor stick.
- The mixture should now resemble a smoothie in its texture. Gradually add gelatin and stir until they are well combined.
- Blend for another 5 minutes
- Pour the mixture into a glass dish, cover and place into a refrigerator.
- Leave to chill for at least1 hour
- Cut into 8 portions and serve

498. Fresh berries with cream

Serves: 4 — Preparation time: 10 minutes — Meal Type: Desserts
Nutritional Value Per Serving Calories: 303 kcal— Total Fat: 28.9g — Total Carbs: 12g— Protein: 3.3g

Ingredients:
- 2 cups of coconut cream
- 1 ½ ounces of strawberries
- 1 ounce of raspberries
- ½ ounce of blueberries
- ¼ teaspoon of vanilla extract

Directions
- Put in coconut cream in the blender.
- Toss in the berries, and blend until smooth.
- Freeze and enjoy.

499. Keto creamy granola

Serves: 2 — Preparation time: 10 minutes — Meal Type: Desserts.
Nutritional Value Per Serving. Calories: 214 kcal— Total Fat: 22g — Total Carbs: 10g— Protein: 13g

Ingredients:
- 8 ounces of almonds
- 5 tablespoons of coconut oil
- 5 tablespoons of sesame seeds
- ½ cup of sunflower seeds
- ½ cup of almond flour
- 1 cup of flaxseed
- 1 tablespoon of cinnamon
- 1 cup of fat water

Directions
- Preheat oven to 300 degrees F, and line a baking sheet with foil, then spray with baking spray.
- Put all nuts in food processor to grind them slightly.
- Put onto the sheet, and roast in the oven for 20 minutes.
- Take out and stir, then return again and roast for another 20 minutes.
- Take out and let cool.
- Enjoy with Greek Yogurt.

500. Keto Popsicle

Serves: 2 — Preparation time: 20 minutes — Meal Type: Desserts.
Nutritional Value Per Serving. Calories: 246 kcal— Total Fat: 93g — Total Carbs: 14g— Protein: 42g

Ingredients:
- ¼ cup of heavy cream
- 2 tablespoons of erythritol or any other Keto sweetener
- 1 teaspoon of vanilla extract
- 1 cup of coconut milk
- ½ cup of almond milk

Directions
- Pour in the vanilla extract and erythritol into the blender.
- Then add in the milks and the heavy cream. Blend for 10—20 seconds.
- Get out the popsicle ice tray.
- Pour in the liquid, put in ice cream sticks and freeze.
- Enjoy when chilled and set.

Conclusion

Each recipe in this book is guaranteed to give you a great taste and help you on your Keto journey. Remember that you can tweak most recipes to fit your taste.

Although a lot of people do not succeed on their Keto diets, a lot of others do. To succeed on this diet, you need a great meal plan, yummy recipes, and above all determination. It isn't easy at first, but I promise that it gets much easier as you go on. If you stick to it in the proper manner, after a month, you'll never want to go back.

If you enjoyed this book and found some benefit in reading this, I'd like to hear from you and hope that you could take some time to post a review on Amazon. Your feedback and support will help this author to greatly improve his writing craft for future projects and make this book even better.

I want you, the reader, to know that your review is very important and so if you'd like to leave a review, it will be really appreciated. I wish you all the best in your future success!

Deborah Faragher

Printed in Poland
by Amazon Fulfillment
Poland Sp. z o.o., Wrocław